The
Sunny Side of Winters

The Sunny Side of Winters

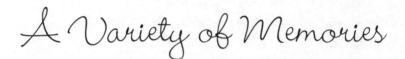

A Variety of Memories

Mike Winters

BOOKS

First published in Great Britain in 2010 by
JR Books, 10 Greenland Street, London NW1 0ND
www.jrbooks.com

A catalogue record for this book is available from the British Library.

ISBN 978-1-907532-02-3

1 3 5 7 9 10 8 6 4 2

Printed and bound in Great Britain by Clays Ltd, St Ives plc

To my wonderful wife Cassie, who lived many of these stories with me, and my daughter Chaney and son Anthony who, in spite of my spending so much time touring – or perhaps because of it – have grown up to be great human beings. And with thanks also to my lovely daughter-in-law Erin and supportive son-in-law, Kevin.

Contents

Foreword

Dear Reader,

I had a problem explaining exactly what kind of book this is, so, I asked my wife, Cassie, who had helped considerably in correcting this book how she would describe it. She had no problem. She is always direct, and always has an opinion.

'Very readable,' she began. 'It is a series of individual stories of various famous people whose lives interacted in one way or another with you, Mike. So, this isn't a regular autobiography; I am not certain it could even be called one. With each story a little of your life is revealed, but it is the stories themselves that made it such an enjoyable experience.'

I have very little to add to Cassie's comments other than the stories are as true as a good memory permits. Quite truthfully, some of the memories seem like yesterday. I hope you like the book.

Fondest thoughts,

Mike Winters

1

It's All About Timing:
The Genesis of a Double Act

How did Bernie and I get into show business? And why? It's difficult to say. But as I reflect, one reason may have been the thought of working with beautiful show girls and meeting glamorous actresses.

While we were still at school, I had a crush on two actresses, Gene Tierney and Rita Hayworth. Being three years younger than me, Bernie probably had different tastes. But he was certainly interested in girls, even at that age. while we were living in Blackpool to escape the bombing raids on London, thirteen-year-old Bernie arrived home for supper one day and announced to Mum that he was going to get married to Pipina, a local girl of fourteen.

Mum shook her head, her expression showing what she thought of the idea. She said mockingly, 'Really? How nice for you. I hope you have somewhere to live, because you aren't living here. I don't know how you expect to keep a wife when you can't even keep yourself. You'll have to get a proper job. No more hanging around at the arcades on the front where you don't earn enough to buy yourself lunch. Food costs money, doesn't it? You'll be paying for two. May I ask how?'

She shook her head again with an unmistakable sign of annoyance. 'Now, you silly sod, unless Pipina is going to feed you tonight, sit down and eat your supper.' Mum placed her hands on her hips and gave him one of her withering looks. 'I won't charge you for the meal,' she said, 'because you're just a bloody stupid schoolboy.' Bernie sat down without a word.

Mum never had to mention the subject again, and I'm sure she and Dad had a laugh about it later that night. When Bernie thought over what Mum had said, the part about the food hit home. Bernie loved his grub, especially the way Mum cooked it. Both Pipina and the thought of marriage were forgotten.

Another reason why Bernie and I were attracted to a life in show biz was more basic. We hated getting up in the morning! We believed actors and entertainers stayed in bed until midday. Oh, how mistaken we were! As youthful dreamers, we didn't understand there were such things as rehearsals, sometimes over an hour's drive away, that started at 10am. And, if you were lucky enough to make movies, you could get called to the set at seven.

I admit there were many times later in our lives when we slept until at least twelve o'clock. But on those occasions, we had been working in cabaret until past midnight, and didn't get to bed before two in the morning. And of course, if you don't have a job there is no need to get out of bed early every morning. We had quite a few periods like that. But even if we had realized such things, it wouldn't have made any difference. As I look back, it seems we were destined to embrace a life of show biz in one form or another.

I was born in Islington, north London. My sister, Sylvia, was three at the time, and brother Bernie came along three years later. Our mother, Rachel Bloomfield, was a member of the Blumenfeld circus family. Her immediate family consisted of five brothers, two of whom became professional boxers, and one younger sister, my Auntie Lily. Mum was even tougher than her brothers. Beautiful as she was, and blessed with a wonderful sense of humour, she was fearless. No one told her what to do, not even her elder brother Jack, who stood six foot two and became heavyweight champion of Great Britain and the Empire – when we still had one.

My father was Samuel Weinstein. London born, son of a Russian-Jewish immigrant, Dad had spent some time at school in Paris before running away to sea at fifteen to work on a Swedish tramp steamer. He'd been a professional boxer, a bodyguard to a top London gangster, and a bookmaker – with the brother of the founder of Ladbrokes as his partner. Dad was known in gambling circles as someone you didn't mess with.

Perhaps our mother's circus family history accounts for Bernie's and my attraction to show business. Anyway, at the age of nine, Bernie entered a talent competition in Margate, where the whole family was on holiday. He told no one about it. Copying the impressions I did of film and radio stars at home to entertain my sister, Sylvia, and Mum and Dad, Bernie went on to the open-air stage and won first prize.

The impressions he did weren't very good. . .Well, he had copied me, and mine weren't very good either. But Bernie's desire to perform was evident, and he had natural stage presence. His talent lay dormant for quite a while after that initial success. But, as they say in show business, it's all about timing – and as we'll see, in Bernie's case it was bad timing, or at least bad time-keeping, that was to set him on the road to a career in show biz.

When the German bombing raids on London began, we went to live with my Auntie Lily and Uncle Phil in Oxford. I managed to pass the entrance exam for the City of Oxford School, where I soon became a keen rugby player and was picked for the Second XV. I also began learning the clarinet, after Mum and Dad bought me one as a present for my fourteenth birthday, and eventually I became quite good. So, in the spring of 1941, my clarinet tutor arranged an audition for me at the Royal Academy of Music. He and I travelled to the Academy in the Marylebone Road, in London, where I played the adagio movement from Mozart's Clarinet Concerto. I had the music in front of me as a guide, but I had memorised it and didn't need it.

The three music examiners seemed to like my playing. Then one of them placed a sheet of music on the stand in front of me and asked me to play it. The piece wasn't terribly difficult, and I began confidently. I sounded good, but I soon knew I was messing up. Not being terribly good at sight reading, I was playing the right notes but giving them the wrong time value. If a note was supposed to be held for a beat, I might hold it for a beat and a half. Notes that should be held for two beats I would make last for three. Half notes, quarter notes, they were all over the place. I just played them quickly and hoped they were right. It may have sounded interesting, but it wasn't what was written. I returned to Oxford in a state of depression.

I shut the experience out of my mind. Then, just before term's end, I received news from my tutor. To his surprise and mine, the Royal Academy of Music had awarded me a scholarship, with a year's grant. It seemed they liked my tone and natural ability, and believed that with hard work and application I would overcome my sight-reading inadequacies.

It meant leaving Oxford and returning to London. Mum wanted me to go on to university and take Law. Dad was in favour of me coming home and studying music. So the final decision was left up to me. Of course I wanted both! I would particularly miss playing rugby for the school – by now I was a regular in the First XV. But to be a music student in London sounded pretty exciting. And who knew for sure if I would get into Oxford University? One needed a pass in Latin, and my Latin was. . .well, I was in the bottom three every term.

We were a pragmatic family. Mum always said a bird in the hand is better than two in the bush. On one hand, I might get into university. On the other hand, I had was a definite offer from the Royal Academy of Music, and it was something I wanted to do. It wasn't too difficult to decide. To help confirm my choice, Dad was having a bad financial patch, and the grant would be a help.

So, at fifteen, I began life as a music student. I had mixed emotions. I would have to find a rugby club to join, but I was pleased to have left Oxford and begin a whole new experience.

My first couple of terms at the Academy weren't an unqualified success. In Oxford, as a young clarinettist, I had been a big fish in a small pond. Now, at the Academy, I was surrounded by clarinet students of high calibre. One of those students was called Johnny Dankworth. He was in the Academy's first symphony orchestra and he was damn good. I soon realised I was a very small fish in a big pond. Quite honestly, I was lucky to find a place in the second orchestra.

Although I loved classical music, I also loved jazz and swing. So instead of practising Mozart's Clarinet Concerto I spent time learning to play Artie Shaw's Concerto for Clarinet. For the uninitiated, Artie Shaw was a swing band leader, and a great clarinettist. I became a big fan. My interest in jazz unfortunately distracted me from my classical music studies, and it showed.

Another distraction came in the form of a beautiful, dark-haired cello player named Helena. I wasn't yet sixteen and I had a big crush on her. The Royal Academy of Music, unlike my school in Oxford, was co-educational. Having girls in my class was embarrassing. Having a lovely young girl sit next to me gave me all sorts of thoughts, and music wasn't one of them!

The raven-haired beauty Helena sat next to me during sight-reading music class. While she aced every exam, I floundered and failed, and came bottom of the class. Helena so distracted me that I couldn't count time even with single crotchets. My thumping heart had its own beat. I should have moved seats, or asked her to move, but that wasn't possible because I hadn't the courage to speak to her. Besides, sitting close to her was exciting and I liked it.

We smiled at each other, and she occasionally wished me good morning. I nodded and quickly looked away. For some nonsensical reason I didn't want to show my hand. Let her think I wasn't interested. What the hell was the matter with me?

She moved on to a higher class. Obviously, I didn't. In fact I was lucky there was no lower class to which they could drop me. I still had a secret crush, though, and wanted to get to know her. But how?

A few weeks later, I talked a fellow student, David Wald, who loved jazz and often ate at Helena's table in the canteen, into taking me along. Of course, I was cool and didn't give him a clue as to how I felt about Helena. David and I lunched together a couple of times at her usual table, but Helena didn't appear.

Then, one lunchtime, I was in luck. Helena was there, and there were two empty spaces. With smiles all around, David and I placed our full trays on the table and sat down.

Helena smiled, and I smiled back. In fact, I think I may have smiled at her too many times. She began smiling back with a baffled look on her face. You see, I had decided to discard my 'playing hard to get' plan – I doubt if she was even aware of it. Now I was trying my new plan, the smiling, friendly boy next door – though it probably came across as the smiling idiot from hell.

We lunched together a few more times. David wanted to know what I kept smiling at. And I noticed Helena obviously wasn't making eye contact. I cut down on the smile offensive.

I was determined to speak to her, but I was a little worried about her name. Of course, I knew it, but for some unknown reason I could never be sure if it was pronounced Hel-en-a, or Hel-ane-a. At lunch, on this particular day, I compromised and used neither. With only a half smile, I leaned across the table, and in a confident voice said my first words to her. 'I say, would you mind passing me the pepper, please.' I gave a silent sigh of relief.

She smiled graciously, displaying beautiful, even white teeth, and passed me the pepper. I mumbled a thank you to the side of her head, as she had turned to speak to the young man sitting next to her. It couldn't be her boyfriend, could it? Not this thin chap with glasses and a growth of hair on his chin one could hardly call a beard? I asked David in a whisper if the fellow was Helena's boyfriend. He nodded an affirmative.

They were the only words I ever spoke to her. It's a wonder I still remember them. Maybe it's because I never spoke to her again.

She didn't leave the Academy, and neither did I. We ate together a few more times, but never alone. We joined in other people's conversations, but I never addressed her personally. I don't believe I smiled at her again, and finally, I stopped lunching at her table. I don't think she even noticed.

Fortunately, the second half of my year at the Academy was far more positive. My friend David Wald decided to form the Royal Academy Swing Quintet. It would play at local weddings, bar-mitzvahs, engagement parties, confirmations – in fact, any event that would pay us to play.

Bill Stevens, who was in the second orchestra, but in my opinion good enough for the first, was our trumpet player. Our bass player, also from the second orchestra, was a big strong guy we called Bud. I was on clarinet. Johnny Dankworth would have been a far better choice, but his reputation had already reached beyond the Academy, and it was said he had even played at professional jazz clubs. David didn't have the nerve to ask Johnny.

I had met Johnny a few times at the Academy, and had talked about swing bands. He liked the Woody Herman Band and the Duke Ellington Orchestra. I was so impressed by Johnny that I automatically became fans of the two bands. Johnny was always friendly, but I didn't blame David not having the gall to ask him to join his Quintet. Johnny was in a different league.

David lifted a lot of arrangements from jazz records. With Bill on trumpet and me on clarinet, we made a good sound. David gave us basic charts for the latest pop tunes, and Bill and I would do the vocals. We were all set, except for one major factor – we didn't have a drummer.

The percussionists at the Academy didn't want to play jazz. Some would argue it wasn't really music, just a primitive rhythm with undisciplined, discordant sounds. Anyway, we needed a drummer. Someone who could swing, and who would work cheaply. I knew just the person. And Bernie, his drums, and his timing, changed our lives.

The year before I began at the Royal Academy, Bernie at the age of twelve was already as tall as me. He had taught himself to play the ukulele, but he hadn't started playing drums yet. He was more interested in his social life than music. Bernie wore an American Stetson hat, garish American ties, and spoke with an appalling cockney accent, which I barely understood. He was friendly with some of the roughest young villains in London. Not that Bernie was a villain, he wasn't, but these anti-social young men liked him. He made them laugh.

Bernie's best friend was a champion amateur boxer, Danny Sewell, of whom great things were expected, though he later had to give up his dream of boxing fame for health reasons. He was a local boy and well respected by the local villains. He and Bernie had a couple of things in common. Although Bernie wasn't an amateur boxer, and had no interest in turning professional, he could fight – he and I had sparred together since we were kids. Dad made sure we knew how to take care of ourselves.

Both Bernie and Danny shared a fondness for the excitement and the glamour of the West End, and in spite of their youth and complete lack of money, they hung out 'up West' until past their normal bedtime. They weren't bad boys, their parents would never stand for that, but it was wartime. You grew up quickly in those days. At the back of most young men's minds was the realisation that at seventeen-and-a-half you would be called up to serve your country.

Danny had an elder brother everyone called Chuck. He was a few years older than me and was serving in the Royal Air Force, training to be a pilot. I was impressed. He was impressed by me in turn; I was a local boy who had made it to the Royal Academy of Music. Chuck told me of his ambition to be involved in something creative when the war was over. We hit it off, and over the years always celebrated each other's success.

Danny eventually moved to California, where he made a name for himself as an actor and producer. Chuck became an actor too. His tough looks were made for the gritty movies and TV shows of that time, set in the fictitious, gangster-infested streets of London. Now known by his real name, George Sewell, he played tough-guy roles on either side of the law. He was a tough villain in the movie *Get Carter* with Michael Caine, and starred as a tough cop in the hit TV series *Special Branch*.

Bernie, Danny and Chuck were frequent visitors to the Tottenham Palais de Dance. They loved the sound of the big swing band. Chuck had aspirations to play the drums and Bernie caught the bug. He decided he wanted to be a drummer. Dad, who really could not afford it, bought Bernie a full-size drum set. The die was cast.

The German bombing of London had been tamed, although the era of the doodlebugs was about to begin. The residents of our block of flats were grateful for the respite from the sound of bombs falling, the wail of air raid and ambulance sirens. Yet they would have probably welcomed it all back if it stopped the maniac Winters boy practising his drums night and day!

They had occasionally suffered the sound of a clarinet practising scales. But that seemed like a golden age of celestial music compared to Bernie's almost non-stop crashing and banging, which ended only when Mum, at breaking point, would scream, 'Stop that bloody row!'

My mum's youngest brother, Uncle Mick, was the youngest of the five Bloomfield brothers. I think perhaps Uncle Mick, a debonair man-about-town, was Mum's favourite. He was Bernie's favourite too. For years Bernie would sleep with Uncle Mick's large army boots under his bed. Bernie kept them, and wore them as props when playing an eccentric comedy character on television and on the stage. He kept those beloved boots until he died.

Uncle Mick was six feet two inches tall, a large man with a big, generous heart and a wide circle of friends. One of those friends was George Firestone, the drummer of the London Palladium Orchestra. Lessons for Bernie were arranged, and his playing began to improve. Now as I mentioned earlier, the embryonic Royal Academy Swing Quintet had no drummer. It was time for little brother Bernie to step in.

The very thought of Bernie joining the Academy band was treated like a gift from heaven by my mother. She had been thinking of evacuating Bernie back to our Auntie Lily in Oxford – anything to escape the noise of the drums. But if he was in a band, working at night, sleeping late in the morning, he wouldn't be able to practise all the time. The flat would be practically drum free! Mum implored me to get him into the band.

David Wald, the leader of the group, was a brilliant pianist. He was only fourteen and had already won national contests, including the Stanley Black Award for Arrangers. Unfortunately, he was a little shy and didn't want to be the front man. As he pointed out, three of the most famous American bands were fronted by clarinettists – Artie Shaw, Benny Goodman and Woody Herman – so he decided I would be the one standing in front and doing all the talking.

The band began getting gigs. Mostly these were at functions that wanted background music, old standards and waltzes. We didn't like it – we wanted to play more contemporary music – but we were poor students, we needed the money. Very rarely – we couldn't often afford it – we would pay a young 'pro' musician with a big reputation to sit in. Guitarist Malcolm Mitchell and tenor sax player Ronnie Scott, of Ted Heath Band fame and co-owner of the legendary Ronnie Scott's Jazz Club, were two such players. I really enjoyed those gigs.

Things started to unravel when we started playing exclusively dance music. The more lucrative bookings – weddings, bar-mitzvahs and confirmations – began drying up. Whatever the cause, we lost our bass player. Schlepping a double bass on and off buses, up and down the Tube stations, was no fun. None of us owned a car – we didn't know how to drive anyway. So the Royal Academy Quintet was history, but the Royal Academy Quartet, with young Bernie on drums, was ready for whatever was going. And what young people wanted was dance music.

We soon came across an unexpected hitch in that department. Without a bass player the tempo relied solely on the drummer. The piano was important too, but it didn't drive the tempo like drums did. And David, classically trained, wasn't that kind of pianist. He had a great technique and feel for thick, melodic chords, and a penchant for flowery right-hand improvisation, but pounding out rhythm wasn't his thing. We depended on a solid drummer.

Bernie could swing. He could take good solos. What he couldn't do was keep a solid beat. For dancing, that's imperative. Solid tempo. Strict time. Otherwise, a quickstep could end up as a foxtrot.

Admittedly, that never happened with Bernie on drums. What happened was worse. A slow, romantic foxtrot was liable to end up as frenetic quickstep. And you couldn't dance cheek to cheek to a quickstep!

At first, people actually stopped dancing and gathered around the bandstand in bewilderment. I had to say something, so I began ad-libbing. I explained, 'It's our drummer, Bernie, ladies and gentlemen. He sometimes gets this uncontrollable urge to do a drum solo. So stay where you are. Bernie is going to start as he and I play our version of Woody Herman's "Golden Wedding".'

This was a piece Bernie and I played at home, to the annoyance of our neighbours in the adjoining flats, and to the delight of our dad, who was without doubt our biggest fan. We never played it the same way twice. It was just a bit of fun that gave Bernie a solo, and allowed me an opportunity to finish with a few flashy cadenzas and go for a high top C.

That night, the first time we'd done it in public, Bernie opened with the exciting tom-tom beat, and the crowd was intrigued. I began playing the theme that led into Bernie's solo. He surpassed himself. The crowd were excitedly swaying to the rhythm. I came in after Bernie's solo and went for a big finish, but got worried about the high C and finished with a top A. The crowd went crazy anyway. We were a big hit.

The Quartet went back to playing dance music, and Bernie's tempo gains were only marginal for the rest of the evening. Unfortunately, the problem didn't go away. Bernie's tempo problem would return at other dances, and we had to cover the problem by giving our duet performance again. On some nights we would play some of Artie Shaw's Concerto for Clarinet, and talk to each other using imitations of famous celebrities. We even got one or two laughs.

After one such evening, I was approached by a RAF sergeant air gunner who asked if I would like to play for the Allied Forces at the Stage Door Canteen in Piccadilly. Had I heard of it?

Of course I had heard of the famous Stage Door Canteen. It was where service personnel would go to be served food by famous actors and entertainers who would also perform. And of course I would be happy to play there. What did I have to do?

The air gunner said he would arrange everything. All I had to do was turn up at the stage door at around seven on Tuesday, and bring what music I might need. And not to forget my clarinet. Ha ha!

Before he left, I asked if I could bring Bernie to play drums. He looked at me with astonishment. 'Of course. You have to play that duet, that tom-tom bit you did tonight. It was great.'

I told Bernie about the Canteen gig, and what the sergeant had said. Bernie shrugged. 'So he said we were great, eh? I don't think Gene Krupa would be too worried if he heard me play.'

'And I'm doing impressions of Artie Shaw and Woody Herman. It would really mean something if they wanted to do an impression of me.'

'They couldn't play that bad,' Bernie grinned.

'Watch it! With you on drums, and your sense of tempo, you would make anyone sound bad.' We laughed, but there was no doubt about it, we were both excited and looking forward to the experience.

From that first appearance at the Stage Door Canteen, I felt this would turn out to be a defining experience in our lives. The servicemen loved us. Mr Thackeray, the director of the Canteen, invited us back. Then back again. We were becoming a regular part of the scene.

With the confidence only applause and appreciation from an audience can give, Bernie and I decided to do more comedy impressions. We would steal gags and ideas from double acts. Our prime source was Jimmy Jewel and Ben Warriss. And whatever we did on the stage, the international servicemen and women encouraged us with their enthusiastic support.

Off stage, we rubbed shoulders with international film stars like Paulette Goddard, Michael Wilding, Anna Neagle and the soon-to-be-famous Terry-Thomas. To the mature, sophisticated people we met backstage in the Green Room, we were just two talented kids who'd done well in front of an entertainment-starved bunch of young servicemen and women, who were determined to enjoy themselves come what may. Bernie and I were young and cute, and no competition to the established stars. Bernie, aged thirteen, and me at sixteen, were thrilled and awed just to be at the famous Stage Door Canteen and to mix with those famous people. Sometimes, if there were no entertainers available, we might appear three times in one week. Of course, we didn't get paid – nor, as far as I know, did anyone else. It made it a little awkward sometimes finding artists to appear. A paying gig took precedence over patriotism!

Mr Thackeray asked me if I would bring in my own trio and play more music. I shouldn't give up the comedy, of course, but the foreign servicemen didn't speak English too well, and they absolutely adored our playing. 'So, dear boy, more music would be just the ticket,' he said in his characteristic manner.

One evening, after our first set – we were now making two appearances a night, giving latecomers a chance to see us – a guest in the Green Room whom I didn't recognise came over and spoke to me. He seemed important by the way everyone treated him, but he was unknown to me. Anyway, he asked Bernie and me if he could sit in on drums in our next set. Young and good looking, he spoke with an American accent, and he had a charismatic way about him. He introduced himself as Bonar Colleano Junior. The 'junior' impressed us. It sounded big time. We assumed he was a star from the States we hadn't heard of yet. Bernie had no objection to Bonar using his drums; I just hoped he could play and keep proper time.

During the set, he asked if I would play 'Golden Wedding', the drum and clarinet duet Bernie and I did. I gave him the beat. He attacked the tom-toms and he was pretty good. Not as exciting as Bernie, but not bad at all.

After we finished playing, he asked me to join him at a nightclub for a drink – a soft drink in my case, as I didn't yet drink alcohol. I had however begun sporting a pipe, which I thought made me look older, though never put in any tobacco. As for nightclubs, I had never been to one. I was a struggling music student. I told

Bonar I was broke and couldn't afford the high life. He shrugged it off. He would take care of everything.

Bonar pointed out that Bernie was too young to come along, so Bernie packed his drums and caught the bus home. Meanwhile, carrying my clarinet case, I took a taxi for my first visit to a sophisticated West End nightclub.

When we got there everyone seemed to know Bonar, and I couldn't help wondering why he wanted me along, someone who couldn't afford to buy a drink even if he wanted one. But I was enjoying myself. The plush seats, the soft lights and the pretty waitresses fascinated me. There were a few sexy-looking young ladies sitting alone at the bar – though if I couldn't afford a drink, I most certainly couldn't afford them.

Before I was halfway through my Coke, Bonar, after a word with the leader of the five-piece band, came back to our table and told me we were going to sit in for a couple of numbers. I was hesitant. 'I don't know, Bonar. Are you sure no one will mind?' He reassured me. I grabbed my clarinet case and followed him to the stage.

The couple of numbers expanded to four. Everyone seemed happy, especially Bonar. He obviously loved to play the drums.

We went on to another night spot, not as smart or sophisticated as the previous one, but with equally cute waitresses. The professional girls looked a bit older, the room was decorated in a darker red, and the tables closer together. It had a naughty atmosphere. I saw quite a few American officers, and a couple of British naval officers. There were a lot of middle-aged civilians, business types, sitting with glamorous ladies, who were unquestionably born in an earlier decade than their companions. The band sounded good, though the musicians were either too young or too old for the services, or I guess, medically unfit. I made no resistance when Bonar said we were going to sit in. We played about six numbers. The audience seemed to enjoy it as much as we did. We swung. The pianist and the trumpet player could really play.

Bonar and I stayed late. He drank whisky, and I stayed true to Coke. It suddenly hit me; I had missed the last bus home! I would have to borrow my cab fare, and at this time in the morning it would be expensive. This was embarrassing. My problem was solved when Bonar asked me if I had ever been to a Turkish bath. 'No,' I answered, not knowing for sure what a Turkish bath was.

'You'll love it, Mike. It's kinda late, and I gotta be up early. I'm filming. Gotta get to Pinewood. We'll spend the night at the baths.'

'Sleep in a bath?'

'No, pal. Don't worry. You're with a Colleano.'

The Turkish baths of Jermyn Street were an all-night haven for wealthy playboys, stars of entertainment, knights of the realm, leaders of industry, magnates of finance. . .and now Michael Winters, clarinet student. One could luxuriate in the steam room, have a massage and take a dip in the cold pool. If one so desired – and paid, of course – one could spend the night sleeping on a cot like those in a hospital, and wake in the morning feeling refreshed, rejuvenated and reborn.

It worked for me! After we had been served a cup of tea and a biscuit in the morning, Bonar was off. I thanked him for a great night. He said he'd see me on Friday, my next show at the Canteen, and we'd paint the town. I made my way home via the Tube and bus, reliving last night's experiences. It was obvious to me now why Bonar had invited me to go clubbing with him. I was the key. The young classical clarinettist from the Royal Academy of Music who played jazz was the hook allowing him to sit in with the club's band. I wasn't some tipsy playboy who thought he could play. I didn't want to use someone else's instrument, like Bonar did. I had my own clarinet. I had credibility. So, I had been of use. I didn't care. I liked Bonar and I'd enjoyed myself.

Mum was in the kitchen cooking when I got home. It smelt good, like everything she cooked. After planting a kiss on her cheek, I asked if Dad was home. He had gone to the Newmarket races, she told me. Bernie was asleep in bed. I was told not to wake him. It was so lovely and quiet right now. She moved away from the cooker and sat on one of the two chairs placed either end of the small kitchen table, from where she looked me up and down. 'Bernie told me you were going to a nightclub with an American movie star last night. Some actor called Colly, Boony Collarno, or something.'

'Bonar Colleano,' I told her with a smile. My parents never seemed to get famous people's names right. I too have always had a problem with names.

'I've never heard of him. What did he want with you?' Mum asked suspiciously.

'He wanted me to play clarinet at the clubs, so he could get to play the drums.'

'Clubs! There was more than one?' She changed the subject. 'D'you fancy a cuppa tea? A bacon sandwich or something?' I grinned and nodded vigorously. Mum got up and went to the refrigerator that Dad had bought after a good day at the race track. 'Put the kettle on,' she instructed as she took out the bacon. Mum had her own dietary laws – you could eat bacon at home though not ham or pork. While I drank my tea and devoured a wonderful bacon sarnie, Mum interrogated me. 'How old is this actor? Where did you spend the night? Did you have your own bed? Did he touch you?'

I got the message. 'Touch me! My own bed! Mum! He isn't a queer. And if he was, and he isn't, he didn't try anything on with me.'

I relayed to her what Bonar had told me last night. He had been born in New York. He came from a circus family. His uncle, the Great Con Colleano, had been the first tightrope walker to perform a forward somersault on the high wire. Bonar had worked in the family's circus act as an acrobat. Now, since moving here from Australia with his family, he'd been doing West End theatre and films. He lived with his family just off Tottenham Court Road. His real name was Sullivan.

'Sullivan?' Mum repeated. 'Irish. Hmmm! That must be why he's not in the forces.'

'I have no idea, Mum. I didn't ask. It's possible, I suppose.'

'How old is he?'

'I don't know. I don't go around asking people questions,' I answered irritably. 'About nineteen or twenty.'

Mum seemed satisfied. 'Your Uncle Mick, and Jack too, go to the Turkish baths in Jermyn Street.' She smiled sweetly. 'He sounds a nice boy,' she said. 'No harm in being careful. There are a lot of strange men running around the West End. You're a handsome boy. Be careful who you mix with, men and women. Remember, if you lay down with dogs, you get up with fleas.'

Bonar and I did the club circuit a couple of times more. I stayed a couple of nights at his parents' flat when I missed the last bus. But it wasn't something you could keep on repeating. The novelty soon wore off, although I saw Bonar a few times at the Canteen and Bernie kindly let him use his set of drums.

Most nights Bonar was with pretty young lady actresses. One was rather young, about my age. He said we should make up a foursome, but we never did. It was understandable. Although Bonar was extremely generous, with little regard for money, his career hadn't yet taken off and he had to watch his spending. Paying for me, who didn't drink, was one thing, but taking me and an extra girl out to supper was another story.

Now I was no longer doing the nightclub circuit with Bonar, I had no problems getting home after a show. Apart from my lack of progress at the Academy, my immediate problem was keeping the Quartet together. When Mr Thackeray asked me to form my own trio at the Canteen, I'd naturally asked David to join me. He came a couple of times, but since he was working for nothing and didn't enjoy the twee, showbiz atmosphere, he declined to continue.

It wasn't only the Canteen that David had a problem with. By now, both he and Bill were fed up being sidemen for the Mike and

Bernie show. I didn't blame them. At any time I expected David to tell me and Bernie the comedy routines had to go.

Things came to a head one night. The Mike and Bernie segment wasn't going down too well with the crowd, who only wanted to dance. They stood sullenly around the bandstand, waiting for us to play some proper dance music.

Suddenly the crowd split in two as the organiser of the dance came bursting through, heading straight for me. In a loud, angry voice he demanded we stop playing. Pointing his finger at me he bellowed, 'What is this? No one can dance to this rubbish. Pack up and leave. And don't even think about asking to be paid.'

So the Quartet folded. Bill got a job at the Croydon Palace with the resident dance band. David and I went on with our studies, though mine weren't to last much longer. At the end of the summer term I lost my grant. Dad was on a losing streak too, and paying for me to remain at the Academy was going to be a problem. I somehow knew I would never be the clarinettist I wanted to be, and I didn't have the desire to study and practice. I accepted that my days at the Academy were over. The war was still on. It was an exciting time. I really didn't know or particularly care what I would do next.

Bernie and I still appeared at the Canteen, but strictly as entertainers. We did a six-minute spot, including our clarinet and drum duet and a series of impressions. We did well, but we had grown six months older since our debut. Now I looked old enough to be in uniform, although I was still well under age. I was becoming a little concerned about my future. I called Bonar and asked if he would meet me for a chat. I needed some advice.

We met at Olivelli's, a famous showbiz restaurant near where he lived. He insisted he take me for lunch. We both ordered lasagne. Between mouthfuls I told him of my dilemma.

'I'll probably be called up soon, but if I got a part-time job to help pay the fees and went back to the Academy, I might get a deferment so I can finish my studies.'

'So what's wrong with that?'

'I don't like the idea of avoiding being called up. And quite honestly, Bonar, I don't want to be just another clarinettist. I'll be wasting my time at the Academy.'

'Hey kid, everyone thinks you're a pretty good clarinet player, including me.'

'Yes, pretty good! That's not good enough. There are an awful lot who are pretty good. And most of them are far better musicians than I'll ever be.'

Bonar remained silent for a moment, thoughtful. 'What do you want to do?' he asked finally.

I was slow answering – I too was thoughtful. 'Something to do with the theatre, I think. A writer? Director? Performer? I don't really know for sure.'

'I see.' He took another mouthful of lasagne and sipped a little red wine from his glass. 'Look, Mike, I really can't give you advice. Hell, I'll probably screw up my own life.' He paused as a thought hit him. 'Maybe that's it. If you're gonna screw up, make sure it's your screw-up, and not somebody else's. Get it?

'I've watched you and Bernie work together, you've got somethin'. Sure, you're raw and amateurish, but you'll learn. You got plenty of time. The war is gonna end one day, maybe in a year or two. You and Bernie will still be kids.' He leaned forward in order to emphasise what he was saying. 'Base your act around your instruments. Learn to dance. Build the comedy slowly, OK? Show talent first. You guys will do just fine. Don't rush things. Remember that. Always give yourself time. The great acts always seem to have more time than their competition. OK? Hey, I'm sorry I couldn't be more helpful. I'm not good at givin' advice.'

I shook my head. 'Are you kidding? You've just given some great advice. I tell you, Bonar, I will always remember what you told me. Providing I remember it!' I added.

Bonar smiled. He knew I was kidding.

Later, after I had done my National Service, we met now and again as Bernie and I began our slow climb up the entertainment ladder. I watched Bonar's success with pride. Within a year or so, he had a personal hit in the movie *Way to the Stars*. There were many more movies and successes to follow, and he married an actress named Tamera Lees, although they were divorced in 1951.

We didn't see each other for several years; then, in the autumn of 1952, we bumped into each other on the corner of Oxford Street and Regent Street. We were both trying to hail a cab. He was going to his mother's flat off Tottenham Court Road and I was going to Warren Street to see a car dealer. As they were on the same route we decided to share.

Within minutes an empty taxi pulled up. As soon as we were sitting in the intimacy of a London cab, I congratulated Bonar on his movie career and told him Bernie and I were playing a few small theatre dates, though we were struggling to get laughs.

'That's OK,' Bonar began, 'but don't play the dumps for too long. You get a dump mentality. You end up doing well on them, and dying if you get a class date.'

Changing the subject, I said I was sorry to read about his divorce from Tamera. I casually mentioned I had met a girl I thought might be the one for me. His advice was familiar.

'If you think you love her, marry her. If it doesn't work out, so you've screwed up. Tough. At least it's your screw-up.'

We reached his destination first. He went to pay the taxi driver. I gave him a 'don't argue with me' look. 'Forget it. My treat for all the advice you haven't given me,' I said with a grin.

He smiled back. 'Cute,' he said, and with a wave he was off. That was the last time I saw him.

Bonar died in car crash in Lancashire six years later, in 1958. He was only thirty-four. It happened after an evening theatre performance. If he hadn't driven his sports car quite so fast he may have still been with us, but as they say, it is all a matter of timing.

As the story goes, he lost control of the car because of his speed. It seemed he was solely responsible. I can't help remembering his words to me: 'If you're gonna screw up, make sure it's your screw-up, and not someone else's.'

I often think about Bonar. About the good advice he gave me, and how in such a short time he was such an enormous influence on my life.

2

Royals Are People Too:
The Royal Variety Performance

I was deeply saddened to read of the death of Sir John Dankworth, and called his wife, Dame Cleo Laine, to leave a message conveying my sorrow. After putting down the phone it dawned on me that I had known Cleo even longer than I had known John, whom I had met when we were fellow students at the Royal Academy of Music in London.

I first met Cleo when she was in a singing group. We were both very young. I can't remember any details, but from the one show in which I saw her perform, her talent was obvious and I believed she would do well. I never imagined I would know her and her husband all my life.

I used to go and see the Johnny Dankworth Orchestra whenever possible, and we occasionally met at Ronnie Scott's Jazz Club in Soho. One night, John introduced me to Quincy Jones and Ben Webster, a famous tenor player from the Duke Ellington Band, and for that evening I felt like a real musician. Johnny was a fellow Water Rat, and was a special guest when Bernie and I were honoured on the TV show *This Is Your Life*. Our paths have crossed many times.

Cleo, John, Bernie and I met again in November 1961. Cleo was pregnant, and all four of us were booked to appear together at the London Palladium for a Royal Variety Performance. This next story recounts my experiences of that show and the circumstances leading up to it...

M y mother always taught me to treat prince and pauper alike. My sister Sylvia, brother Bernie and I grew up with that advice instilled in our heads. However, when Bernie and I were booked for a four-week run playing the Moss Empires – the premium theatres in Britain – we were excited to find ourselves working with a pair of real live aristocrats.

Baron and Baroness van Pallandt were from Denmark. They looked aristocratic. He was over six feet in height, good looking, with reddish hair and a tidy beard; she was tall and slim, blonde and extremely attractive.

They were quite famous, not as aristocrats, but as singers, in which role they were known as Nina and Frederik. Their recent recording of a folk-style song, 'Little Donkey', had turned out to be a monster hit. Now they were topping the bill at major theatres all over the country.

I would have been even more excited had they been British aristocrats. Had it been the Duke and Duchess of Bedford or Norfolk making a hit pop record, that really would have been something. But that they were Danish was definitely not to be sneezed at, and I was looking forward to working with them. There was another reason, though, why I wasn't quite as excited as I might have been. Six months earlier, to our delight and surprise, Bernie and I had signed to appear in the pantomime *Puss in Boots* at the London Palladium.

To play the London Palladium had been a dream of ours from the beginning of our career. In 1961 we had made it. We were given a twelve-minute spot as a supporting act to Shirley Bassey. But in the first house on Monday, the opening night, we overran by three minutes. It wasn't really our fault. I blame the audience, and my wife, Cassie. Bernie and I were struggling at first, until she broke the funereal atmosphere by laughing loudly at one of our ad libs. The audience suddenly seemed to realise we were funny. Cassie was obviously enjoying herself. The audience decided to do so too. We were the hit of the show – at least, of the supporting cast. Shirley was in a class of her own.

Second house, brimming with confidence, we overran four minutes. The chairman of Moss Empires, Leslie McDonnell, was waiting for us in the wings. 'Boys, you were great,' he said putting his arms round our shoulders. 'You went over your time both houses. Do that again tomorrow night, don't bother to be here on Wednesday.'

Before the Tuesday night show, though, Mr McDonnell came to our dressing room. 'Boys, I want you to spread tonight. Shirley has a throat infection and is cutting a couple of numbers. I'd like eighteen minutes from you. OK? Don't go crazy on me and go way over time.' He went to the door, turned and gave us a grin. 'Have a good show.'

And we did. We were the talk of the business. Without doubt it was our performance with Shirley Bassey that got us the booking for the pantomime at the Palladium, and a television appearance on *Sunday Night at the London Palladium*, hosted by Bruce Forsyth.

In our early days, we'd gone to see the shows at the Palladium, getting in without paying by using our Variety Artist Union card. The management permitted us to stand at the back of the stalls to watch the show. We went to see our idols Jimmy Jewel and Ben Warriss many times, wondering if one day we too would appear in a big production on that famous stage. Well, come December

1961, for sixteen weeks that is exactly what we would be doing. Unlike Jewel and Warriss, we wouldn't be top of the bill – we would have to wait a few years for that honour. In *Puss in Boots*, we had fifth billing. It was a terrific cast. Headlining was Frankie Vaughan; second top was Joan Regan, followed by Jimmy Edwards and Dick Emery. Then it was us. Bern and I were thrilled to be in the same show as such famous entertainers. Little did we know that another show business surprise awaited us, one that would excite us even more.

We had been working with Nina and Frederik for a few days when we received a letter from Joe Collins, our sardonic and sophisticated agent, who was the father of probably the most famous sisters in show business, Joan and Jackie Collins. His short but thrilling letter told us we had been chosen by Bernard Delfont to appear in the Royal Variety Performance of 1962 at the Palladium, in front of Her Majesty the Queen.

The letter said we should call Joe in the morning when we got to the theatre. He knew we'd be there. Every morning, Monday to Friday, from eleven to one, we practised our musical instruments and tap dancing, went over any comedy ideas we had and checked our mail.

Before we called Joe, we talked things over. We were excited, euphoric, anxious. What routines should we use in front of the Queen? Joe had written that we would only get a four- or five-minute spot. It took us that long to say 'Good evening'. And what if the Queen didn't like us? We knew it wouldn't mean the Tower, but would it kill our career?

'We can't be blue,' Bernie said. Being 'blue' in the Sixties wasn't like today. The word 'kinky' was considered too blue for television.

I said, 'What are you talking about? We aren't blue.'

'I know, but I meant vulgar. We are sometimes. Like when we use enduendo.'

'You mean innuendo. So we won't do the vowels routine.' That was a routine when Bernie mistakes the word 'vowels' for 'bowels'. It was vulgar, no argument, but it was funny too.

'Supposing there's another double act on the bill. Or what if Des O'Connor is on and he does some of our gags?' Bernie could be a big worrier.

'Will you stop it? They won't book another double act that would clash with us. Bernard Delfont knows what he's doing. And as for Des. . .so he's on. So what? Let's call Joe. Got any change?'

Bernie did the talking while I put my ear close to the telephone. I heard Joe warn us to make sure we kept it clean, otherwise the press would kill us. He told us Bob Hope, Eartha Kitt, Cliff Richard and Rosemary Clooney were some of the big names on the show. But we shouldn't worry about that, just make sure we did a good job.

Oh, and we should let Nina and Frederik know we'd miss the Saturday show in Liverpool, as it would be an early call for us on the Sunday, with rehearsals all day. The show was being televised, and Joe didn't want us to drive down overnight from Liverpool arriving exhausted; we had to be on top form. He would arrange with Phil Solomon – Nina and Frederik's representative – to release us for that one Saturday night.

After the phone call, we cut our practice short. Over coffee in the Kardoma café, we worried over the enormity of the opportunity. Millions of people would see us on television. We were moving up to the big time.

Bernie put down his coffee cup and grinned at me. 'So, we're working for the Bernard Delfont office, eh? Do you remember, it was Keith from that office who told us we had no chance in show business? We were too foreign looking and sounded too Londonish. We'd be eaten alive up north. We should give it up.'

'You're right, Bern. That had to be about eight years ago. We certainly proved him wrong,' I said with a smile.

'It's water under the bridge.' Bernie lifted his coffee cup. 'To the Queen.' I joined him in the toast. 'The Queen.'

That night, in between shows, we knocked on the door of the stars' dressing room and received a pleasant 'Come in' from the middle-aged lady who was Nina's dresser. Nina and Frederik, in expensive dressing gowns, sat drinking coffee. The room looked so different to ours. A vase filled with flowers and a bowl of fresh fruit sat on a fancy coffee table – not a part of the usual furniture of a dressing room.

We proceeded to tell them our good news. We also explained that unfortunately we would miss the Saturday performances in Liverpool. Nina understood. Driving overnight wasn't the wisest thing to do before such an important show. Frederik (we never called him Baron, and Fred just didn't sound right) didn't seem too pleased. Nevertheless, he smiled, offered congratulations and said something would be worked out.

The weeks went by in a flash. We were engrossed in preparing for the big night. Nina and Frederik were as friendly and charming as ever, and Bern and I couldn't have asked for a better run-in for the Variety Performance.

The audiences were just right. Not rock 'n' roll, not too old or stuffy. We kept trying new lines, and were getting close to deciding what material we would use.

The event was building up in our minds. It was hard to believe we were actually going to appear in front of the Queen. This was the genuine article. She was the Queen of England, and of a fair bit of the rest of the world too.

Lying in wait beneath the haze of glorious anticipation were the many inescapable details we had to take care of. Tickets! Joe warned us to arrange to get our personal tickets NOW. Suddenly, we discovered more relations than we knew existed, all wanting tickets for the royal show. Naturally, the tickets weren't free. Far from it. They were very expensive – it was for charity, after all. Not one relation mentioned paying for tickets. They didn't want to embarrass us. We were stars appearing at the London Palladium in front of the Queen. Many family members had been part of the fight game, and were used to getting complimentary tickets from boxing promoters, who were often close friends of the family. I could imagine my uncles discussing the thought of paying to see Bernie and me in a show – 'Offer my nephews money to watch them perform? Come on! They don't need my few quid. Would I ask them if it was me? Do me a favour! It's family.'

Then there were the expenses. Our musical arrangements needed to be reworked for the Palladium orchestra. We were recommended one of the best. He was. He was also one of the most expensive.

Without question, we needed new suits. We had always made certain we wore smart suits on stage. You dressed up not down in those days, and the theatre bookers were strict about it. When Cissie Williams, possibly the most powerful woman in the business, first came to watch us to see if we were good enough to play the prestigious Moss Empires, she told Evelyn Taylor, our agent at that time, 'I'm not mad about their act, but I have to book those suits.'

So we travelled back and forth to London for fittings. The West End tailor was busy. He didn't have a lot of time to finish our suits. But it was imperative they should be ready for the show. We turned his original high price into an astronomical one.

Our wives insisted we dress like stars. Naturally it followed that, as the wives of stars, they too needed to look good. We gave them no argument. This was going to be a night we would always remember.

As we approached D-Day, Bernie and I continually discussed the upcoming show. The material we had decided upon looked good. We were feeling reasonably confident, but we were relieved there wasn't another Royal Variety Performance in the year. We didn't think we could afford it!

The week before the performance, we received a letter from Joe Collins. Philip Solomon didn't want to release us on the Saturday night prior to the Palladium. We had signed a contract and he was keeping us to it. What about our appearance before the Queen? Solomon didn't want to know. It wasn't his problem.

We got Joe Collins on the phone. I asked Joe what would happen if we just didn't turn up for the Liverpool show.

'You could be sued for breach of contract, but between ourselves, what he'll get won't be worth a cold cup of tea. No one is going to ask for their money back if you two aren't on the show. Let's be honest, who knows you?' Being subtle wasn't one of Joe's strong points.

He continued, 'Don't worry too much about it. I don't think he'll take you to court. Worst comes to worst, he'll put in one of his own acts for the night as a replacement, bump up their salary, which they won't get, and you'll have to pay for it.'

'What kind of money do you think that would be?' Bernie asked.

'About a quarter of your salary. Maybe a little more. What can you do? You signed the contract and you aren't fulfilling it. At least it's better than paying a lawyer. That could cost you a fortune. Just do well on the Royal Variety Performance. A few pounds one way or another won't mean anything.'

Oh really? A quarter of a salary we had already spent! Bernie and I grinned at each other. But we had no real money problems. We had work in the book, as they say in show biz. Joe was right. All we need worry about was the Royal Variety Performance.

The sky was overcast, and it was cold. A typical November morning in London. But it was far from a typical morning for me, because I was on my way to the London Palladium for the Royal Variety Performance.

My drive from Putney Hill, where Cassie and I lived with our sixteen-month-old daughter, Chaney, had been practically traffic free. The rehearsal call had been for ten o'clock. I arrived, after parking virtually across the road from the Palladium's stage door in Carnaby Street, at nine fifteen. Bernie was already there. He was always the first to arrive, and the first to leave. I have known him to wash and change so quickly he would leave at the end of the show the same time as the audience.

The stage door keeper – I would get to know him well during the pantomime season – told me which dressing room I was in. As I made my way down the corridor my heart was racing. Hard to believe I could be so nervous, but then again I knew I would be performing that evening in front of Her Majesty the Queen.

As soon as I met up with Bernie in the dressing room, though, I lost my nervousness, which was replaced by excited anticipation. We were sharing the room with four other artists: Dickie Henderson, Frank Ifield, Andy Stewart and Norman Vaughan. I knew them all personally except Andy, who did most of his work in Scotland. Frank, an Australian, had done a four-month summer season with us in Jersey a couple of years back. Though he was unknown at the time, his hit record, 'I Remember You', had since catapulted him to incredible success.

I only knew Norman Vaughan slightly at the time, but we later became great mates. He, like Jimmy Tarbuck, could always make Cassie and me laugh. Dickie Henderson was from a famous theatrical family that included his sisters, the glamorous and talented Henderson Twins. Bern and I had worked with Dickie at the New Theatre, Cardiff, where he topped the bill. He was friendly, supportive and encouraging. Dickie and I got on well together.

Before our band rehearsal, Bern and I sat in the stalls listening to Cleo Laine run through her music. We had known Cleo early in her career and were fans. Soon it was time for our 'band call'. The conductor of the orchestra – it was too big to call it a band – was Jack Parnell, the former drummer of the great Ted Heath Band. Bernie and I had done a television show with the band about four years earlier on the first teenage-targeted TV series, *Six-Five Special*. After a warm greeting, Jack counted in the orchestra to start our dance music. We hardly recognised it, it sounded so good. The song 'On the Sunny Side of the Street' was normally played by a provincial theatre pit band of seven or eight musicians. This was the Palladium Orchestra, with seventeen or so top musicians. The musicians sight-read the arrangement perfectly, and Jack got them to master the two difficult tempo changes in our routine with only one extra run through.

We would do our full routine for the lighting and TV cameras later, but there wasn't anything more for us to do for at least a couple of hours. We stood in the wings as Eartha Kitt began to go through her music. It sounded great. But we couldn't hang out in the wings for long. Should we go across the road to the Italian cafe at the top of Carnaby Street for a cup of tea, or join Frank Ifield and Cliff Richard who were sitting in the front of the stalls, watching the band call while awaiting their turn? Our decision was made for us when our dad quietly walked up behind us and put his arms on our shoulders. 'Hello, boys. How's it going?'

Was I surprised? Yes and no. He had told us he would drop in for a minute during the morning, although Bernie and I knew his minute could mean the whole morning. But what did surprise me was how he got backstage.

'How d'you get in?' Bernie asked after we'd both given Dad a quick hug.

'No problem. I just gave the stage door keeper a friendly nod and walked right in. Mind you, it helped that Harry Secombe and a couple of fellers were going in at the same time,' he said with a grin.

I could understand why the stage door man hadn't stopped Dad. Only five foot eight, but solidly built, he wasn't the kind of man you would want to pull up. He was wearing his expensive raglan sleeve raincoat – we rarely saw him in an overcoat. His grey trilby was pulled down slightly over one eye, and a cigarette dangled from his lips. He looked the type of man who knew his way around.

We thought we would show him around backstage. Rosemary Clooney and her musical director stood talking outside the dressing room she shared with Sophie Tucker and film actress Edie Adams. Sophie Tucker had been the favourite of our late mother, who had died just a couple of years before. As we passed, they looked up and gave us a friendly 'Hi'. Bernie and I said 'Hi' back, with a broad smile, and moved on. Not Dad. Over he went and introduced himself.

'Hey, boys, come here,' he called out after a minute. Over we went, and like two schoolboys we stood there as Dad introduced us. Rosemary was absolutely charming. 'I did a sister act, you know, when I started. Although we weren't real sisters. Not like you two guys.'

'We're not sisters either,' I said. Everyone laughed. Dad asked her if she had any children.

'Yes, I do. I have five.' She smiled at our surprise. She looked so trim, so young.

'Five kids, eh!' Bernie said, adding, with his goofy face on. 'Do you have any other hobbies?'

'Hey, Buster, that's Bob Hope's line!' It was smiles all round.

We took Dad for a cuppa at the Italian cafe across the road. Then Bern and I went back to run through our routine. Dad lit up yet another cigarette – he smoked around eighty a day – and went home via Oxford Street Underground. He'd see us later, after the show. Dad's visit and the chat with Rosemary Clooney had jazzed us up. We were ready for the show right then and there.

Our run-through went really well. We even had the band laughing. The dress rehearsal went even better. There were a few people sitting in the stalls, including a couple of reporters, who would give their reviews on this dress performance and not bother to attend the evening show. We got a few laughs. Quite an achievement making members of the press laugh, but our high spirits were short lived. As we sat in the dressing room after the dress show talking to Andy Stewart and Dickie Henderson, the producer's assistant came into the room with a message for us.

'Mike, Bernie. Mr Nesbitt would like a word with you.' We followed him back to the centre of the stalls, where legendary producer Robert Nesbitt sat with his secretary behind a table-like contraption which had been set up across the back of the seats in front of him. On top of the makeshift table top stood an ice bucket holding a bottle of vintage champagne, a dirty ashtray, a clipboard, and a hand microphone that enabled him to call out lighting and stage instructions. He put down his champagne glass and gave us a quick smile. We stood awkwardly in front of him with our backs to the stage, where the Great Magyar Pusztal Troupe, in full costume, were marking moves while stage hands busied themselves clearing the stage.

'Ah! Boys,' the great man began as he watched the stage with half an eye. 'Just a couple of notes for you. You'll have to cut the reference to Jack Parnell's ears. It might upset deaf people. And . . .' He stopped, distracted by something he'd seen on stage. 'That trick there. They'll close on that. It'll save a minute or so,' he said to his secretary, who made a note on her board. He turned his eyes back to us. 'That Roger Moore gag is out. Too blue. You don't need it.'

'But, Mr Nesbitt, that gag leads us into the Spanish routine,' I said, not quite controlling my frustration.

'My dear boy, you can't do that Spanish line about virgins in front of a royal audience. So, that line is out. It's an old gag anyway, boys. Better off without it. Was that it?' he asked his secretary.

She flipped a page and looked at her notes. 'Nothing else,' she told him.

'Right. Thank you, boys. You'll do fine. Good luck tonight.'

We were dismissed. Mr Nesbitt was a man of excellent taste and an expert at his craft, a gentleman of the old school. I liked him. But not at that moment when he cut our material.

The Jack Parnell 'ears' bit was designed to establish Bernie immediately as a buffoon. As I started to say 'Good evening', Bernie would point down at Jack, who was wearing prominent earphones to keep contact with the television director, and would say, 'Hello, Jack. You've done well. Big band. They all work for you.' Bernie was going to point to the earphones and say, 'Sorry about your ears. I hope they get better. Can you hear me all right?' How could that offend anyone?

Admittedly, the Roger Moore gag was kind of risqué:

Mike: When I travel to New York, I always stay at the Plaza.
Bernie: So do I. Last time, Roger Moore the famous actor was staying in the next room.
Mike: Are you sure?
Bernie: Yes. All night long I heard the girl in the next room calling out, 'Roger, more. Roger, more.'

And as for the Virgin Islands gag? You decide:

Mike: I have travelled extensively. Where have you ever been?
Bernie: I've been to the Sandwich Islands. I didn't find any sandwiches. Went to the Canary Islands. Didn't find any canaries. Went to the Virgin Islands, Didn't find any –'
Mike: Stop! I'm not interested.

Too blue? Anyway, it was cut. We were aware that once the cameras were on us, nobody could censor our routine. But, if Mr Nesbitt or Bernard Delfont so ordered, our entire routine could be edited out of the television broadcast. Even worse, we would have made enemies of two of the most influential men in show business.

So we had a problem. Our whole routine needed new material. Our total spot was only six minutes. The dance routine was three, leaving three minutes to get laughs. It was enough time, but it had to be smooth. We didn't do one joke after another like a solo act. We had to have a subject, a continuous thread. Ours had been travel. That's why we had the gags about Roger Moore in a New York hotel, and Bernie visiting the Virgin Islands.

Bernie and I spent the next couple of hours rearranging our 'spot'. All references to Jack Parnell's ears were out, as were the Roger Moore and Virgin Islands gags. We replaced them with a routine in which I showed off how fluent I was in French, while Bernie pretended to both speak and understand it. There was no punch line; the laughs, hopefully, would come from the conflict between my arrogance and Bernie's lovable ignorance. At least it was clean!

We were on early, the first comics in the show. Somewhat of a warm-up act, so to speak. The first two acts received polite applause, as did Cleo Laine and Johnny Dankworth, who immediately preceded us. Under normal circumstances they would have wowed the audience. But a Royal Variety Performance isn't normal. The audience were so conscious of being in the presence of the Queen that they spent nearly as much time watching her reaction to the artists as they did watching the artists themselves.

Then it was our turn. Our music began. We said a quick prayer to our late mother, as we always did. Then, with pumping hearts, we strode on to the stage. For the first minute, the audience treated us with the utmost respect. No distracting whispering, no excessive coughing, no giggling – certainly no giggling. There wasn't even a rumour of a laugh. Our opening routine consisted of Bernie, standing slightly behind me, continually interrupting me by repeating everything I said, then apologising profusely each time I told him not to do it. Behind my back he would confidentially tell the audience I was 'sensitive' and 'rinsed my hair', asking them 'not to upset me'.

We had done this opening many times. It always got laughs. Maybe not big laughs, but some. Not this time. The audience reacted as if we were acting the death scene from Shakespeare's *Romeo and Juliet*.

As we got into our French routine, however, the good Lord was kind to us. The smiling Queen leaned forward and laughed. When the audience saw this, they too began laughing. It wasn't a roar, or a swell, but it was laughter.

The dance routine went very well. Perhaps the audience were relieved to see we had some tangible talent, or were just pleased to see us finish. Who knows? We didn't care why they applauded, as long as they did. We left the Palladium stage, perhaps not as conquerors, but definitely not defeated.

Back in the dressing room, Dickie Henderson, Frank Ifield and Andy Stewart gave us a 'Well done' and a thumbs-up. Andy then went one better. He poured two large measures from a nearly full bottle of whisky. 'Yew deserrve a drrink, lads. They were bloody tough, but ya gottem in the end,' he said in his thick Scottish accent. He poured himself a small one, a little courage before he entered the arena. 'Come on, lads, drrink up. It's good. It's from the Heelands. To the Queen.'

We raised our glasses for the toast and took a large swig. Bernie and I were both whisky drinkers, and had been known to down a few after work. I say 'whisky drinkers' – this was one hundred per cent fire water!

We sat watching the show on the small dressing room TV. After each act finished, Andy suggested we toast their health, to which we readily agreed. When he went to stand by for his performance, he left us the bottle. It was a long show with many performers. The other occupants of the dressing room only had one or two drinks, while Andy seemed unaffected by the whisky. But as the evening wore on, Bernie and I grew more and more sloshed.

The show was coming to an end. It was time for the finale. The performers lined up across the large Palladium stage in a straight line, with the dancers behind them, for the ensemble curtain call and the bow to the royal box. The best-known stars stood in the centre of the long line, the lesser names on the edges. Bernie and I were on the extreme end of the line, the side furthest away from the Queen. I didn't mind. The whisky had relaxed me. Some drinkers who have had a tad too much become all floppy, others act as if they have a stiff back and neck. Bernie had taken on the latter set of characteristics. His body was rigid as his eyes unwaveringly stared at the royal box. A smile was fixed on his face. I was sober enough to know that he was not.

The curtain fell. It was over. But no, not quite. Bill Mathews, the stage manager, came over and told us we were to be presented to the Queen. We were to go through the backstage pass door into the theatre and wait on the stairs leading to the circle and the boxes. Someone would be there to show us exactly where we were to stand.

'Great,' Bernie enthused. 'We're going to meet the Queen, Mike. I thought she liked us. Come on, let's go.'

Bill Mathews studied Bernie. 'Are you all right?'

'Right as rain,' Bernie answered, smiling happily.

'Good,' Bill said seriously. 'Now pay attention, I'm going to tell you how to address Her Majesty,'

'Address her? We're not going to post her, are we?' Bernie said giggling.

I told Bernie to be quiet and listen to what Bill had to say. Bernie became all attentive, putting on a false look of concentration. Bill explained: 'When you first meet the Queen, call her "Your Majesty". Thereafter – if there is a thereafter and she speaks to you – call her "Ma'am", pronounced "Marm". Got it?' We quickly repeated the instructions, and off we went.

I watched the royal party as they came down the stairs. The Queen stopped and had a few words with Cliff Richard, then moved on to spend a moment with legendary band leader Edmundo Ros. The party reached juggler Rudy Cardenas, and Her Majesty spoke briefly with him.

She was so close. She was smaller and far prettier than I had thought, and had a great figure. Prince Philip was much taller than I realised, and he too was better looking in the flesh than in photographs. Bernie, standing next to me, one step down, followed the Queen's advance, his smile seemingly permanently engraved on his face. As the royal group reached me, I wet my lips and took a deep breath.

Bernard Delfont made the introduction. I smiled and said, 'Your Majesty,' and bowed my head slightly.

'You have a good French accent,' she said smiling. She had a beautiful smile; in fact, she was an extremely beautiful woman.

'Thank you, Ma'am,' I answered, pronouncing it 'Marm' as instructed.

'Do you speak French?' she asked.

'Not as well as I would like to.'

'I know what you mean,' she said with a smile. Bernard Delfont moved closer to her side. It was time to go. She gave a charming nod of her head, smiled again, and moved on with Delfont at her side. Prince Philip, and the Marquis and Marquess of Milford Haven, who made up the royal party, followed on.

Bernie was waiting, his smile still fixed on his face like a scar. He had eyes only for the Queen.

Bernard Delfont duly introduced Bernie, whose joy was palpable. With great enthusiasm he said, 'Hello, Your Worship.'

I didn't know whether to laugh or cry. Should I say something? I looked at the Queen's face. She was smiling good-naturedly. Thank goodness. Delfont shook his head in amusement. Prince Philip frowned, the Marquis and Marquess looked puzzled. I must have looked relieved.

'Your brother told me he speaks French. Do you speak any foreign languages?' Queen Elizabeth asked.

'No, Mum. I have enough problems speaking English proper. . . I mean properly.'

The Queen and Delfont couldn't help laughing. Bernie's obvious pleasure at meeting the Queen was completely disarming. Ma'am. Mum. In one way, a flattering mix-up. Bernie's next remarks brought smiles to the whole royal party.

'We're working here this Christmas,' he said, pointing to a poster displayed on the wall at the bottom of the stairs. 'We're in pantomime, *Puss in Boots*. You should bring the kids.'

The Queen smiled kindly. Delfont moved in closer and murmured, 'Ma'am.' That was the code for 'Let's move on.' Before they did so, Bernie gave what I considered to be the funniest, most outrageous, but well-intentioned remark of all. He leaned in towards the Queen, and said confidentially, 'I'll get you tickets.'

The memorable evening came to an end. What with the excitement and the whisky, Bernie and I were absolutely exhausted. Cassie and I said our goodnights and went home. She made us an omelette sandwich, I poured her a glass of champagne and myself a large whisky, and we toasted the Queen. It had been quite a night.

The next day I bought the daily newspapers looking for reviews. I feared the worst. That first minute without laughs stuck in my mind. I needn't have worried. Most papers didn't even mention Bernie and me, and the one that did had reviewed the dress rehearsal. 'Mike and Bernie Winters had the orchestra laughing at rehearsal. I tip them to be the surprise hit of this year's Royal Variety Performance.'

His prediction was wrong – we weren't the hit of the show by any means. But we were happy to settle for doing OK. Our wives insisted we had been successful, and that was important to us. Bernie and I thought the Queen had liked us. I guess she must have, as we were invited to appear in front of her again, though we had to decline as we were going to be in Australia. I was very disappointed. I would have liked to have once again met Her Worship.

3

Mike and Dud: Dudley Moore

Bob Hope was an American superstar, but he was born in Eltham, on the outskirts of London. He belonged to the exclusive group of English comedians who have become not only international stars, but American icons. Charlie Chaplin, a Londoner by birth, and Lancastrian Stan Laurel are two who come to mind.

There have been other English comedians and comedy actors who have been successful in the United States, in both television and movies, stars like John Cleese, Ricky Gervais, Eddie Izzard, Billy Connelly and Rowan Atkinson. And TV shows like *Are You Being Served* and *Keeping Up Appearances* – still shown in America – are very popular, though perhaps the most popular of all has been the Benny Hill Show.

I knew Benny well. Bernie and I worked with him, and he was a very nice fellow. I have never met Ricky Gervais or Rowan Atkinson, but I did meet John Cleese years ago at the start of his incredible success. I told him he was the second funniest comedian in Britain – the first being my brother Bernie. John smiled and thanked me. He knew I was serious.

Dudley Moore, in my opinion, could have reached the exalted status of Bob Hope, but his career was cut short by illness and an untimely death. I regret I never got to know Bob, although he was a fellow Water Rat. However, I was fortunate enough to know 'Cuddly Dudley', the main character in my next story. It begins in London...

Dudley Moore and I could have been great friends. Don't get me wrong, we were friendly, but we never really got to know each other. It wasn't our fault, just circumstances.

We had a lot in common, and in the Seventies when I grew my hair long people thought we looked alike. We were both dark, the shorter member of a comedy duo, and – excuse my blushes – kind of cute. Admittedly, there was a difference in our heights; I was taller by about seven inches. But as far as the public was concerned we were both known as the 'little one' of the act.

In our youth, Dud and I had trodden a similar path. Dud won a scholarship to study music and piano at Magdalen College, Oxford. I attended the City of Oxford School, and won a scholarship to the Royal Academy of Music, London, to study clarinet. Although both of us were classically trained, we played jazz, and earned a living playing in jazz clubs at some time in our lives, though never together.

And when we did eventually meet, we found we shared a penchant for pretty girls and fast cars.

Dud and I met at an afternoon cocktail party thrown by a model agency for a trendy designer whose name completely escapes me. I had been given an invitation the previous night at Ronnie Scott's Jazz Club by my old pal, Ronnie himself, who couldn't make it. It was at the Valbonne Club, one o'clock to four.

I knew the Valbonne well. It was owned by my good friend Louis Browne, also known as Louis Curzon, a photographer of lovely young socialites and beautiful models. A tough job, but someone had to do it!

I figured the press would be there, but it wasn't the thought of the press that enticed me to go. I never sought publicity; in fact I mostly tried to avoid it. The press was never too kind to Bernie and me. The reason I decided to go was because my wife Cassie had gone to Malta with my son and daughter for ten days. I hadn't been able to go with them because at the last minute Bernie and I were offered a week in cabaret in Sheffield. I had two days and nights to wait before Cassie and the kids got back. I was on my own. So, last night it had been Ronnie Scott's, and today it was a cocktail party!

The party was much as expected. The cocktail turned out to be wine – never a martini, Manhattan or genuine exotic cocktail in sight – and the people there were only interested in their own business. For the first fifteen minutes or so, people spoke to me, some a little impressed by my TV reputation, but once they established I was nothing to do with the fashion industry their interest in me evaporated.

I said 'Hi' to Anne Scott (no relation to Ronnie), organiser of the fashion parade that was to take place. She smiled pleasantly, but was quickly swamped by well-wishers, sycophants and business associates, which made conversation impossible. I eyed the pretty ladies floating around, and saw one or two famous footballers doing the same. Good-looking girls in provocative costumes walked round offering tasty hors d'oeuvres from small, round trays, while husky young men, maybe male models picking up a little extra cash, wearing tight, black trousers, white shirts and black bow ties, circulated the room carrying glasses of red and white wine on substantial oblong trays.

The large room featured a bandstand, a tiny lake with a live alligator swimming in it, and a smallish dance floor which, at night, would be packed with beautiful people doing the latest moves to the current disco hits. The back of the room was dominated by an elegant bar and tables covered by plum-coloured tablecloths, while a few plum-coloured booths made up the dining area. They were all taken.

Louis Browne's table was slightly elevated and tucked away in a corner, from which the whole dining area could be observed. I saw Louis sitting talking to a familiar face. I went over to my old friend, who was very pleased to see me, but surprised I had never met his companion, another well-known entertainer. He introduced me to Dudley Moore.

Outside the club, the March afternoon was bright and invigorating, but inside it was like a midnight carnival, the darkness punctuated by coloured lights. Loud music, not quite drowning the high level of conversation, encouraged some couples – the men in bell bottoms, the women in mini skirts – to disco dance.

We managed to talk above the noise. The subject was motor cars. As it turned out, all three of us loved fast, stylish, well-designed cars. At that particular time I owned a Jenson Interceptor, while Dudley had a Maserati. 'The lines of a car are like the lines of a woman. When they are right it is a thing of beauty,' Louis opined.

'The roar of a V8 engine has the power of Beethoven's Fifth Symphony,' Dudley observed.

'Pulling away at four-point-nine seconds to sixty mph has the exhilaration and passion of Artie Shaw's clarinet solo on "Stardust",' I claimed. It all sounded fascinating to us. By that time Louis had ordered champagne for Dudley and himself, and a whisky for me. We were on our second glass – or was it our third?

As the fashion show was about to begin Louis left us to be introduced. 'Do you want to me to mention you're here?' he asked. Dud and I shook our heads, and answered, 'No. Thank you, but no.'

Photographers were busy snapping away, garbled voices came over the microphone from the stage. The fashion show ended, guests were beginning to leave, but Dud and I were too engrossed in analysing the pros and cons of the Ferrari – a car I've never driven, at that time or since – to notice.

As the afternoon wore on Dudley and I began talking comedy. Understandably, our tastes were different, as evidenced by the styles of our acts. Pete and Dud were part of the new wave of comedy, like Monty Python. They acted, playing funny characters in sketches. Bernie and I were from the traditional school of duos: a slick, know-it-all straight man and a simple, lovable buffoon who always triumphed in the end.

In spite of our differences, though, we both thought Ken Dodd a unique stage talent. We enjoyed the television comedy of Leonard Rossiter and Stanley Baxter, and thought Kenneth Horne's *Round the Horne* radio show very funny. We agreed that Jack Benny was the greatest all-rounder, a master of the four main show business media – stage, movies, radio and television. Dudley's favourite medium was movies, an apt choice considering the success he made in it. I voted for the stage.

We could have spent the whole evening discussing show biz, but we had to talk about jazz too. On that subject we were practically on the same page. We both admired Errol Garner, while Dud loved Oscar Peterson. I was a fan too, but preferred the delicate style of Bill Evans. Dudley liked the more modern clarinettists; Buddy De Franco was mentioned. I had no problem with that, but I loved Artie Shaw and Benny Goodman.

Louis came back to join us and we suddenly realised the club was empty. He generously asked if we wanted anything. 'Thanks, Louis, for the champers. The time's just flown,' Dud said. He added, grinning, 'I gotta go. Gotta meet Suzy. Mike, it's been a pleasure. Pity we couldn't find anything to talk about.'

I felt sure Dudley and I would bump into each other again in the near future, perhaps at some showbiz function. But it didn't happen. It was about five years before I set eyes on him again.

I had been living in Miami Beach for three years, trying – without much success – to make my mark as a writer. I had read of Dudley's break-up with his partner, Peter Cook. By that time Bernie and I had broken up too, so I knew how emotionally tough it could be.

But by then Dudley had gone on to become an internationally famous film actor.

I can't say I was surprised at Dudley's success. When I saw him in an earlier film, *Foul Play*, starring Goldie Hawn, playing only a supporting role, he was magic. And who could have played opposite the gorgeous Bo Derek in *10* better than Dudley? No one.

His mega hit, *Arthur*, came out in 1981. After seeing it at least two or three times, my son Anthony became a fanatical Dudley Moore fan. I had no idea how that would come back to haunt me!

The following year, Dudley's latest movie, *Six Weeks*, co-starring Mary Tyler Moore, was being premiered in selected cities across America. Miami Beach was one such city. Anthony had read that the star of *Arthur* was going to be staying at the Fontainebleau Hotel the following day. I realised the mistake I had made in mentioning to my son that I knew the film's star when he insisted I take him to meet Dudley Moore.

I pointed out that tomorrow was a school day. Anthony brushed that off. 'I'll take the day off,' he told me. Should I be strict and insist he go to school, I asked myself. I decided to consult Cassie, who said, 'If you don't take him, he'll only go to the hotel and try to see his idol anyway.' I was unconvinced until she added, 'Just imagine it was a rugby international, England versus Australia, and your dad could take you to meet the players.'

So I told Anthony I would take him. We would leave for the hotel at around ten in the morning. That evening Anthony went out with his pals, no doubt telling them his dad was a pal of Dudley Moore and was taking him to meet Dudley tomorrow in person.

I felt kind of pleased with myself that my son could brag about his dad's connections. I didn't have the slightest doubt that Dudley would remember me and I would have no problem in seeing him.

The following morning around ten, as I was saying goodbye to Cassie, the doorbell rang. Anthony, who had been ready for at least two hours, rushed to open it. He quickly returned with a thin, tallish youth of similar age to himself. My son calmly said, 'Dad, this is Kevin. He's coming with us. He doesn't believe you know Dudley Moore.'

'Really Kevin, that's nice. Why bother to come then?' I asked with a tight smile.

'Oh, he's joking.' Cassie said sweetly.

'No I'm not,' Kevin said in a nauseating nasal whine.

'Ha ha,' Cassie laughed. 'Have fun. Bye,' she said ushering us out.

At the Fontainebleau, the valet took my Pontiac Trans Am Firebird, with twin removable sun tops. Kevin wasn't impressed with the car. He said, 'I woulda thought you'd have a Rolls or Jaguar.' I wasn't too keen on Kevin.

At reception, I asked to be put through to Mr Moore's room, only to be told he wasn't taking any calls. Explaining that I was an old friend from England, I was informed again that Mr Moore was not taking any calls. I tried one more time as Anthony and Kevin moved ever closer to me, listening to every word: 'Would you try to reach one of the management team, please.' After a moment on the house phone, the reception clerk told me the line was busy and had been for at least the past half-hour. He added that it was like a mad house up there. Maybe I should come back in an hour. Things should have quieted down.

I moved away from the counter and tried to think of a plan. I heard Kevin tell Anthony, 'I told you he doesn't know Dudley.' The only plan that came to mind was to throttle Kevin.

'Let's go and get a Coke or something. We'll come back in a little while. We have lots of time,' I told them with forced joviality.

'Why don't we go straight up to his room? If you know him, he'll want to see you, won't he?' Kevin said with a supercilious smirk. I hated to admit it, but the obnoxious boy had a point. I went back to the reception desk and spoke to the same clerk as before, with Anthony and Kevin in close support.

'Excuse me,' I began politely. 'Could I have Mr Moore's room number, please?'

'We are not giving out that information, sir.'

'Well, how can I let him know I am here? I'm a close friend.'

The desk clerk nodded patiently. 'Where is your pass, sir?'

'I don't have one. I didn't know I was coming.' I couldn't hide the frustration in my voice.

I turned and glared at the large woman crowding me from behind. The whole reception area was packed. 'Come back later,' the clerk said, moving away.

I pushed through the crowded area with my two young, equally frustrated companions on my heels. I stopped once we had space and said in a voice that advised no argument, 'We're going for a Coke. I have to think.'

'He doesn't know him. I told you. Where's his pass?' Kevin said to Anthony in a half whisper. But I heard him. I stared right at him and said, 'Listen Kevin, I bloody well do know Dudley Moore, and before this bloody day is over I will prove it. Until then, you keep your bloody remarks to yourself. Understood?'

Kevin shrugged nonchalantly and said, 'OK,' with complete indifference. I felt sympathy for his teachers at school.

'Let's go and get that Coke,' I said. The hotel coffee shop was full, so we went to the pool area where the boys had Cokes and I had a coffee. Kevin leaned closer to Anthony and in the half-whisper technique he knew I could hear, said he was hungry. Pretending I hadn't heard, I suggested they go and look around the pool area and then we'd grab some lunch. That went down well. There were lots of good-looking girls hanging around at the pool.

After shooting my mouth off to Kevin about how I would prove by the end of the day that I knew Dudley, I had to do some serious thinking. I couldn't let my son down. How could I get a pass? Who would be allowed in? Who did I know who could help? Who had clout? I racked my brains. Suddenly, I had an idea.

The boys arrived back. Now they weren't just hungry, their short walk had morphed their mild hunger into raving starvation. I gave

Anthony twenty dollars and told him to go to the snack bar and get a couple of hamburgers, French fries, hot dogs. I'd see them in five minutes or so. I had to make a phone call.

I quickly found the line of telephones. Within no time I was through to the *British Tourist*, a local newspaper owned by my British friends John and Irene Bell. A one-time reporter for the *Daily Mail*, and deputy editor of two leading tabloids – the *National Inquirer* and the *Globe* – John was now proud owner and lead writer for the *British Tourist*, the premier newspaper for the vast British tourism business in Florida. I was in luck. John was in, and I was put through to him immediately. I explained my predicament. He wanted to know why I hadn't used my press credentials.

Many years ago, before my showbiz career took off, I'd briefly been a cub reporter on the *North London Observer*. I had to smile as I told him. 'John, it's over thirty years since I was a reporter. Even if I still had my press card I doubt if it would be accepted as anything but an historical document. Now, John, can you get me out of trouble? I've got to get in to see Dudley.'

I listened to what he had to say, only interrupting once, 'Of course I know him.' Then I added, 'Don't you start about if I really know Dudley. I've had enough trouble with Kevin, Anthony's school friend. Can you help me?'

His answer was encouraging, but I said nothing when I went back to the boys. They were stuck into their hamburgers, the French fries piled high, dollops of tomato sauce laid thick on the side of the plates, and both had a large Coke at their elbow. It smelt great. I excused myself and headed for the snack bar, returning with a cheeseburger, fries, lots of tomato sauce, a pickled cucumber and another large Coke. The boys had finished eating when I got back to the table.

'Shouldn't we get back to the reception now?' Kevin asked Anthony. I was eating my cheeseburger but I jumped in to answer. 'As soon as I'm finished, Kevin,' I answered with my mouth still full.

I looked at my watch. I still had half an hour to kill. 'Could you get me a coffee, Anthony?' I asked, handing him a five-dollar bill.

As he got up to leave, Kevin had something to say. 'What about Dudley Moore? When are we gonna see about that? You said we would meet him. That's what you said.'

'He's right, Dad. That's what you said.' Now Anthony was teaming up against me.

'Do me a favour, just get me the coffee. You'll meet Dudley, don't worry about it.'

I was playing for time as I secretly prayed John would come through for me. Fortunately, Kevin went with Anthony for the coffee so I didn't have to look at his nasty, suspicious face. Was I being unfair? Probably, I told myself. In a couple of year's time I would look back on this and laugh.

When the boys returned, I casually drank my coffee, ignoring the silent pressure emanating from them. Finally, my cup was empty. I could delay no longer. Hopefully John would not be late.

Anthony and Kevin eagerly walked ahead towards the reception desk, occasionally stopping to turn and check if I was still behind them, silently urging me to hurry. At the reception area, I stopped and looked around. The two lads eyed me with suspicion, no doubt wondering what I was up to. I looked at my watch. John was late. Only a few minutes, but a minute was a long time. I didn't think I had a minute before Kevin or Anthony would ask again, 'When are we going to meet Dudley Moore?'

Seconds before disaster struck, the cavalry arrived. Coming through the large, glass automatic doors strode renowned newspaperman John Bell. 'Sorry I'm late. Let's get going,' John said as we quickly shook hands. He immediately went to the now quiet reception desk, with me and the boys on his heels.

'Press,' he told the receptionist – a different clerk from the one I had spoken to – flashing his open wallet. 'I've got a promotional interview with Dudley Moore and the kids.' He jabbed his thumb in our direction. 'What floor?'

'Five,' the clerk answered, glancing at the press pass on display in the wallet. 'You'll go through security on the floor.'

'Right. Let's go,' he added to us as he set off for the lifts.

The boys were excited but silent, in awe of John's authority. On the fifth floor, two police officers were waiting at the top of the corridor. John walked straight towards them, wallet out and open. He paused as he reached them.

'Press. The kids are doing a publicity interview. What's the room number?'

'You'll see a cop outside the door. Show the card and go right in. There are still a lot of folks in there. Have a nice day.'

There was no problem at the door. We were in. The large, beautifully furnished room was only part of a magnificent suite. To our right, tables were spread with a bountiful buffet, making me wish I hadn't eaten the cheeseburger. To the left was a line of about thirty people, mostly kids, queuing to be photographed with Dudley, whose diminutive figure stood at the top of the line in front of a large poster promoting his current movie. He was practically surrounded by associates and bodyguards.

The two boys stood as if hypnotised, peering at the barely visible actor.

'Go on, join the queue. Get your photo taken,' I told the boys. John and I watched them join the end of the line.

'They're the final two,' John observed. 'We got here just in time. Let's eat something. I didn't get time for lunch. Had to meet you,' he said, giving me a wry grin.

While John ate, I took a quick minute to open a door behind the buffet table and take a peek inside. It was a gorgeous bedroom, one of two in the suite. No one seemed to notice me and I went and joined John. I couldn't resist taking a plate from the table and helping myself to a portion of smoked salmon.

Anthony and Kevin were nearly finished. First, a beaming Anthony stood next to Dudley while the photographer did his job. With what looked to be a genuine smile, Dudley shook my son's hand. Then the photographer handed the instant photograph to Anthony, who stood to the side to wait for his friend. It was the same routine for Kevin, but Kevin didn't beam, he looked shell-shocked. He quickly snapped out of it as he and Anthony, proudly holding their photographs and giggling together, made their way back to John and me. I saw Dudley exhale in relief. I guessed he must have been doing this photo routine all morning.

The two boys happily showed us their photographs. John suggested we leave. 'OK guys, time to go.' I said. The boys looked at each other and began whispering. This time, Kevin made sure I couldn't hear by stepping back a little. The conference ended and Anthony said, 'Dad, you haven't spoken to Dudley. Kevin still doesn't believe you know him.'

He had a point. If I knew Dud I should at least say hello. I looked over towards Dudley, who stood talking to a couple of executive types. Close to him was a large residue of kids who were reluctant to go home. The scene looked daunting, but not too daunting. I had to go over. I needed to get my proof. I began walking towards Dudley. Naturally, Anthony and Kevin were only a breath behind me.

I was close enough to touch him. He had his back to me as he listened to one of the executive types. There was a slight pause in the conversation. I grabbed the opportunity. 'Excuse me, Dudley,' I said. He turned round. His face registered surprise. For a moment his mouth fell open. 'What the fuck are you doing here?' he said as he broke into a big smile.

'I live here.'

'Here in Miami? Great. I mean, what are you doing here, like now? You should have let me know. Why didn't you call me here at the hotel?'

'Ah! Therein lies a story. You were harder to get to see than the Pope.'

'This bleedin' security! I'm frightened to go for a pee in case I can't get back in. So, you live in the Sunshine State, eh? No wonder you're so dark. You look like the Indian owner of my local Seven Eleven store. What car you driving, Mike?'

'A Trans Am with T. Tops.'

'Hmmm! I'm thinking of getting a Corvette.'

At that moment one of the executives pushed in, pointing his index finger at his watch. I took the hint. 'I have to go. I know you must be knackered, but can I introduce you to my son. He's a big fan of yours. Dudley, this is Anthony.'

I introduced Kevin too, who was so excited he could hardly speak, although he managed to ask Dudley to sign his photograph. Anthony made the same request and Dudley obliged. The kids near the scene followed suit, and before we knew it Dudley was mobbed by kids thrusting their photographs at him.

Dudley found a moment to look up at me. His expression was one of humour and mock horror. Needless to say, I gathered my group and got the hell out of there.

I wrote Dud a humorous letter thanking him for his time, and apologising for the extra work we had caused. He replied in kind, writing that he had suffered with a nightmare that night – he was being chased by thousands of zombie-like kids who were trying to get him to sign their photographs.

It made me smile. Zombie-like kids! I pictured Kevin.

We never met again. Our lives now had little in common. If Dudley had visited Miami again I'm sure we'd have got together. I most certainly would have called him if I had visited Hollywood, but I never did.

I read of his illness and subsequent death with a heavy heart. Although we weren't what one would call close, I felt very sad at his passing away. I wish I had known him better. I will always think we could have been great friends.

4

Making a Good Impression: Cary Grant

How have I managed to meet so many celebrities? Well, if you go to clubs, restaurants and parties where celebs hang out, you're in with a chance. If you happen to work with them then you've got it made. And it doesn't hurt to be a celeb yourself. Who knows, they may want to meet you!

I always wanted to meet Gareth Edwards. To the uninitiated, Gareth was one of the greatest rugby players of all time. About forty years ago I eventually did meet him. I was introduced to him in a club in Wales where Bernie and I were appearing. After our performance we went for a nightcap to one of the less busy bars, where – unknown to us – Gareth and a few rugby mates were having a drink. One of his party asked us for our autographs, and I noticed Gareth standing there. I wasted no time, and introductions were made.

To me he was a legend – a superhuman giant of immense courage, outstanding skills and unbelievable strength. But when we met I found him quietly spoken, unassuming and, surprisingly, only my height, although far more powerfully built. We chatted for a while; then, after handshakes all round, Gareth and his band of fellow rugby players moved on to another club and another bar. I doubt if Gareth remembers the event as clearly as I do...I'm not the greatest scrum-half Gareth ever saw play!

I met Cary Grant, the subject of my next story, in a rather unusual way. It was in a theatre, but we weren't working together. I had been a fan since I was a kid, but I never thought I would get to know him, let alone call him a friend.

Cary's showbiz career was ending and mine was just making its mark. I knew I would never reach the same dizzying heights of fame and success that he had attained, but then, very few did. And as Cary once said to Bernie and me as we discussed why we ended up in show business, 'I don't think fame was the spur, it was the desire to partic-ipate and earn a living doing it.'

For many years, there have been rumours and gossip about Cary's sex life. Had he swung both ways? Who cared? Certainly not Bernie or me. What goes on in the bedroom is private – that's why you close the bedroom door! But I digress. Let me tell you how I first met Cary...

L ike lots of kids who end up on the stage I did impressions. Radio was the easiest and certainly the cheapest way to hear famous voices, but I was a fan of the movies and chose to imitate the voices of famous film stars, greats like James Stewart, James Cagney, Edward G. Robinson – and Cary Grant.

It didn't bother me that nearly every other kid who wanted to be a performer did the same impressions. Many did them far better than I did, although my Edward G. was pretty good. He was one of my two favourites. The other one was Cary Grant.

When Bernie and I, still in our teens, began doing a double act, another of the impressions I did to fill in time was Frank Sinatra.

Way back in the Forties Sinatra was extremely thin. For my Sinatra impression, I was spotlighted in green, and would suck in my cheeks to look thinner. Bernie would take off my hat and stick it on top of the microphone (we both wore trilbies, an idea pinched from the top comedy team of our time, Jewel and Warriss). Bernie would then point at the microphone and announce, 'You've heard of Frank Sinatra, well, here's Stank Tomato.'

The music would begin. I adjusted the front of my hair, trying to copy Sinatra's style, and began singing. Unfortunately, I didn't sound anything like him. To the tune of Cole Porter's 'I Get a Kick Out Of You', I sang special lyrics I had written: 'I get a pain from your looks. The size of your smile looks just like the Nile, your teeth are green, white and blue. Yeah, you make me sick, yes you do.'

Bernie and I would repeat the last line singing to each other. We ended on a big, loud high note. The audience reaction to the number, in fact, to the whole ten minutes of our act, was at best complete indifference, at worst, outright audible hostility.

Understandably, we soon found ourselves out of work. So we changed the act, basing the comedy around our characters. I was the pompous musician and Bernie was my simple but lovable assistant. Gradually it began to work. Thanks to a successful television series, we eventually graduated to the top of the bill. No more Sinatra, Edward G. or Cary Grant. I never attempted them again.

Over the next twenty-five years, Sinatra put on weight and was no longer the skinny teen idol. He was becoming a legend. Edward G., still a wonderful actor, no longer played those dynamic roles of gangsters and historical figures. He was becoming one of that prestigious group known as 'character actors'. And Cary Grant? He was different. He had become a movie mega star. A Hollywood icon.

At the end of 1967, Bernie and I began a twelve-week run starring in the pantomime *Aladdin* at the Bristol Hippodrome. Bristol was an important date. It was quite an honour for us to be starring at such a prestigious theatre; built in 1912, the Hippo-drome was second only to the London Coliseum in its grandeur. And Bristol, it so happened, was Cary Grant's home town.

The pantomime was proving a big success. For the first few weeks we played six evening shows and five matinées a weeks to near-capacity houses. Then the kids went back to school and we began playing only three matinées a week.

The Saturday matinées were fine, filled with noisy, enthusiastic families with lots of young children. They laughed and yelled at our humour; they loved and cheered Bernie, who played Aladdin, and they booed and hated me playing the evil Abanazar. I relished it. But as the show neared the end of its run, the weekday matinées were invariably less well attended. The audience consisted mainly of senior citizens who seemed to enjoy our work but didn't react with the same noisy enthusiasm as the youngsters. It was tough for Bernie and me working without the reaction we were used to. If the house was only half full it could be even tougher. The old adage is true – you can't make empty seats laugh.

On one such dreary weekday matinée, we welcomed the interval with sighs of relief. It had been rough going. Getting a laugh out of the half-empty house was like striking gold in your back garden – rare, very rare.

In our dressing room, Bernie and I were slumped on our chairs drinking our customary interval cup of tea, served by our 'roadie' Eric. There was a rap on the door. Eric opened it a fraction to see who was knocking. 'It's the house manager,' he told us.

'Show him in,' Bernie called out. The door opened wide and the smart, dignified figure of the house manager in a dark suit and white shirt stood filling the doorway. 'I'm not stopping. Just want to let you know Mr Cary Grant is out front watching the show with his manager, Mr Bill Weaver, and they would like to drop backstage after the show just to say a quick hello. Will that be all right with you? Mr Grant said it would only be for a minute or two. I know you like to relax between shows, but I told them I was sure it would be OK.'

OK? Cary Grant! Was he kidding? Of course it was bloody well OK.

The news gave us both new energy. The realisation that Cary Grant was actually sitting out there watching us was surreal. Bernie and I grinned at each other. Both of us had the same thought – what a damn shame it was this bloody house. Why couldn't they have been here on Saturday when we had paralysed the audience?

The call for the start of Act Two came over the speakers. I was on practically at the start for my scene with the Emperor of China's daughter, Princess SoShy, played by a young actress in her first major part. Princess SoShy said her lines to her handmaiden, who then shuffled off, Chinese style, leaving the Princess sad and worried over Aladdin, whom I had purposely trapped in a cave.

I, the wicked and treacherous Abanazar, now made my entrance. I strode on to the stage, and for some reason unknown both to the audience and myself, I began moving my shoulders stiffly from side to side. In my demented head I thought it captured Cary Grant's walk, but on reflection I suppose I looked more like a drunken sailor.

My first line to the Princess was, 'Ah, my sad little Princess. Moping over that pathetic imbecile, Aladdin, are you?' To which she replies, 'Yes, I am waiting for Aladdin. He will come back to me. You'll see.'

That was the dialogue as written. I knew that. I had written it. But I was overwhelmed by the desire to do my Cary Grant impression.

'Judy, Judy, Judy,' I said to the Princess in my Cary Grant voice, now moving not only the shoulders but my upper torso too. The Princess looked at me as if I had taken leave of my senses, but I wasn't finished yet. 'I don't like that dress you're wearing, Judy. Quite truthfully, it doesn't suit you. It's more Sophia Loren or Ingrid Bergman. And please, don't call me Abanazar. Call me Abby. Yes, Abby. It's far more me.'

The Princess was transfixed in horror. Her eyes were signalling panic.

During my monologue the audience sat quietly staring at me, no doubt wondering why I had changed my voice and sounded a little like Cary Grant. And why did I keep calling Princess SoShy Judy? I think they agreed with me about the dress. It was too flamboyant. She wasn't tall enough to carry it off.

I could hear the sound of programmes being searched through. Maybe the audience was checking to see if Act Two was a different show. Besides the sound of rustling paper, I heard the distinctive sound of muted laughter coming from halfway up the stalls.

Taking the cold, stiff hand of the shell-shocked Princess, I patted it reassuringly and said in my own voice, 'Forgive me, my sweet Princess SoShy, I am afraid I have this rare disease called Cary-grantitis.' I expected a giggle from the stalls, but was surprised and delighted to hear a swell of laughter from the whole theatre. The audience had twigged that Cary Grant, the local boy made good, was sitting somewhere in the audience.

There was a new and exciting atmosphere in the theatre now. I played the rest of the scene straight until my exit. As I neared the wings, I began moving my shoulders again, and as I was about to exit, I stopped, turned and called out to the Princess, 'Goodbye Judy, Judy, Judy.' This not only got a big laugh, it got a round of applause too.

The pattern was set. Whenever Bernie and I were on together the ad-libs flew, and we did impressions of film stars, all pretty badly, without rhyme or reason – James Stewart, James Cagney, Edward G. Robinson, Charles Boyer, Charles Laughton and Clark Gable. Bernie threw in Hylda Baker for good measure.

The audience loved it. Most of them were sixty-five or older; heck, they probably remembered the silent movie stars too.

After the show we quickly changed and put on dressing gowns. We waited expectantly for Mr Grant and his manager while they were being introduced to our co-stars, Avril Angers and Sheila Hancock. I didn't doubt we'd have plenty to talk about tomorrow in between shows.

Within minutes, the main man was at our open dressing-room door. Accompanied by Bill Weaver, a nice-looking man of average height and build who appeared to be in his mid-forties, he looked just like. . .an older Cary Grant. The house manager introduced us. Mr Grant said he hadn't stopped laughing. He told us to drop the Mr bit. It was Cary and Bill.

As soon as they came into the dressing room, the house manager said diplomatically, 'I know you're pressed for time, gentlemen. Shall I have your driver come round to the stage door in, shall we say, a few minutes?'

Bill and Cary exchanged glances. Cary said, 'Oh, I think ten minutes will be fine. We'd like to chat with the boys a bit. If that's OK with you, Mike, Bernie? We know you want to relax.'

'Relax? After that show who wants to relax? We all need a cuppa tea,' Bernie said.

The house manager smiled. 'Love to, but I must get back. Your car and driver will pick you up at the stage door in about ten minutes. I'm sure the boys will see you out.' He said his goodbyes and made a quick exit.

'Nice guy,' Bill remarked. 'Very English. You guys are just naturally funny. You know, Mike, that was the worst Cary Grant impression I ever heard. But I gotta tell you I nearly fell off the seat laughing. You should keep it in the show.'

'Sure,' I answered. 'If you guarantee Cary will be in the audience every time.'

Bernie chipped in, 'Don't encourage him, Bill. He's only the straight man. If he gets too many laughs it makes me look bad.'

'That's easy to do,' I quipped back.

Bernie, his teeth purposely protruding, pulled a funny face and responded with one of his trademark catch phrases, 'Shut ya mouf.'

Cary and Bill laughed.

'You have a great rapport on stage. The way you follow each other's ad libs is impressive. I guess it helps being brothers,' Cary said.

'Oh yes,' Bernie cried out as he threw his arms around me. We pulled apart and Bernie said, grinning, 'I can't stand him really.' He leaned across and pinched my cheek. 'He's such a choochie face. You gotta love him.'

I was saved further brotherly embarrassment by a rap on the door. Eric, our roadie, came in. Seeing we had company, he said, 'Excuse me,' and went to leave.

'Don't go, Eric. Let me introduce you,' I said with a hint of pride. He didn't seem in the least impressed, he just smiled politely as they shook hands. 'Do you want your tea now, boys?' he asked. 'Would your friends like some? And bacon sarnies for everyone?'

'What's that?' Bill asked.

'A bacon sarnie, my dear friend, is a part of English soul food,' explained Cary. 'It's a pile of thick bacon, not the crispy stuff we get back home, in between two thick slices, not too thick mind you, of fresh bread.'

'Not too good for the waistline, I would imagine,' Bill observed.

'Maybe not,' I said, 'but they're delicious.'

'And,' added Bernie, 'of course, we only eat kosher bacon.'

Smiling, Cary said, 'Come on, Bill, we can't say no to that offer.'

Eric closed the deal. 'Right. Four bacon sarnies it is then. Four teas. I'll bring sugar separate. D'you like it strong, Mr Cary, Mr Bill?'

Before Bill could speak, Cary said, 'The same as the boys.' Here we were, two mature men, and nearly everyone referred to us as 'the boys'.

Off Eric went to get the grub. I suggested we sat down. Unfortunately, we only had three chairs. We offered two of them to our guests, explaining Eric would fetch us another one when he returned. Cary raised his hands. 'Don't worry about it. I'll sit here.' He hoisted himself onto the dressing-room table that ran the length of the room, and rested his back against the walled mirror. He looked perfectly at ease, ankles crossed, legs dangling, showing black silk socks encased in shiny black moccasins. Still standing, I looked at him. For a moment I could hardly believe that Cary Grant, the movie legend I had admired since I was a schoolboy, the megastar I had actually tried to impersonate on the stage, was sitting on the table of the dressing room I shared with my brother.

Bernie broke my reverie. 'Tell me, Cary,' he began as he plonked himself down in the empty chair. 'You come from Bristol, but you don't have the accent. Did you go to school in America to get your voice. . .you know, the way you speak? Or did the studios give you lessons? I read they sometimes do that.'

'That's true,' Cary said with half a smile on his lips. 'But not with me. When I arrived in the States, I wasn't an actor then. I wasn't Cary Grant then either, I was still Archibald Leach from Bristol, with an accent so thick you could cut it. I was a sorta acrobat, so I didn't mind too much when Americans said they couldn't understand me. But when I started to go to auditions and began getting small acting parts, I made up my mind that even if the audience didn't like me they would certainly hear and under-stand me. I practised speaking, making sure I finished every word. It came out kind of staccato. Of course, working with Americans, then living in Hollywood and hearing other actors, my accent got modified. But I never lost the clipped pronunciation and I always tried to finish every word. The good thing is, I'm easy to imper-sonate. Right, Mike?'

'How would he know? He's the worst I've ever heard,' Bill said with a grin.

'Yeah? I'm the big shot here, see. Don't be a wise guy, Bill, or I'll put the finger on ya, see,' I said in my best Edward G. Robinson. Cary and Bill applauded. In a voice like Groucho Marx, Bernie said with a big grin, 'Terrific. That's the best James Cagney I've ever heard.'

The dressing-room door swung open as Eric entered backwards carrying a tray. The tantalising smell of bacon filled the room. Eric put the tray down on the table alongside Cary and handed out the plates, then opened the paper bag holding the hot sarnies and told us it would be easier if we helped ourselves. I got off my chair and hoisted myself up on to the full-length table so that the food tray sat between Cary and me. I followed Cary's example and took a sandwich.

There were no complaints, and not much chat, as we munched away. After his second bite, with his mouth half full, Bill said, 'They're great. I didn't know bacon tasted like this.'

After ten minutes or so Eric came back, carrying an extra chair and a bottle of malt whisky. 'How was the sarnie?' he asked our visitors.

'Terrific!' Bill said enthusiastically.

'Boy!' said Cary. 'It was great. Better than I remembered.'

Eric nodded his head appreciatively. 'Yes, they are good, aren't they. It's only a little café, but they do a good job.'

Eric was unique as a roadie. To start with, he was an imposing figure. About six feet two inches tall, with a mane of thick, brown, wavy hair, he had the aura of a college professor who played rugby. He was obviously well educated; in fact, Bernie and I continually asked him how to spell difficult words. Eric had been recommended by a make-up girl who worked on our television series. We liked him, and he seemed to enjoy working for us. Bernie and I didn't pry into his private life. We tried to keep our own private lives private too.

'May I make a suggestion, boys?' Eric asked. 'You have an hour or so left before the next show. You overran nearly ten minutes. . .'

'It was all that messing about in the second half,' Bernie said.

'Yeah,' I agreed. 'They turned out to be a great audience.'

Bill said, 'I don't want to sound big headed, but I think we had something to do with that.'

'We? What the hell did you bring to the game, Mr Weaver?' Cary said, then added with a mischievous grin, 'Mike did an impression of *me*.'

'So it was you, huh? I wondered who it was.'

I grinned at the good-natured jibe and asked Eric what his suggestion was.

'Would Mr Cary and Mr Bill care for a drop of Glenfiddich?' He displayed the bottle.

'Whisky?' Bill sounded negative. He glanced at his elegant wristwatch.

'What are you doing, Bill?' Cary asked. 'We've got time.'

'A malt whisky after bacon cuts the fat. It's good for you. Try a small drop,' I said.

'Just a small one then, to cut the fat.' His pleasant face broke into a smile. 'Must watch the waistline, you know.' He gently rubbed his modest stomach.

I said, 'OK, Eric, Glenfiddich it is. To cut the fat.' I gave Cary a sideways look. He winked at me.

Bernie and I rarely, if ever, drank alcohol before or during a show. Our dad, whom we loved and respected, gave us that ruling. For the most part we kept to it, and never displayed booze in our dressing room. But with a special guest like Cary, plus the fact there was at least an hour before show time, Bernie and I did imbibe a couple of small shots each, and we tried to keep Cary and Bill's glasses topped up. As far as I remember no one was slurring their words.

I wish I could remember all we talked about that evening, but I can't. I do however remember a story Cary told us about drinking. He was doing a movie, I think he said it was called *Kiss and Make Up*, though I could be wrong. Anyway, here's Cary's story as I remember him telling it:

'One of the actors was a real pain in the ass. Always loaded. After each of his scenes he would take a swig from his hip flask and his breath smelt like a brewery. Not at all pleasant. I hated playing a scene with him. I had to do something about it. And I did. I got this doctor pal of mine to make me the strongest, tasteless liquid laxative he could. Then, at the first opportunity, I mixed it in the guy's flask.

'Believe me, the guy was up and down like a jack in the box. At the end of the day's shooting I told him he looked pale. Was he OK? The poor guy told me he must have eaten something that upset him. He asked me if I thought he should see a doctor. He said he felt like shit, which was an apt choice of words, I thought. He wanted to know what to do.

'I asked him if perhaps he'd been hitting the bottle too hard? He nodded guiltily. I put on my serious face and spoke gravely. "I don't like the look of your eyes, old sport." I shook my head sadly.

'"What is it, Cary? Should I go to the hospital?"

'I put my hand on his shoulder. "We mustn't panic" – I put on a "full of wisdom" face – "I've had some medical experience." Sure, I've played doctors in movies, I look good in a white coat with a stethoscope accessory, but that's it.

'I said in my doctor mode, "I have seen this look before. I believe you may have the early stages of cirrhosis of the liver. Of course, I can't be sure without a full medical examination, but I strongly advise you to cut out the booze entirely for at least two weeks." The movie would be wrapped by then. "I can't say this more forcefully, do not drink anything but water for at least fourteen days. You must give your liver a chance to regenerate. Your very life may depend upon it. Do as I say, and I expect a vast improvement within a week or so. If there is no improvement consult your own doctor for a diagnosis."

'Would you believe, the guy bought it. True, I was pretty good playing the doctor. Strangely enough, once the guy was cold sober, he wasn't a bad actor.'

The time had passed so quickly I was surprised when Eric came into the room again – I hadn't even noticed him leave – reminding

Bernie and me it was fifteen minutes to curtain.

Eric turned to Cary and Bill. 'Your car is waiting at the stage door, Mr Cary, Mr Bill.'

'Right. Gosh! We're sorry. We've stayed much too long,' Bill said as he stood up.

Cary got up from his chair. Stretching his arms momentarily, he said, 'Weren't we dropping in for a quick visit? Five or ten minutes, I believe. Perhaps I'm wrong, but haven't we been here nearly two hours? I don't blame you, Bill. It was that damn bacon sarnie. It affects the mind. It's too good, it should be illegal. . .Bernie, Mike, thank you for your hospitality. We're leaving right now. You guys have to get ready.

'Come on, Bill,' he said, moving to the door. 'Come on, Eric. Show us the way out of here.'

I thought they had gone when Cary popped his head round the door again. 'It was really fun, thank you. And please, say goodbye to Sheila and Avril.' As he finally left he was muttering to himself, 'Judy, Judy, Judy.'

Bernie and I were ready within minutes for the evening show. It was a full house, the audience receptive, but it didn't have the magic of that second half of the matinée. No ad-libs, and no Cary Grant, in person or impersonated.

I wondered if I would ever meet up with Cary or Bill in the future. Like most embryonic show business friendships, the very nature of the work made it a 'when or if we meet again' relationship. Bill had told Eric last night he and Cary were leaving for London today.

I hoped I would bump into them again. Maybe in London? Hollywood? New York? I was wrong. Our paths did cross again, but it was in Leeds, in good old Yorkshire.

I like Leeds. One reason is that one of my best friends, Ian Brill, lived there, and it was Ian who was responsible for the Winters brothers meeting with Cary Grant again.

Bernie and I were playing a week at the Wakefield Theatre Club, one of the new and luxurious nightclubs that had sprung up during the Sixties in the North of England. It was only a twenty-minute drive from Leeds – at least it was with the way I drove in those days. I was staying with Ian Brill in Leeds at what he called the Border Cottage, so named because quite a few young ladies had come across there.

On the Saturday of that particular week, Ian, in his position as chairman of the Yorkshire Variety Club, was promoting a fundraising ball for various charities. As the saying goes, everybody who was anybody was going to be there. Invitations had been accepted by Princess Alexandra, Roger Moore, Douglas Fairbanks Jr, Morecambe and Wise, Dickie Henderson, David Niven and an assortment of local big shots. The guest of honour was flying in on a private jet, courtesy of Fabergé, for whom he was spokesperson.

Ian knew Bernie and I were working on the night of the ball, and had arranged with his friend, Steve Burtle, the Wakefield Theatre Club's owner, for us to go on stage half an hour later so we could at least spend some time at the function. We were doing record-breaking business at the club and the act was going down really well, so Steve was happy to accommodate us.

On Saturday night, Bernie and I arrived at the Adelphi Hotel in our separate cars. We entered the magnificent ballroom with its large crystal chandeliers glittering above us, and saw the glamorous women in eye-catching gowns, wearing sparkling jewellery. We mingled for a short time, then were directed by a uniformed steward to join the welcoming committee for the guest of honour.

There were twelve of us on the committee: all the showbiz stars, and the most important of the movers and shakers. We stood in a wavy line about twenty feet away from the large wooden double doors. Bernie and I were positioned a couple of bodies right of the centre. Bernie was on my left standing next to Roger Moore, and I had my good friend Dickie Henderson on my right.

Without any preamble, the doors opened and a uniformed major-domo stepped through. He banged his heavy stick on the floor, but it didn't quieten the crowd. When he spoke in his loud, stentorian voice a hush gradually descended over the room.

'My Lords, Ladies, Honoured Guests, Ladies and Gentlemen, please welcome your guest of honour, Mr Cary Grant.'

There was an enthusiastic swell of applause as Cary entered, accompanied by Ian Brill and one of the directors of Fabergé. Cary's beaming smile swept along the welcoming committee line. Without apparent hesitation, he stepped ahead of his two escorts and walked straight over to Bernie and me.

We shook hands warmly and Cary leaned in a little closer. 'I'm so glad you two are here. I try to dodge these affairs, but I knew you'd be here so I thought it might be fun even without the bacon sarnies.'

'I'll ask Ian to get a bottle of Glenfiddich for later,' I said before, as if on cue, Ian came over to lead Cary away to meet the rest of the committee.

It had been quite a thrill being greeted by Cary like that. I felt the other members of the committee looking at us as we spoke to him. They must have wondered why he had he come over to us first. I didn't care. I felt good about it. I knew I was basking in reflected glory. Yes, it was shallow, absolutely juvenile. But what can I say?

Bernie felt the same way. We had to be honest. If Cary had gone over to Morecambe and Wise first, would we have felt a touch of envy? Probably. But, on reflection, I feel what Bernie and I really got out of it was realising that someone we liked and respected held us in high regard too.

Before dinner, Bernie and I got a chance to talk to Cary and his friend from his Hollywood days, another famous movie star, Douglas Fairbanks Jr, whose father had been a silent movie legend. A photographer took our photograph and said we were the four best-looking men in the room. Cary said, 'I agree, but don't let Roger Moore or David Niven hear you say that.'

We broke up when the announcement for dinner came. Bernie and I went to our table. Another announcement was made. Would we all be upstanding for the entrance of Princess Alexandra?

As soon as the Princess had sat down, the magnificent voice of the major-domo instructed everyone, 'Please be seated.' Bright music filled the room. Waiters and waitresses appeared, eager to serve the first course, a salad. It was the only course Bernie and I had time for. We had to go.

In between courses, we made our way to the head table and politely made our excuses to Princess Alexandra. We went over to Cary, who was on the Princess's right hand, to say a personal goodbye. 'Pity I can't come with you, I'd love to see your act. If I was there, Mike, you could do that terrible impression of me.'

'Please, don't come. It wouldn't be fair to the audience,' Bernie said with a grin.

But there was no time to chat. As we turned to leave, Cary placed a hand on my arm. 'Just a second, Mike. Do you remember the movie in which I said "Judy, Judy, Judy"?'

I thought about it for a moment. 'I haven't a clue.'

'How about you, Bernie?' he asked.

'No,' Bernie answered.

Cary stared into space for a moment. 'You know, boys, I've been racking my brain ever since I saw your pantomime. That impression you did of me, Mike, you kept calling the Princess "Judy, Judy, Judy". Remember?'

'Of course,' I said.

'Well, I can't remember the film I said it in. Still, you fellows have to leave. Sorry to have held you up. Have a good show.'

I hadn't taken two steps when he added, 'Hey! Maybe I never said it.'

I turned and looked at him seriously and said, 'Maybe it wasn't you. It could have been Archibald Leach and he forgot to tell you.'

Cary let out a laugh that made the other guests at the table look at us. 'They're funny guys,' he explained as he shook his head at us in amusement. 'Take care, you two. We'll meet up again. Good luck.'

Over the next couple of years we exchanged invitations to visit, but we never did. More's the pity.

5

More Than Two, Two of a Kind: Eric and Ernie

I think it's fair to say it is easier for singers to become international stars than it is for comedians.

Besides language barriers, comedy is basically a local thing. A London comedian may not appeal to a Birmingham or Newcastle audience, and vice versa. The audience may even have problems just understanding the comedians' accents.

The movies and television have widened our familiarity with American speech, but a mixture of slang spoken in a British accent is still a problem for most Americans. It's worth noting that in Miami 60 per cent of the population speak Spanish. I've been told California, New Mexico and Nevada aren't far different, which makes it tough for a British comic!

Bernie and I worked abroad. We played in Australia and Canada, and did a one-night gig at the Hilton Hotel in Chicago. We even got an offer to play Las Vegas, though we passed because the terms weren't good enough.

Our closest rivals, Morecambe and Wise, the subjects of my next story, also had a shot at playing the States. They appeared on the highly prestigious *Ed Sullivan Show*, which was shown across America. I didn't see the show, but by all accounts they did very well. I thought they were going to make it into the international star bracket, but it didn't quite work out that way. Perhaps it was because, for reasons only known to Ed Sullivan and Eric and Ernie themselves, they were introduced to America as two comedians from Ireland! I can't imagine Eric's Lancashire accent with an Irish brogue, though it might have been fun.

But I don't think it concerned Eric and Ernie too much whether they were international stars or not. The phenomenal success and affection they enjoyed in their home country would be enough for anyone.

My relationship with Eric and Ernie goes back a long way, as does my story about that relationship. Yes, it all began a long time ago. . .

A s a member of the honourable company of double acts, I can say in all honesty that I never met a fellow member of our august group I didn't like.

A few years ago, maybe four or five. . .well, it may have been nine or ten, even fifteen, perhaps twenty. Twenty-five? For goodness' sake, it was over thirty years ago. . .Anyway, around that time, two sets of double acts dominated the show business scene. One set undoubtedly had the advantage on television, the other had the advantage in live theatre.

I was recently asked during a magazine interview if Morecambe and Wise were our rivals. Of course they were. All double acts out there at the same time as us were our rivals. We were all pursuing the same dream, but the cold reality was that first we had to get work. Getting booked for a show was tough, and the competition was even tougher.

When Bernie and I began there were many well-known and successful double acts. But they weren't our rivals. . .they were, to use boxing terminology, in a different weight class. We competed with the novices – the up and coming. And there were some good acts in that weight class too. Bernie and I had to work pretty hard just to stay in the fight.

You may have forgotten, or never have known, the names of those double acts who worked at the local theatres fifty or so years ago, but many were well worth watching. Acts like Earle and Vaughan, Sid and Paul Kaye, and Daley and Wayne, always seemed to be working and played top theatres. But the very top rung was held at that time by Jimmy Jewel and Ben Warriss, deservedly so in Bernie's opinion and mine. We thought they were great and in those early days we copied them quite a bit.

Another couple of acts we admired, and who had earned them-selves big reputations strictly by their theatre performances, were the polished Len and Bill Lowe and the hilarious Sid and Max Harrison.

Bernie and I got to know Sid and Max when both acts were playing in Blackpool. They were appearing at the North Pier Theatre, which had a midweek matinée. Luckily for us, the venue we were playing didn't. On several occasions we took the long hike along the North Pier to catch their act. We knew how difficult it could be in Blackpool to attract an afternoon audience into a theatre if the weather was good. But each time we saw Sid and Max perform they had the audience in stitches, no matter what its size. That included Bernie and me. We were big fans.

Other strong acts began moving up the ladder – Hope and Keen, Little and Large, Cannon and Ball. All solid stage performers. But probably the biggest name in the group of up-and-coming double acts was Morecambe and Wise. Bernie and I always tried to watch other double acts. Strangely enough, though of course we had heard of them, we had never seen Eric and Ernie work.

The opportunity of seeing them in action came in 1953 after we had read in a trade paper that Alan Jones, an American movie star famous for singing 'The Donkey Serenade', was playing at the Winter Garden in Blackpool for a whole week. Second top of the bill was Ken Platt, a funny North Country comedian, and also appearing were Morecambe and Wise.

It just so happened, on the Saturday night of that particular week, that Bern and I had a cabaret gig on the outskirts of Manchester, which wasn't a long drive from Blackpool. Show time was ten o'clock, but there was a rehearsal for our music at six with the club's pianist.

Bernie came up with the idea of driving up together on the Friday. It would save money, he said. He had it all worked out. 'We could catch the show at the Winter Garden, then go for a bite to eat and a drink. There has to be dancers, or a girl act in the show. You might pull,' Bernie added with a smile. 'You normally do.'

I shook my head at him, half in exasperation and half in amusement. He was trying to get me at it. Did he really think he could con me? It was obvious, he wanted to go to Blackpool.

He went on trying to convince me it was a good idea. 'More-cambe and Wise are on the bill. I think we should watch their act. See what they're doing. You never know, it might —'

'Bernie, please,' I said, interrupting him. 'I don't care if I see Morecambe and Wise or not. I don't particularly want to see Alan Jones either, and be honest, neither do you. I know what this is all about. Why can't you be straight with me?'

Bernie shrugged sheepishly. 'I thought it was a good idea.'

'Of course you did. And it is. I don't care if you want to see Jean Bayliss.' Jean was a singer, a pretty redhead. 'I know she's in the show. And I know you've been seeing her for a bit, if you'll excuse the expression. Come on, Bernie, I've nothing against Jean, she's a nice girl. Tell you what, we'll drive up on Friday, see the show, see what all the fuss over Morecambe and Wise is about, and you can see Jean.'

'What will you do on your own?' Bernie asked, as if he cared.

'Don't worry about me. I'll be OK.' I didn't bother to tell him the Beau Belles were also on the bill. Something told me I would do just fine.

Bernie's romance with Jean soon faded out. But I suppose it was because of her that Bernie and I got to see Morecambe and Wise for the first time.

We went to see the Alan Jones Show, and compared to the one we did the following night in Manchester, it was stupendous. Alan Jones pleased his fans, Ken Platt got a lot of laughs from the North Country audience, and Morecambe and Wise did OK. By any standards they were talented. To use an adjective management used about Bernie and me, they had potential. You have to understand, all those famous catch phrases they became known for – 'short fat hairy legs', 'you can't see the join', 'the play what I wrote' – didn't exist at the time. I enjoyed their act, but I wasn't knocked out. In fact, I preferred Earle and Vaughan. There were three reasons why. One, Kenny Earle was the best-looking comic in the business. Two, Malcolm Vaughan had the best singing voice of any straight man, except perhaps for Dean Martin, and he was American. Three, and most important of all, Ken and Mal were good pals of mine.

We had been friends from the days when Bernie and I first began touring. If they followed us into a theatre we would leave a note letting them know which gags we had used that might clash with their material. The compliment was reciprocated. Sometimes, if one act had a gag that would fit into the other's routine, permission was given to use it. We agreed a gag or two didn't make an act. It was finding the correct balance between the two performers that was important. Mind you, good material was pretty important too!

A few months after our trip to Blackpool, Eric and Ernie once again entered our horizon. We were living at the time with our parents in their flat in North London.

Bernie, unlike me, who had spent more time living in Oxford and Norwich than London, had many friends in the capital and a pretty active social life. He had more dates than a palm tree.

One evening, he came home earlier than usual. Mum, Dad and I were listening to the radio, while I tucked into a slice of bread pudding Mum had made.

'You're home early, son,' Dad remarked as Bernie entered the sitting room.

'Yeah. I'll be going out later. Mervyn [our cousin] and I are going to the Stork Club. I told Merv I'd meet him at the Regent Palace about eleven,' Bernie said giving Dad a grin and Mum a hug. He took out a cigarette, lit up and turned to me. 'Have you heard about Morecambe and Wise?'

Dad showed more interest than I did, but then, he was a little obsessed with our career. He turned down the volume of the radio so he wouldn't miss anything. At that moment, Mum returned and handed Bernie a plate of bread pudding the size of Buckingham Palace, sitting down at the table on one of the hard-backed chairs.

'If you want any more, help yourself. Do you fancy a cuppa tea?' Mum asked.

'Leave it. I'll make some later,' Dad said impatiently. 'Bernie was just telling Mike something important to do with the act.' He looked at us expectantly. 'What about Morecambe and Wise?' he asked Bernie.

Bernie put his cigarette in one of the many ashtrays scattered around the room. He took a bite of the pudding, and when his mouth was practically empty answered, 'They've got a TV series coming up. What d'you think about that, Mike?'

'Hmmm!' I was surprised. 'Should be interesting.'

'What d'you mean, interesting? It's a disgrace. It should be you two. You're much better,' said Dad with conviction.

'Have you ever seen their act?' I asked him.

'No. What's that got to do with it? I'm your father, I'm entitled to be biased.'

Bernie and I never got to see their TV series. We were in Europe doing shows for the American military for most of 1954. Somehow the news that the Morecambe and Wise TV series hadn't been a success reached the small band of British acts working in Europe, commonly known as 'The Zone'. It is true, bad news travels fast!

I can't say I felt sorry for them, or pleased that a rival's show had flopped. I didn't know them personally at that time, and I had no opinion on the show because I hadn't seen it. In fact, they weren't on our minds. We had to please American servicemen now. English television and Eric and Ernie were another world.

While I was in Paris, my girlfriend Cassie Chaney came to visit. It opened my eyes to how much I had missed her. She was an artist whom I first met while she was still a student at St Martin's School of Art, in the heart of London, and we'd been going steady on and off for a few years.

After graduating, she became a fashion sketch artist for major houses. She was offered a place with Norman Hartnell, a top designer, but turned it down, and when not designing or sketching clothes, she found time to model for *Vogue* magazine.

In the summer of 1955, Cassie spent her holiday with me in Llandudno, Wales, where I was working in a summer season show with the wonderful comic Norman Evans. Llandudno can be a romantic place – at least it was for Cassie and me. We became engaged.

After the show finished, I was immediately booked to go to Germany to begin another tour of the Zone. Cassie's parents thought it wise to wait a year before we got married as Cassie wasn't long out of college. Not only that, they weren't too happy about her marrying a struggling entertainer with little money, and as far as they could see, one with few prospects. Strangely enough, in spite of their reservations about the future, they liked me, and I them. They were pleased I had agreed it was wiser to wait. It made sense, gave me a chance to save some money.

When the summer season at Llandudno ended, I said a sad goodbye to Cassie and left for the Continent. There I was now, in the autumn of 1955, staying in a cheap hotel in Kaiserslautern, Germany, wondering what the hell I was doing with my life. Was this the career I wanted? Playing American military bases, not making enough money to marry the girl I loved?

I had to wait until Christmas for Cassie to fly over and spend the holidays with me. After only a few weeks I found myself dreading the next few months. To break the monotony after a show one Saturday night at an officers' club, I sat in on a poker game.

Dad was a brilliant poker player. When we played poker together he memorised every card played, and worked out in his head the odds of buying the card he wanted. He tried to teach us, and though we never mastered his skills, we became pretty good poker players. I didn't have much stake money that night, and within a short time I was out of the game. But the American officers were nice enough guys, and they invited me back any Tuesday or Saturday, their poker nights. I borrowed from Bernie, went back twice the following week and lost. I just didn't have enough money to stay in the game.

I decided I would give it one more go, but I needed more stake money. I got an advance on my salary. Just one more game and that would be it. Just one more, win or lose. All I needed was a little luck. I knew I was a good poker player. Hadn't I been taught by a master – my dad?

On the next Saturday night, after our show, I took a taxi to the officers' club. It was a little late, which was OK by me. It meant the players had been drinking longer and weren't so alert. The game was in full flow, with six players. There was no objection to me joining them. An extra chair was pulled up and the players moved a little closer together. I think most of the guys were pleased enough to take the money again from the Limey. Not this time, I thought to myself. Not this time!

That evening I won enough money to pay all my debts, take a week off work and go back to England. I arrived on Monday, and on the Friday of that week, 21 October 1955, Cassie and I got married at Kensington Register Office in London. It was the anniversary of the Battle of Trafalgar. Cassie and I have been battling ever since, but we're still together and, unlike Lord Nelson, the hero of Trafalgar, neither of us has lost an eye or an arm.

As if getting married hadn't changed my life enough, the following year, 1956, Bern and I got an unusual booking. We had been working with famous, mature stars such as George Formby, Joseph Locke, Albert Modley and Anne Shelton, who were all very nice people, but their audience wasn't right for us. This new booking was in Sunderland and was unusual because we had no idea what the top of the bill looked like, or exactly what he did. Our agent said he was a new singer, and what difference did it make what he looked like? We would still get paid if he looked like a frog, or come to that, sang like one!

When we got to the Sunderland Empire and met the star, a teenage pop singer by the name of Tommy Steele. We'd had no idea what to expect, but he was certainly no frog. A golden mane of hair framed a good-looking face highlighted by large blue eyes and a bright, infectious smile. This was his first theatrical date. Before he took that initial walk on to the stage, Bernie had slapped some make-up on Tommy's impish face. What did Tommy know about stage make-up? Nothing, and why would he? No one had taught him. This was a night for firsts.

Tommy was a revelation. He had that indefinable magic that makes a superstar. For Bernie and me too it was a first. At last we were playing to a young audience. They liked us. Not only did they like us, Jack Good, a recent Oxford graduate and later a television producer for the BBC, liked us too. He was looking for young comics for his new teenage-targeted show, *Six-Five Special*. He booked us.

Working with Tommy in theatres and appearing in the unorthodox *Six-Five Special* was great fun. We even appeared in the movie spin-off. Of all the shows we did in that series, the one that stands out in my mind is our appearance with the Ted Heath Band. We sat in with them and played Duke Ellington's 'C Jam Blues'. Bernie, on a second set of drums, did a terrific drum contest with Jack Parnell, and I, on my trusty clarinet, had a twenty-four-bar solo.

Unfortunately, the magic carpet came back to land and we were dropped off. There were conflicts behind the scenes at the BBC over the show's future. Jack Good was replaced by Dennis Main Wilson, who in turn was replaced by a third producer, Russell Turner. So we left, along with Main Wilson and a number of the original cast, including Freddie Mills and Jo Douglas. Letting us go may not have been the wisest decision the BBC ever made. The show came off the air at the end of the season. But we'd made our first move into TV.

By the mid-Sixties, Jewel and Warriss, although as great as ever, were no longer the force they had once been. Fame and reputation earned from live stage performances were no longer viable. Neither was it still possible to become a big star through the medium of radio alone. Times had changed. Now the key to the magical kingdom of stardom and success was television.

It was only a matter of time before we met Eric and Ernie in person. We were at a showbiz function in the spring of 1963, among lots of the current crop of ATV (Associated Television) stars and a mixed bag of well-known entertainers. Bernie and I saw comic Dave King, a close friend, talking to his former writers, Sid Green and Dick Hills. Eric and Ernie were in the group. We walked over casually and joined them. No introductions were made.

Somehow it was assumed we all knew one another, which in some strange way we did, if only by reputation.

At first, the conversation was inevitably about show business, but it quickly moved on to football. Eric was a big fan, as were Bernie and Dave King. Dick Green and I tried to inject some rugby into the conversation but with little success. It was all good humoured and I liked our main competitors. They, like us, were now names.

Eric and Ernie's new series, *Two of a Kind*, written by Sid Green and Dick Hills, was original, fresh and funny. Meanwhile, thanks to our appearances on *Sunday Night at the London Palladium* and the support of our producer and mentor, Philip Jones, we were about to get our own series.

Later in 1963 we began recording *Big Night Out* in Manchester. And although Eric and Ernie's show was far better received by the press, *Big Night Out* dominated the ratings. In 1964 *Big Night Out* was followed by *Blackpool Night Out*. This time it was live, not pre-recorded. Our regular writers, Brad Ashton and John Morley, and I put together a variety-type show, with short comedy sketches, lots of quick gags, a little slapstick, and a carefree holiday atmosphere. Clever, subtle, television-structured comedy wouldn't work in a live, theatre-based TV show. Live meant we couldn't stop and do it again. Whatever happened, happened, and in front of the whole country! And for two years, the thirteen-week Sunday night show was one of the ten most watched TV shows in Britain, regularly reaching the top three in the ratings.

Bernie and I were grateful for our success and, like Eric and Ernie, we weren't worrying what another double act was doing. . . the four of us had enough to worry about. Television is bloody demanding. But we were no fools. We knew how good *Two of a Kind* was.

Both acts got on with their domestic lives during off-TV periods. Bernie, though, was something of a workaholic, so we played a few cabaret dates. One such date was a beautiful club in Luton, about thirty miles from London.

On the Saturday, Bernie went with our brother-in-law, Leslie Wise, to see Arsenal play. I intended to go to Esher and watch my old team play rugby, but Lenny Weston, one of the owners of the Luton nightclub, had an extra directors' box ticket for Luton Town's home game. Instead of going to watch rugby, I accepted Lenny's offer.

The game was forgettable, but the afternoon certainly wasn't. Eric Morecambe was there. He seemed to know everybody, and his humour, charm and wit created a wonderful atmosphere in the directors' lounge at half-time when we tucked into the sandwiches and assorted cakes, washed down with coffee or, in my case, tea.

I only got a few moments to chat with Eric. To my pleasure, and I think to his too, neither of us went anywhere near show biz. Appropriately, we talked football, as well as cricket, another game we both enjoyed.

After the match – which Luton won – Eric came over to Lenny and me as we were having a drink while waiting for the crowd to clear before leaving the ground.

'Excuse me, Lenny, I need a quick word with Mike before he leaves,' Eric said, then turned to me. 'Mike, would you like to pop down to the players' changing room for a quick hello? I think they would really appreciate it.'

'Yes. I'd love to,' I said enthusiastically.

Eric grinned. 'Right. Come on, lad.'

I excused myself and followed Eric to the changing-room door. He paused, and we heard the players' boisterous voices. Eric pushed open the door, then threw his arm round my shoulder as we walked in. 'Hello lads,' he called out. The players went quiet as they looked up at Eric and me standing there like two old pals.

'Who said we didn't get on?' Eric said, grinning as he gave my shoulder a squeeze.

The boys loved it. They saw the surprise on my face, and guessed correctly that Eric had set me up.

We congratulated the team on their win and left everyone with a smile on their face. Their fondness for Eric was palpable, and was obviously reciprocated. It was no surprise to me that in a few years' time, Eric became president of the club.

The next time our paths crossed was in Yarmouth in 1967. Three years earlier, at the Wellington Pier, we had broken the town's attendance and box office records. Throughout the twelve-week season, every seat was sold except for two on a Friday, first house. If we had known there were going to be two empty seats, we would have bought them for Siggi and Cassie, our wives, and risked being heckled! There was no doubt in my mind that we had done such phenomenal business because we had such great co-stars – Matt Monro and Jimmy Tarbuck. Now, for the first time Bernie and I were doing a summer season on a percentage deal instead of a guaranteed salary.

Why? I'll explain. We wanted Joe 'Mr Piano' Henderson to be in the show – he was just right for the audience we brought in. But Bernard Delfont wouldn't pay for Joe, saying we already had a great act in Mike Yarwood (which was true). Joe was too expensive, and – according to Bernard at least – we were getting paid so much there was nothing left in the budget.

Our agent Joe Collins, reached a compromise. Joe Henderson would be in the show, and the amount we got paid would depend solely on how much money we brought in at the box office. It was a gamble, but Bernie and I decided to take it. We signed the contract in January 1967, to open at the Britannia Pier in June.

In February, we learned the names of our competition, and began to worry. Rolf Harris, who was very popular, had his show practically across the road. Further down the beach, at the Wellington Pier, our friend Val Doonican was appearing. He was sure to do big business. If Rolf and Val weren't enough competition, playing at the ABC Theatre, which had the biggest seating capacity in town, were our friendly rivals, Morecambe and Wise.

John Powles, the manager of the Britannia Pier, was one of the best in the business, and he could see Bern and I were worried. Could we even start to follow the success we'd had three years ago? And, of course, this time we were on a percentage.

It wasn't just the money. It was pride too. For the first, and as it turned out, the only time, we would be in direct competition with Morecambe and Wise. We knew they would do big figures, their advance bookings were impressive. Not so with us. The advance was mediocre.

We opened in early June. The house was packed for the opening night, and we couldn't have asked for a better reception. The show was a hit, but the bookings for the following few weeks didn't reflect it.

John, our genial theatre manager, visited our dressing room every night to keep us abreast of the local news and let us know how our bookings were doing. He always tried to keep up our spirits. 'Don't worry, boys. It's early days yet. Everyone loved the show. You wait and see. Val and Rolf have their own audience. They won't affect us. Most of Val's crowd will come to see you as well. We'll do him, and Rolf too. Come on, Mike, you know how it is here. It's word of mouth. You're practically a local boy.' (I had lived in Norwich for four years and had worked both Norwich and Yarmouth markets.) John opened the dressing-room door as if to leave, but stopped. 'As for those two at the ABC. . .You've opened already and the town is behind you. You'll do them as well. You'll see.'

John, in his colourful way, wasn't entirely wrong. We ended up with another record-breaking season, and I'm pleased to write that Rolf, Val, and Eric and Ernie were successful too. I'm even more pleased to write that they weren't quite as successful as Bernie and I.

Just off the front in Yarmouth there was a small eating and drinking joint, a sort of tavern, where some of the theatricals, or 'pros' as we in the business say, used to hang out after the show. It was a fun place. Bernie and I went there when our wives were in town. It had the air of a place with a considerable history, and it must have been well over a hundred and fifty years old.

After two big houses Bernie and I decided to go and have a meal at the tavern. Eric and Ernie and their wives, Joan and Doreen, had the same idea. Our wives were home in London – Cassie with our six-month-old baby boy, Anthony, and Siggi with her four-year-old boy, Ray.

Bernie and I didn't want to intrude on the two couples. We went to sit at a separate table, but they wouldn't hear of it and we joined up. After a round of drinks, Ernie said to Eric, 'This place looks as if Lord Nelson – a local lad, you know – might have spent some time here. I wonder if he ever did come here.'

'Ask Mike. When he was younger he knew Nelson. Didn't you Mike?' Eric said drolly, adjusting his glasses in his inimitable style.

Bernie chimed in, 'Mike knows all about the Nelson Eddies, I can tell you that!' (For the uninitiated, 'Nelson Eddies' – commonly referred to as 'Nelsons' – is cockney slang. 'Nelson Eddy' rhymes with 'ready', which means ready money. So when you get the 'Nelsons', you get cash – sometimes, 'under the table'.)

As the night progressed and the wine kept flowing, someone came up with an idea to have a cabaret. Eric and Ernie, Bernie and I obliged. We gave an impromptu cabaret with a difference. . . Bernie teamed up with Ernie, and I teamed up with Eric.

Double acts are a separate tribe with their own unique characteristics. Eric and Bernie had much in common, as did Ernie and I. Maybe that is why rivals can so easily be friends. There is an affinity between double acts. They share similar experiences, the most common of which is the true value of a straight man. The value of a straight man is really only known by the comic of the partnership. As Ernie once said to me, 'A straight man is the comic's labourer. We are there to make the comic funnier. The straight man's personal talent is often subjugated for the good of the act. If it doesn't get a laugh, it's out.'

Ernie was right, of course. It goes without saying that Eric knew how good Ernie was, just as Bernie knew he was always funnier when I was at his side.

Historically, successful double acts split up. Laurel and Hardy had their problems; Abbott and Costello, and Martin and Lewis, eventually split. The more closely the lives of a duo are entwined, the more likely, for one reason or another, it seems that they will reach a breaking point. Those acts who keep their private lives separate seem to fare better. But who can be sure? It happened to Jewel and Warriss too. And, in 1978, it happened to Bernie and me.

But as far as I know, not one comedy half of a big double act became more successful working alone. Even Jimmy Jewel, though he became a successful actor, never reached the stature he had when he was part of Jewel and Warriss. And only Dean Martin, of the straight men, retained his superstar status.

Bernie and I felt a deep loss when Eric died in 1984. I was living in America at the time, and I hadn't performed for five years, but the show business world I had known all my adult life suddenly changed when Eric Morecambe died. A great comic was no longer with us.

For Ernie, the loss of his partner must have been devastating. I had suffered more than anyone knew, other than Cassie, when Bernie and I split. But Eric was gone altogether. No second chance to give or accept an apology, no opportunity to make that call and talk over the great new script or that bit of material that you didn't fancy doing. It must have been a very sad time. I was glad Ernie had the love and support of his wife Doreen.

Ernie lived part of the year in Florida, so it was natural we would see each other. Over the next few years we would occasionally meet in Miami Beach for coffee and to talk show biz.

Around this time, I had my first book published, *I Only Talk Winning*. Ernie had done a pantomime in England and was contemplating his future. There was no doubt he was a terrific performer and a big name, but how and where to harness his talent needed thought. To develop a single act wasn't for him. The age of variety theatre was long gone. To play cabaret, where good, clean comedy was a non-starter, wasn't for him either.

A few more years passed with the speed of light. I had two more books published. Ernie and I sometimes met on the 71st Causeway and sat looking at the Intracoastal Waterway as we got a mutual fix of show biz. 'Did you ever see the Michael Winner film, *The Cool Mikado*?' I asked Ernie. It was a disastrous venture into the movies Bernie and I had made in the early Sixties.

He laughed. 'Oh yes. You should have bought the negative and destroyed it along with all the copies.'

I sounded like Mickey Mouse. I was never crazy about doing films. Not enough control.'

'I know what you mean. Eric and I felt the same way about the films we made. We didn't know the medium well enough. We thought it would be more like TV. Now, if we'd had Eddie Braben and Ernest Maxim with us, a good script and a proper budget, we could have cracked it.'

'You don't want much, do you!' I said, half humorously. 'You and Eric had it all with the BBC. What Bern and I would have given for three weeks rehearsals. We were lucky to get six days. Three weeks! How did. . .'

'That was because of Eric's heart attack,' Ernie said, interrupting me.

'I know, but Bernie and I were doing a week-to-week turn around, live. Live, my friend.'

'We thought you were nuts. Why did you do it?'

'Because we *were* nuts.' We laughed. It was amazing how much show talk we had in us.

I came up with a new subject for us to talk about. I had written a TV show format. It was based on current show business. Reviews of shows, interviews with stars, newcomers, film clips, a little gossip too. I thought Ernie, alongside two or three young, attractive colleagues, would make a great anchorman.

Ernie liked the idea and came up with a few suggestions. Why didn't we host it together? It sounded interesting. Neither of us wanted another partner, but the idea sounded fun. What's more, it seemed commercial, which was not to be sneezed at. Ernie took the concept to his agent, Billy Marsh, one of the few remaining denizens left in Sir Bernard Delfont's organisation. But Billy blocked the idea, for what reasons I never knew. Ernie went into a West End show shortly afterwards. I heard it was well written and Ernie was good in his part, but unfortunately the play didn't run.

My third novel, *Razor Sharp*, was published, and I began working with Center Stage in Orlando. Walter Bowen, the CEO, and I wrote and produced programmes for cable TV and home video. One series was nominated for an ACE – an Award for Cable Excellence. In retrospect, I wish I had done that TV show with Ernie. I bet it would have been good for us both. I think it would have been a big success too.

Ernie and I didn't get the chance to repeat our Florida sessions after that. I did see him in England a few times after that, though. One summer's day, he and Doreen were together in their boat on the River Thames, not far from their home, when Cassie and I passed them on a craft going in the opposite direction. We waved as we passed. They seemed very happy and contented.

As one grows older it is natural to suffer the loss of a dear family member or close friend. But it is never easy. Ernie passed away in 1999, by which time my brother Bernie had been gone for eight years. First Eric, then Bernie, and now Ernie. They were all gone, leaving a large empty space in the halls of the earthly kingdom of double acts. I sometimes ask myself, why am I the last man standing? But as Eric Morecambe would say, 'There's no answer to that.'

6

A Lot of Balls — Footballs, of Course: The TV All Stars

There are millions of football fans, with millions of opinions — which is as it should be. Having opinions on the game, the teams, the players, even the referees, is a football fan's right. Having opinions on managers too is par for the course.

It doesn't matter if some think the opinions are ludicrous. One could argue that the so-called experts don't know it all. If a fan was made English team manager, with the help of a couple of his mates from the local pub team, and advice from the senior players, who knows what the result would be? It would save a ton of money in salary. And I don't think the new manager would pick players and play them out of their regular positions!

I'm not seriously advocating selecting a fan for manager, though the idea intrigues me. However, I do suggest waiting to see how we do in the World Cup first.

Opinions! We all have them. It's only a bit of fun, like comparing past legends with new ones. Was George Best a better player than

Wayne Rooney? Would you put Bobby Moore or Bobby Charlton in today's England team? I bet you have an opinion! It's only an opinion, of course. But it's fun debating it, isn't it?

We all have different opinions about players. When I was a kid, about eleven years of age, just before I got the rugby bug, I saw Eddie Hapgood and Laurie Scott playing for Arsenal. I've seen some great full-backs over the years, but I still rate those two players as a great defensive duo. Here is a list of twenty British footballers I consider great, selected only from those I have personally seen play: Stanley Matthews, Tom Finney, John Charles, Jimmy Greaves, George Best, Ray Daniels, Danny Blanch-flower, Dave Mackay, Jim Baxter, George Eastham, Alan Ball, Jimmy Armfield, Denis Law, Noel Cantwell, Jimmy Logie, Gordon Banks, Billy Bremner, Bob Wilson, Bobby Moore and Joe Mercer.

I know my choice leaves out lots of wonderful players – most of the English World Cup-winning team, for example. Nevertheless, it's a pretty impressive list, and I'm lucky to have seen them play. But let me add, no matter how good a single player may be, it is the skills and efforts of the whole team that win trophies.

Football, like most sports, can be addictive. I spent many years giving up my free Sundays to play football. I loved it. However, my wife resented it. Should I have spent my free Sundays for the best part of seven months a year playing football, or should I have spent them, at least many more of them, at home? I refuse to answer on the grounds of self-incrimination. After fifty-four years of marriage to the same woman – we married very young – I have learned when to zip it! Let's begin the chapter...

From the age of eleven I'd played rugby. I loved it. But when Bernie and I started doing our act together, I soon found playing rugby and show business didn't go together.

Besides the risk of injuries (although this also applied to playing football), it was very rare to find other theatricals who played rugby. This made casual, friendly seven-a-side games virtually impossible. And I couldn't play rugby on Saturdays, the traditional day for rugby matches, because in pantomime there are matinées every Saturday afternoon. But if I couldn't play rugby on a Saturday, I could play football on a Sunday. That was one of the reasons why, in 1957, during a pantomime season at the King's Theatre in Portsmouth, I formed the TV All Stars football team.

There was already a football team for show business people – actors, entertainers and so forth. Aptly named the Show Biz Eleven, its founder and manager was a music publishing executive named Jimmy Henney. The team played their matches on Sunday afternoons. I had turned out for them a few times, and Bernie more regularly – he loved the game. We trained at Queens Park Rangers' ground in London alongside regular members of the team such as Sean Connery, Ronnie Carroll, Des O'Connor, singers Gary Miller, Glen Mason and Toni Dalli, skiffle player Chas McDevitt, Roy Castle, Pete Murray and Dave King. They were all pretty fit and some of them were quite useful players.

I enjoyed the chance to train with them, but I was still only really interested in rugby. I kicked the ball with my toes, rugby style, not with my instep as footballers do. I couldn't head a ball correctly, even though I practised on my infrequent trips to the training ground. In fact, I had no football technique or skills at all.

On the plus side, I was fast, strong in the tackle, and in good shape. Bernie on the other hand had some skills but needed to get fitter. Playing regularly and training would fix that. Which brings me to the main reason I formed the TV All Stars.

On one winter Sunday at the start of our pantomime season in Portsmouth, Bernie left at the crack of dawn and drove over a hundred miles to a town somewhere in Bedfordshire to play in a charity football match. I don't remember the name of the town, but I do remember telling Bernie not to go. The road conditions were too bad. Reports were scary – ice and snow. But Bernie had told

Jimmy Henney he would be there, and he didn't intend to let the team down. So off he went in his white Volvo. In the event, all went well and he returned safely, pleased with the way he had played.

I called Jimmy during the week to let him know I was available to play on the coming Sunday, and said I'd be there with Bernie. The game was being played at Ruislip, on the outskirts of London, which meant that Jimmy, using the influence of the company he worked for, Francis, Day and Hunter, would be able to contact the press and get the game some media coverage. Some of the big names, who passed on playing if it meant a long drive or the weather was too bad, would show up for the game on such occasions.

On match day, Bernie and I drove to the ground together, arriving with little time to spare. The weather was mild and the small stadium looked nearly full – the charity would do well. We made our way to the team's changing room and began chatting to our mates, who were in various stages of changing into their kit.

I caught Jimmy's eye, and he smiled and came right over. I could see by the number of star names in the dressing room it would be unlikely I would get a game, but I was still surprised at what he had to say.

As expected, he told me, sorry, but I wouldn't be playing. OK. But when he told Bernie the same thing I got angry. Bernie was dumbfounded, literally at a loss for words. 'Hold it,' I told Jimmy. 'Bernie schlepped all the way from Portsmouth last week in the effing ice and snow, and now, because all the big names have turned up, you're dropping him! That's not right. How about dropping one of the players who didn't show up last week?'

Jimmy apologised to Bernie, and explained that the crowd wanted to see the big names. Pete Murray, the popular BBC disc jockey, who was listening to the heated, but muted, discussion, offered to play a half a game and give the other half to Bernie. A very nice gesture, but Bernie was over his shock, and was now burning. Those who knew Bernie will agree that when Bernie burned it was not pleasant to behold. And if you added a little alcohol to the fire you might have a nasty explosion. Fortunately, on this occasion there were no intoxicants available.

Bernie remained relatively calm. 'Thanks Pete, but Jimmy should have made that suggestion. And why should you give up half a game? What's wrong with one of those other geezers playing a half? And my brother Mike should get half a game too. He's better than some of that lot.' Bernie turned to Henney, eyes blazing, and jabbed him in the chest. 'You've taken a diabolical liberty with me. I was good enough for you last week, wasn't I? You can stick your effing team up your arse. Come on, Mike, let's go.'

There was a deathly hush in the room as we left, and little conversation in the Volvo as Bernie, lips tight, drove us back to Portsmouth.

In a way, I understood Jimmy's point of view. Bernie and I were relatively new members of the team. Most of the regulars were established star names and pretty good players too. Bernie, even with his few skills, was still a novice at football, as I was. We weren't much value as players and at the time we weren't a big name act. Having star names in the team brought in the crowds, who brought in the money that paid the expenses for the team and supported the charities. I understood Jimmy Henney's reasons, but I didn't agree with what he had done. He shouldn't have dropped Bernie.

As we neared Portsmouth, Bern and I discussed the situation. I told him to forget about Jimmy Henney and the Show Biz team. 'I'll form our own team. Who needs Henney? I'll organise it. You can be the captain. We'll make the rules. No star system. Every one gets a fair shake. Look, Bern, all we want is a game of football, right?' Right!

The next morning I arranged a match with the local Johnson & Johnson factory, followed by a weekday game against the local police team – one that developed into a weekly fixture. We were known as the King's Theatre Team. By the third game, I changed the name to the TV All Stars to promote our growing number of famous players. If people came to watch and we raised money for charity that would be great. But, quite honestly, all we wanted was to get a game of football.

At some of the games against the police, played on bleak, miserable afternoons on an uneven, bone-hard or swamp-like field, in bloody cold or wet weather, no one did turn up to watch. We didn't care. We still enjoyed the game. The police team were as crazy as us theatricals. They were terrific guys. Their captain – I think his name was Sergeant Pilgrim – deserved a medal for getting his boys out there no matter the weather, to play on what we laughingly called the pitch. If we were a man short, he would give us one from his side to even things up.

The players included show business mates and some of the cast from the pantomime. A young singer, a member of a group called The Viscounts, was our goalie. His name was Gordon Mills, and he talked of turning pro in the future. In fact he became the manager of Tom Jones and Engelbert Humperdinck, and co-wrote 'It's Not Unusual', Tom's first big hit. Gordon became a millionaire. I don't think he missed out too much in not becoming a professional footballer.

Bernie and I also turned out for the local taxi drivers' eleven every Tuesday afternoon. I think the barracking we got from the few supporters of the taxi drivers' team – I'm talking about their kids, who were still on school Christmas holiday – made us determined to improve our skills. I use the word 'skills' loosely!

Sometimes, in the TV All Stars team, because we were short of players, we used family members or anyone we could hijack. But everyone had to have a showbiz connection. My cousin Mervyn Conn sometimes played, but he was an embryonic theatrical producer so he was cool. Another cousin, David Bloomfield, played a few games – his showbiz connection was Bernie and me. And there was my brother-in-law, Leslie Wise (no relation to Ernie.

One double act in the family is enough for anyone!). Leslie would be an enormous help in building the team.

Once the pantomime season was over, Bernie and I went on tour. We still wanted to play and so did the other players, but I didn't have the time or resources to organise things. That's where Leslie came in. He had an office and a secretary, and he happened to be a very good organiser. He also happened to be a very keen Arsenal supporter. Other members of the team were big supporters too, although not of Arsenal. Teams like Chelsea, West Ham and Tottenham had their followers, while the Manchester sides, United and City, and Newcastle and Liverpool were popular. I think there was an Aston Villa fan. I know Crystal Palace had one supporter, Ronnie Corbett.

Bernie, like Leslie, was a big Arsenal supporter. Truth be told, so were the rest of my family. After all, we came from Islington, which is – excuse the local vernacular – a cough and a spit away from the Arsenal ground. There was a lot of good-natured teasing and bragging when someone's team won, but punch-ups never looked likely.

I asked Leslie if he would like to be the team's manager and help organise things as it was too much for me to handle. He was over the moon, and told me he couldn't thank me enough. As it worked out, the team and the charities ended up owing him a big thank you. Bernie and I hadn't started out to raise money for charity. We were thrilled at first if we made tea money for after the game. That was how we started, but fortunately, not how we finished.

Like most of the team, I began taking playing football seriously, and trained as much as possible. It made a difference when I got the chance to play rugby. On rare occasions I would turn up at my old club, Esher, with my boots, and hope for a game either with one of our teams – Esher ran fifteen sides in those days – or with a visiting team who had arrived a man short. I turned out for a

Saracens 'A' side, Cardiff Athletic and a London Irish side. I didn't disgrace myself. The football was keeping me fit.

For about twenty Sundays every year, work permitting, Bernie and I played football, travelling all over Britain and Ireland. In Dublin we played in front of thirty-five thousand people. That made the team feel like they were professional players.

Self-delusion? Of course. First of all, we didn't get paid, just travel expenses. Second, we were nowhere near good enough. We did our best, though, and had a bloody good time doing it. How many professional football sides allow one of their officials to run on to the pitch and throw a bucket of water over their goal scorer? And can you name me a team that has a glamorous actress wearing skimpy shorts run on to the field and administer mock first aid for a mock injury? We had June Cunningham doing that. Not every game, but we always tried to add a little entertainment to the afternoon. Paul Carpenter, a former vocalist with the Ted Heath Band, would do a commentary on the game over loudspeakers. Any celebrities at the ground would be introduced and would maybe say a few words. I remember Lonnie Donegan singing his 1957 number-one hit, 'Cumberland Gap', at half-time in one game. The crowd sang along. Although we played the game seriously, we tried to make it a fun event for the whole family.

Six months after forming the team, we never had problems fielding a full team; in fact the opposite was true. When we had too many players some of the lads would play half a game. We kept it fair. Everyone, including Bernie and me, would take their turn.

There was a good team spirit. We sang on coach trips to and from the games. Our theme song was 'You Gotta Have Heart', from the 1955 hit Broadway show about baseball, *Damn Yankees*, which proved to us that you gotta have heart no matter what the sport is.

An awful lot of theatricals, famous and not so famous, turned out for us over the years, as did many well-known names from the world of sport. I can't remember them all, but here is a list of those I do. The entertainers and actors included Ronnie Corbett, Alfie Bass, Bernard Bresslaw, Tommy Steele, Frankie Vaughan, Tom Courtenay, Anthony Newley, Harry Fowler, Jess Conrad, Andrew Ray, Larry Taylor, Pete Murray, Edward Hardwick, Dave King, John Burgess, Maurice Kaufman and Jimmy Tarbuck. Among the boxers were Dick Richardson, Jack London and Rinty Monaghan (team assistant), while footballers Malcolm Allison, Tommy Docherty, John Toshack, George Eastham, John and Mel Charles, Joe Mercer and Bobby Moore all turned out at one time or another.

As I look back it is hard to believe I actually played alongside all those great players. And Bernie and I were equally fortunate that because of our growing celebrity, and the fact the All Stars were raising money for charity, we were welcomed at some of the biggest football clubs in the country – Arsenal, Newcastle, Cardiff, Chelsea, who in 1962 gave me treatment for a sprained ankle, and Manchester United, when Sir Matt Busby was manager – and allowed to use their training facilities. In later years, when Bern and I were doing a summer season in Blackpool, Matt kindly rented me his summer house on the beach in Cleveleys, Lancashire, where my family and I saw the most glorious sunsets.

Once, during pantomime rehearsals at the Palace Theatre, Manchester, we went training at Manchester United's ground. We were lucky enough to train with Denis Law, who was finally getting fit after suffering a broken leg. Even with his handicap, Bernie and I couldn't keep up with him.

Our pantomime hadn't opened yet, so on the Saturday afternoon we went with Denis to see the club's home game. It was George Best's first-team debut. He was terrific. After the game, with Sir Matt's blessing, Denis took us to the team's changing room to meet George and the rest of the team. I think the team might have got a kick out of meeting us, but it was nowhere near as big as the thrill Bern and I got from going to their changing room and meeting *them*. It was one of those occasions when I truly appreciated being a celebrity, and being fortunate enough to have friends like Denis Law and Matt Busby.

Talking of managers, Don Revie, manager of Leeds United and England, was a good friend to Bernie and me. We weren't yet household names when we were doing our first series of *Big Night Out*, so guest stars were very important. But getting them to appear on the show was something else.

Would a star accept a show in Cannes, in the South of France? If the money was right, you bet. How about Las Vegas? Rome? New York? Yes, yes and yes. On the other hand, how many stars would rush to do a show from Didsbury? Most would ask, 'Where is it, exactly?' They might well want to know who else was in the show. 'You mean those two new boys? Are you saying the TV company can only pay how much?'

Many had other engagements. Some were on holiday and couldn't commit to another date at this time. In other words, they politely declined.

I came up with the idea of using star names from the world of sport. Football fans will remember the 'Revie Plan'. A different playing formation from the one commonly used at the time, the 'Revie Plan' helped pave the way for the changes that have produced today's game. I thought it might be fun if Don Revie came on the show and explained his plan to me, as a team manager, and Bernie, as my star player.

I talked it over with John Morley and Brad Ashton, the show's script writers, who liked the idea and began working on a script. I ran the idea by producer Philip Jones, who thought the concept had merit. Bernie and I were very fond of Philip. We were on the show because, against powerful opposition, he had insisted. If he didn't like the idea I would forget it. The conversation between us ended something like this.

'Well, what do you think, Phil? Do we give it a go?'

'Well, I don't know, matey.' Philip called most people 'matey'. 'It's a good idea, but do you think Revie would do it? It's hard to get top names to do the show. Why don't you phone him personally? It might do the trick.'

I did phone, and it did the trick. Don came on the show.

Just before we began recording, Don warned us he didn't know the script. I told him not to worry about it. Bernie said with a grin, 'We'll probably change it anyway. All you have to do is answer the questions and have fun.'

Don did just that. The sketch was a success. The audience laughed like crazy, and our viewing figures went up.

Bernie and I remained friends with Don until he died. I read somewhere that Don had no sense of humour. Whoever wrote that didn't know Don. He was a strong-minded man, and judging by what I saw over the years, a good family man. He wasn't too bad as a football manager either, was he? Ask Leeds United.

Still on the subject of managers, Bernie and I met many of them. They were all nice guys – at least to us! – but Joe Mercer and Malcolm Allison were special. As joint managers of Manchester City they put together a great team that won the FA Cup. I'm still pals with Mike Summerbee, one of the players. He and some of the team used to come to see us perform.

Malcolm Allison, a former West Ham team captain, suffered with tuberculosis that meant he had a lung surgically removed in 1957. Although he returned to West Ham, his professional football career was cut short. A few years later, Mal opened a small drinking club on Charing Cross Road in the West End of London where a lot of show people congregated, including many members of the TV All Stars. Big Mal's place soon turned into the team's unofficial headquarters.

Mal wanted to coach. He eventually achieved his ambition and became an accredited coach, and eventually a manager. But before that transpired, Leslie Wise talked him into playing for the TV All Stars, something which turned out to be a major asset for us.

Joe Mercer played for Everton before the Second World War, and won five caps in midfield for England before the war cut short his chance of further honours. Along with other big football names like Tommy Lawton, Matt Busby and Bert Sproston, during the war Joe became a physical training instructor for the armed forces. After the war, I remember watching Joe when he captained Arsenal. Leslie, Bernie and I thought he was as good as they come.

When Bernie and I were doing pantomime at the Grand Theatre, Wolverhampton, we formed a theatre football team to play local pub teams, just for fun. Joe, who was manager of Aston Villa at the time, used to drive over from Birmingham, sometimes with a couple of pros, and play for us. We always won on those occasions! Joe was as accurate a passer of a ball as I have ever seen. I admit, perhaps Bern and I had a bit of hero worship going for Joe, but why not? He'd earned it.

In 1971, when Bernie and I were honoured to be the subjects of the TV show *This Is Your Life*, Thames Television invited Joe to be one of the surprise guests. It was one of the nicest surprises Bernie and I ever had.

Turning the clock back from that heady time, 1962 was the year of the showdown between the powerful Show Biz Eleven and the upstarts, the TV All Stars.

Our team was now a serious rival to the established Show Biz team. The fierce rivalry was concentrated around a handful of players. Obviously, there was strong competition between Jimmy Henney and Bernie and me. Some, like Pete Murray, who had switched alliances and was a loyal All Stars player, and Dave King, who played for both sides, didn't give a damn about the rivalry. They just wanted a game of football. But it's fair to say most of the Show Biz team thought we were a joke, and if we ever met they would slaughter us. We were mainly comics who acted that way on and off the field.

They weren't entirely wrong. Our on-field antics were intended to entertain, but sometimes we went over the top after the game.

At an after-match tea reception, Harry Fowler, acting the part of a waiter, wore nothing but a white towel draped over his arm! He was the first off-the-field streaker. The great comedy actor Alfie Bass had a habit of going over to female dignitaries and saying very quickly, 'How's your bum?' Shocked, they demanded, 'What did you say?' Alfie, innocence personified, would answer, 'How are you, Mum?'

The television companies knew a good deal when they saw one. Jimmy Henney and Leslie Wise negotiated a deal for the two teams to play against each other on television, although the negotiations couldn't have been that tough as none of the players received a penny. I guess the only expense might be medical help for our team after the Show Biz Eleven wiped the floor with us.

We had been told that three of their players – Sean Connery, Glen Mason and Des O'Connor – had been on the books of professional clubs. That didn't worry us. Little Ronnie Corbett said, 'How good could they have been? They never made the first team.' Bernard Bresslaw said with a smile, 'If they play as good as Des sings, we've got nothing to worry about.'

Of course, we didn't want to be humiliated. The Show Biz team included former England captain Billy Wright and former Wales captain Wally Barnes, two great players. We had only one former professional player, but at least he was a regular member of the team. Someone who had helped train and motivate us, Malcolm Allison.

The scene of battle was near Croydon Airport. Before the game the two teams met as they checked out the playing field. I got a strange feeling seeing television cameras around the ground and technicians busy preparing for the action to come. Viewers wouldn't see Bernie and me performing comedy, and I wouldn't be playing my clarinet; instead, they would watch us playing football. It was surreal. I was nervous, but quietly confident, believing we would give a good account of ourselves. Our opponents were strutting around the pitch as if they had already won the match, making condescending remarks about us. I think it was Des O'Connor who said to Glen Mason loud enough for all to hear, 'We'll get seven, then we'll let them score a couple so they can save face.' Yeah?

I must confess, some of the good teams we played against took it easy on us. We were show people, not hot-shot amateurs. They didn't let us off the hook completely, but they cut out the full-blooded tackles. I assure you that did not happen once the whistle blew and we kicked off against the Show Biz Eleven.

Friendships were forgotten. I have been in some tough rugby games, but none with the intensity of this confrontation. It was brutal. Pete Murray made a few tackles on Des O'Connor that were felt in the stands. Sean Connery, a big lad, bowled over Ronnie Corbett, who to everyone's amazement got right up and won the ball back. We were not playing dirty, just hard. I went in maybe a little too hard as I tackled Ziggy Jackson, who worked in the music industry. It was fair, but robust. Unfortunately, because of the awkward way Ziggy fell, his leg was broken and he was carried off. It was an accident. It was a bloody tough game.

After what I believe was a perfectly good goal, scored by actor Andrew Ray, had been disallowed by the Show Biz-appointed linesman, we went into our dressing room at half-time feeling aggrieved. Malcolm gave us a short team talk. His confidence was infectious, and we went out for the second half even more determined to win.

The second half was in the same pattern as the first, each team unyielding. It was attack and counter attack. Would this needle match end in a draw? Before the game had started, we might have welcomed that result, but not now. Now victory was possible.

With little time left to play, Malcolm Allison received a pass from our centre-half, Bernard Bresslaw, the famous comedy actor whose catch phrase, 'I only asked,' had swept the country. Big Mal weaved down the field, avoiding a couple of tackles by desperate but tired players. He looked as if he was going to pass the ball to Andrew Ray, who was running into the penalty area, but the former West Ham player had a different plan. From around thirty yards out he took a shot at goal. For a split second there was complete silence as everyone held their breath. Then, the stadium erupted with a massive roar as the ball rocketed into the back of the net. We had scored.

This time the goal wasn't disallowed. Ten hot, sweaty, bruised bodies jumped all over our goal scorer. That celebration was nothing compared to the one ten minutes later when the whistle blew for the end of the match. We had won.

A bunch of comics and an unlikely and unprepossessing group of actors and entertainers had triumphed over the élite footballers of the Show Biz Eleven. Indeed, it was a time not one of the TV All Stars football team would forget.

The injuries caused by the game had repercussions we didn't expect. Producers began inserting clauses into contracts banning the playing of football. At first the ban was half-hearted, but when Maurice Kaufman was injured in a game and had to act his scenes during a TV drama sitting down, or propped up against a wall, it fanned the flames. And then, when Tommy Steele, at the London Coliseum, and yours truly, while doing *Aladdin* at the New Theatre, Cardiff, needed walking sticks to enable us to get through our respective roles, the producers got serious – though on a positive note, hobbling across the stage with a walking stick gave the Abanazar role a new and arcane dimension. Contractually, many of us weren't permitted to play if we were working in a production for fear of a heavy financial penalty. We certainly didn't want to give away a penalty!

A year after the great football victory, I turned out for an Esher rugby side with the evocative name, 'The Old Contemporaries'. I was playing against the Saracens Second XV, who were far too good and fit for me, having not played rugby for quite a while. I got hammered and could hardly walk. Limping into the club-house bar after the game, embarrassed at my abject performance, I tried explaining to a former French international, who had played a blinder for Saracens, 'I was a little off today. You see, I haven't played in quite a while.' He looked at me with pity, and in a thick French accent replied, 'Zat was rather obvious. I wondered if you had ever played before!' I drank my beer and limped away into the night.

That same evening I was working at The Pigalle, a famous night club in London. Explaining to Bernie that I couldn't do our dance routine was awkward. My wife, Cassie, seeing the state of me, sided with Bernie. Unquestionably, I had played my last game of rugby. I had to agree. My livelihood came first. I had a wife and daughter to support. Unhappily I realised I was way over the hill as a rugby player. It was quite a blow.

Bernie and I hung up our boots around 1969. It wasn't that we weren't fit, it was the fact we could no longer shake off minor injuries as we had done in earlier days. Equally important, our work schedule had become far more complicated. We were spending considerable time working abroad: five trips to Australia, which we loved, two to Canada for television shows, and special trips to entertain our servicemen in diverse places like Northern Ireland, Aden and the Persian Gulf.

So the football years were over. The team carried on with a new set of players through the efforts of Hugh Elton. Leslie Wise didn't want to carry on if Bernie and I weren't involved. He concentrated on his business and within a few years he became chairman of a highly successful public company.

Bernie and I had spent nearly twelve years with the TV All Stars. Wonderful and exciting years. Was it worth all the time and effort we put into it? Well, we raised over a hundred thousand pounds for charities all over Britain and Ireland, bought two Sunshine Buses for needy children, and gave many people an enjoyable time. And yes, we enjoyed it too. For me, it was well worth it.

7

Down Memory Lane: Meeting Sean Connery

One Sunday summer morning in the late Sixties, Bernie and I and our good friend, singer Matt Monro, were at Gatwick Airport on our way to a concert in St Helier, Jersey.

The airport was packed with people eager to be off to their various holiday destinations. We found a bench tucked away from the mass of excited and animated travellers and kept out of sight as much as possible.

Worrying I would arrive late at the airport, I had missed breakfast. I suggested we go to one of the cafés for coffee or tea and a snack.

'Don't be silly, Mike,' Bernie began. 'They'll be packed. It'll take all day to get anything.'

'Bernie's right, Mike,' added Matt. 'Anyway, we haven't got long to wait for our flight, and it's only a short trip. We'll stop when we get there.'

'Yeah,' Bernie continued, 'I'll probably fancy something by then. If we go into anywhere here we'll be driven mad signing autographs.'

Matt agreed. 'True. All it needs is one person to ask and we'll be sitting targets. We've got this spot, let's stay here.'

Matt and Bernie were right. It wasn't that we disliked signing autographs; in fact, we were flattered by it. But there was a time and a place, and sitting eating wasn't one of them. And of course, there were those who didn't really want our autographs. They saw other people doing it, it was free, so they would thrust any old piece of paper in our face and say, 'Sign it.'

While Matt was speaking I'd noticed a middle-aged woman peering at us from behind a post that partially hid us from the crowd. Moments later, as I settled back to wait the ten or so minutes before going to our flight gate, the inquisitive woman began walking towards us. She was tall and slim, with neat grey hair. Her face was thin and drawn, making her look a little sickly. She headed straight for me. In one hand she carried an easily recognisable autograph book, in her other hand a Biro.

A genuine autograph collector, I thought, as she was about to hand me book and pen. I smiled up at her and pointed my thumb at my star companions, expecting an excited reaction. I was wrong. She ignored them and handed me the book. 'Sign it, please,' she said, giving me her pen. I quickly did so and was about to hand the book and pen to Matt when she grabbed them from me and moved away.

I looked at Matt and Bernie and we all laughed. 'She runs my fan club,' Matt cracked.

'Bit of a darling. I think she fancied me,' Bernie gagged.

'Well, gentlemen, I think that shows who has the sex appeal,' I said with mock conceit and a modest shrug.

'I admit you and she make a divine couple,' Matt said. The three of us chuckled. It had been weird but humorous too.

Minutes later we left the bench on our way to our flight gate. As if by magic, the eccentric autograph collector was standing in front of us. She waved the book in my face angrily. 'I didn't want your autograph. I thought you were Dudley Moore. Bloody cheek!' She turned on her heels and was off.

'OK, Star, let's go to Jersey. Maybe we can all sign a few autographs there,' Matt said with a smile.

The fact is, signing autographs is an honour, and it's flattering to be asked. But it can be intrusive; sometimes it's a laugh, at other times a drag. It depends where and when. Being famous has its drawbacks. Sometimes it is necessary to adopt strange methods to avoid attention, as my next subject demonstrated to me one afternoon...

When I began my career in show business I thought I had a good eye for spotting talent. Some of my predictions never made it, but I had successes too. I met Sean Connery for the first time before he ever thought about playing James Bond.

Music Corporation of America (MCA) was an international agency representing actors, entertainers, directors, producers and writers. I was on my way down the stairs of the MCA building on Piccadilly, near Hyde Park in London, sometime in 1957 from the second floor after seeing an agent – the small lift was way up on the fifth floor and I decided to walk rather than wait. Sean was on his way up the stairs, probably preferring the exercise rather than suffer the small, claustrophobic lift. The stairs were narrow, barely enough room for two. We eyed one another as we came closer. 'He's a big lad,' I thought to myself.

He was wearing a pair of nondescript trousers and a forgettable shirt, with its top button undone; his loosely knotted tie needed a press, as did his 'off the peg' creased jacket. His black, unpolished shoes looked weary from pounding the pavements, probably going from agent to agent.

The previous night I had watched him in a play on television. I was surprised therefore at his far from sartorially polished appearance. To me, and to most people in the Fifties, just appearing on TV made you famous. To the uninitiated, it made you rich too. Unfortunately, one week's work from television, including rehearsals, followed by maybe many weeks out of work, is not the most reliable way of earning a living. But at the time I didn't know that.

As we were about to pass, without thinking I asked, 'Weren't you on TV last night?'

'Yes,' he answered suspiciously. His Scottish accent made it sound to me like a question. I treated it as such.

I began hesitantly. 'You see, I saw the show, I mean the play, *Requiem for a Heavyweight*. Great. I thought I recognised you. I hope you didn't mind me stopping you, but I wanted to tell you how much I enjoyed your performance.'

His face lit up. 'Not at all. I'm very flattered. My name is Sean. Sean Connery,' he said with a friendly smile. I never dreamed that with a name change that introductory phrase would one day be known around the world: 'My name is Bond. James Bond.'

I introduced myself and told him what I did – one half of a comedy team, presently resting (a euphemism for not working).

'Well, Mike, I don't know how good your act is, but I think you're a very good judge of talent,' he said with a broad grin.

We chatted for a few more minutes. Sean was off to see his agent. 'Glad you liked the play,' he said. 'I'll find out in a minute what the hundred pound suits thought. You know what agents and producers are like.' He started to climb the stairs. 'They know the price of everything and the value of nothing.' With that philosophical gem we went our separate ways.

Over the next few years I read bits and pieces about Sean in theatrical columns, and saw him on TV in an occasional play. I suppose I subconsciously looked out for his name, hoping my talent-spotting skills would be validated. I saw him in *The Crucible* with Susannah York, a favourite actress of mine. I thought they were both terrific.

In 1959, after making a modest reputation for ourselves in *Six-Five Special*, my brother Bernie and I were on tour. While we were in Leeds, where we were playing the Empire Theatre, I saw Sean Connery's name outside a local cinema. He was one of the stars of a movie I hadn't heard much about, *Darby O'Gill and the Little People*.

'Let's go and see it,' I suggested to Bernie. We had the afternoon free and didn't have to be in the theatre until five o'clock.

'I don't fancy it. There's a John Wayne film on at the Odeon. This Darby O'Gill sounds like a kids' film.'

'I don't think so. Sean Connery's in it. He's good. He's going to be a big name. You know I can spot talent.' Bernie gave me a sour look that showed his opinion, but he agreed to see the film. We used our Equity cards and got in without paying.

We left before the film ended. 'Well, we paid what it was worth – nothing,' Bernie complained. 'He might be a good-looking bloke, but he should give up the singing. Going to be a star, is he? Don't hold your breath.'

My faith in Sean had admittedly diminished; nevertheless I still kept a lookout for news on his career. I got some behind-the-scenes information from a friend of mine, Warren Mitchell, a fellow clarinettist, and later the star of the TV series *Till Death Us Do Part*, when we bumped into each other at Ronnie Scott's Jazz Club. Warren, who had played Sean's trainer in *Requiem for a Heavyweight*, let me know Sean had got the leading role after the American movie actor, Jack Palance, dropped out. He also told me Sean had recently signed a long-term movie contract with 20th Century Fox. So I wasn't the only one who thought Sean had what it took.

In 1963, after an absence of six years, I saw Sean in person once again. Bernie and I were on our way to watch Tottenham play Arsenal.

Bernie's new white Volvo pulled into the private car park, reserved for directors, players and special guests. We had passes from one of our pals in the Arsenal team. Bernie parked, we got out and admired his new car for a minute, and were both taken aback when an old, beaten-up van with mud-splattered wheels pulled in alongside the pristine Volvo. Surely the driver of this old banger had no right to be in the private car park. How had he managed to obtain a pass?

The driver's door opened and out stepped a good mate of ours, the popular singer and TV personality Glen Mason. 'Hello, lads,' he greeted us in his Scottish brogue as he started to move towards the double doors at the back of the van

'So you've got a new van? Nice,' Bernie called out with a chuckle.

'Very funny. No, I borrowed it for the day. Didn't want anything flash.' With that, Glen quickly opened the back doors and out jumped Sean Connery.

To say Bernie and I were surprised is an understatement. We had recently seen publicity photographs and posters of Sean starring in *Dr No*, the first James Bond film. Sean, as Bond, looked sensational in the publicity shots. Elegantly attired in a Savile Row suit, and immaculately groomed, he looked just the part of the debonair, heroic James Bond. The Sean that stepped out of the van brought back memories of our first meeting: creased jeans, a well-worn fleece jacket, a tartan scarf thrown carelessly around his neck and a woollen cap pulled down low over his forehead.

For a second we just stared at him. Bernie called out to Glen, 'Tell your friend he shouldn't have bothered to dress up for a football game.'

Sean smiled, but it was Glen who explained. 'We didn't want any autograph hunters driving us mad. You know, spoiling the game. Sean's had a lot of publicity over this Bond film. Have you seen it yet? It's great.'

We shook our heads, and Bernie quietly said to me, 'I hope he doesn't sing in it.'

Sean gave me a nod. 'How are you, Mike?'

'You know each other?' Glen asked.

'I've known Mike a long time. He's a great judge of talent,' Sean said with a wide grin.

One afternoon, a week or so later, Bernie and I sat and watched Sean in *Dr No*. As we left, Bernie said to me, 'You know you said he would be a big star. Well, you were wrong.'

'Wrong?' I queried, giving him a look of amazement.

'Yes,' answered Bernie. 'He's not going to be big. He's going to be bloody enormous.' He added with a toothy grin, 'As long as he doesn't sing.' I couldn't argue with that, could I?

8

What's a Séance Among Friends?
Dusty Springfield

As I've already said, I used to pride myself on being an excellent spotter of potential stars. I recognised Sean Connery's talent, and, during our first show together, I told Jimmy Tarbuck he was going to be a big star. No big deal. Both Sean and Jimmy were practically there at the time.

In 1958 I – well, Bernie and I – predicted that Jackie Dennis, a twelve-year-old Scottish singer with a hip, spiky hairstyle, would become a star. We introduced him to our agent, Evelyn Taylor, who managed him with her customary skill into the Top Ten. Around the same time, I booked a young singer by the name of Gerry Dorsey into a show I was producing. I thought Gerry had a lot of potential. When he changed his name to Engelbert Humperdinck, I guess he proved me right.

And in the Eighties I got my hat-trick of predictions, although I had made my prediction years earlier, just before leaving for America after Bernie and I had gone our separate ways.

I had written a TV comedy show and was looking for the right comedian to star in it before taking it to David Green, Head of Light Entertainment at London Weekend Television. Keith Becket, who had directed and produced *The Mike and Bernie Show* a few times at Thames TV, had read the script and concept, and had sent me a video of a new comic he thought would be ideal for my show. I agreed – the guy was a natural and would make the show and himself a big hit. Unfortunately, David Green disagreed. He didn't think the comedian or my script funny. But I was sure. 'You are an old dancer, David, I'm an old comic,' I told him, 'and this young comedian is damn funny and is going to be a big star.'

As for the young comedian, I think he confirmed my faith in him. The brilliant Rowan Atkinson, creator of Mr Bean, hasn't done too badly, has he?

But if I had been as good at spotting young, inexperienced talent as I'm making out, how come I never spotted the awesome talent of Dusty Springfield? In my defence, she wasn't actually Dusty Springfield at the time. You see…

I knew Dusty Springfield before she was Dusty Springfield.

It was 1955, and Bernie and I were in a show that played exclusively to American servicemen based in Europe. An English producer, Alan Blackburn, paid us weekly – dare I write, very weakly? – to do twelve shows a week. However, to get any shows at all, we had to do an 'expenses only' audition in Kaiserslautern, Germany, in front of the officers and sergeants who managed and booked the various military social clubs in Germany, Austria, France and Italy where hopefully we would be performing. If the managers didn't like our act, and we didn't get any bookings, Alan would have to pay us anyway.

I don't think he was too worried. We could tap dance, Bernie was hot on drums and ukulele, my clarinet playing was magnificent

That's me at seven I think. I used to pretend to be older, now I pretend to be younger!

The City of Oxford High School Second Fifteen. I made the First team a few months later while still under fifteen years of age. Pity my academic prowess wasn't of the same standard.

Bernie with his uke. Who is the goodlooking, smartly dressed, debonair young man standing next to him? Good grief! It's me.

Bernie doing his thing.

Us with our TV producer and friend, Philip Jones.

Us with Eric Morcambe. We didn't even see his lips move
(*Rex Features*).

The TV All Stars football team. Back row, left to right: Pat Sherlock, Hugh Elton, Larry Taylor, Maurice Kaufman, Bernie Breslaw, Jess Conrad, Peter Thompson, Tommy Steele and Lesley Wise. Front row: Mike Winters, Harry Fowler, Bernie Winters, Don Fox and Anthony Newley.

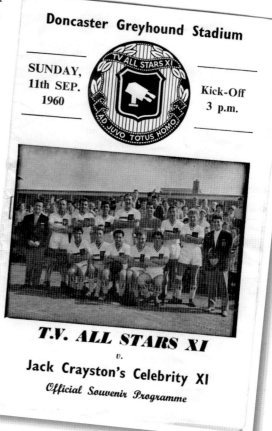

Doncaster Greyhound Stadium

SUNDAY, 11th SEP. 1960

Kick-Off 3 p.m.

T.V. ALL STARS XI

v.

Jack Crayston's Celebrity XI

Official Souvenir Programme

Me on *This is Your Life* being surprised by Johnny Dankworth – and not a clarinet in sight.

The Beatles. Bernie is talking to John while I chat to Ringo. The Beatles did three TV shows with us – and they still remained stars!

With three of my favourite people: Jimmy Tarbuck on the left, brother Bernie and Matt Monroe in 1964 at the Pier Theatre, Yarmouth, Norfolk. We broke the attendance record that year – it still stands.

Taken by Bernie in a car park. All I wanted was a photo of my new Jenson Intercepter. Thanks Bern!

Auditioning for a job at Buckingham Palace. We didn't get it so played two flunkies at the Theatre Royal in Norwich in our first ever pantomime.

Our first major summer season at the North Pier, Blackpool, and the beginning of our friendship with Pauline and Jimmy Tarbuck.

An old photo that I am glad I found of Bernie and me with movie legends Douglas Fairbanks Junior and Cary Grant at a charity event in Leeds.

Training. One of the all-time greats, John Charles, is next to Bernie.

You can see why she was a *Vogue* model: my beautiful wife, Cassie. We have been married three times to each other – civil, Jewish and Christian. We're looking into Muslim, Hindu and Buddhist. Think of the holidays we would get!

Mike & Bernie Winters comedy hosts of ABC Television's BLACKPOOL NIGHT OUT

I loved the old Blackpool postcards. Bossy mothers-in-law, sexy beach girls, indignant wives and stupid, ogling husbands. Where are they now?

One of the pleasures of showbiz was working with Sacha Distel. I was fortunate enough to play a duet with him on TV – me on clarinet and Sacha on guitar. In all due modesty it was bloody good.

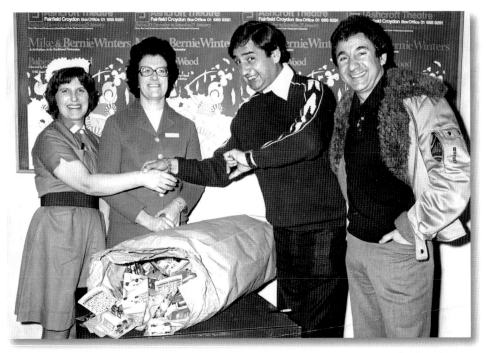

While appearing at the Ashcroft Theatre in Croydon we raised money for local hospitals. It's one of the perks of being a celebrity that you can be useful in helping the less fortunate.

A face that launched a thousand laughs.

I don't know how I sounded that night but I look as if I'm good…Anyway, I couldn't get the sack as I was one of the owners of the club!

A Royal Starlight Supper
attended by
His Royal Highness The Prince Edward C.V.O.
benefiting
Angels In The Outfield's
Joe DiMaggio's Children's Hospital
and
The Duke of Edinburgh's Award International Foundation
to be held at
The Grand Bay Hotel, Coconut Grove, Florida
on Saturday, April 22, 1995

Reception 7:45pm   Black Tie   Dinner 8:15pm

A Royal invitation to a starlight supper in 1995. It was quite an event. Guests included Petula Clark, Barry Gibb of the Bee Gees and his lovely wife Linda, Danny La Rue and David Cassidy. We all had a great time and raised money for the Duke of Edinburgh's Award International Foundation and Joe DiMaggio's Children's Hospital.

– well, pretty good – and we got laughs. Admittedly, we were hardly Dean Martin and Jerry Lewis, the big hit double act at that time. But the American servicemen were starved of English-speaking acts, and if nothing else, we spoke English. The bookers liked us and we got lots of bookings. Alan's gamble on us paid off.

Alan had a show about to start a two-month tour around the US military bases, and he decided we should join it. There was just one minor problem; it was headlined by another comedy team, Roger and Carl Yale, a pair of South Africans known as the Yale Brothers. I asked Alan if Bernie and I would clash with another brother comedy act. 'Don't worry,' Alan explained. 'They're not real brothers, and anyway, you're not billed as brothers. You could be cousins. Who's going to mind? Besides, they're a *real* comedy act.' What could I say?

Also in the show – Alan called it 'the Unit' – was a solo dancer. She was very attractive – I remember her legs very well, but for the life of me I can't recall her name, though I think her first name was Diana. She came from Birmingham, I think.

The Unit also included an Australian magician named Ken Livingston. Imagine a powerfully built, suntanned, blond-haired, brash, confident Aussie. Got the picture? Well, Ken was the opposite. He was quiet, a little shy, of slim build with an air of gravitas, and was a very clever magician.

Backing the show musically, and also doing a solo spot of their own, was the all-girl Iris Long Trio. Neither Iris nor the third member of the trio (whose name completely escapes me – that is, if I ever knew it, as she kept herself to herself and spoke, as far as I could tell, only to the other two girls) sounded like Londoners to us. Bernie thought he detected a slight Lancashire accent hidden by an American drawl probably picked up from working contin-ually for US servicemen. The third of the young ladies had four first names: Mary Isabel Catherine Bernadette. Her surname was O'Brien. But everyone called her Dusty.

She was very sweet and seemed a little young to be working so far from home. I assumed by her name that home was somewhere in Ireland, although she had no brogue. But Dusty told me she was born in Hampstead, in London, and lived in Ealing. Bernie and I liked that. She was a Londoner like us.

The Yale Brothers were South African, Ken Livingston Australian. Now we'd met a girl from Ealing, who sounded and spoke the same as Bernie and I. When you are away from home among strangers, just hearing your local accent can be reassuring. In many cases, you have things in common too. We got on well with Dusty. She was like a little sister.

We had been doing the show for a week or so when we were moved from Kaiserslautern to Munich in Bavaria, where another group of servicemen's clubs had booked the Unit. Bernie and I were excited, but apprehensive at going to Munich. Although the Second World War had been over for ten years, during the war the city had been a hotbed of Nazi sympathisers.

When we got there the destruction from Allied bombing seemed to have been cleaned up. We had to admit it was a beautiful city, with great shops and fine buildings. Nevertheless, in our imagination, we saw Nazis in every shadow. Munich had been famous for its Nazi rallies. The invidious and poisonous seeds of hatred had flourished here. It took a little time for Bernie and me to relax and stop viewing every German with suspicion.

All of the Unit stayed together in a small, modest hotel. We were its only guests so we practically had the run of the place. The breakfast room doubled as the dining room, but most nights the Unit ate at the club after the show. So the rarely used dining room became an after-work social club where we would have a coffee, an iced tea, beer or something stronger, and talk our heads off. The conversation invariably centred around show business, but except for Carl and Roger Yale, no one had enough experience to talk about their memories. After we had squeezed out every drop of rumour and gossip about Elvis Presley and other stars we had never met and didn't know, discussion turned to other subjects, the more bizarre and exotic the better.

After a few late-night conversations, the subject of spiritualism raised its tantalising head. Before we knew it we – mainly Iris and I – were deep into the validity of Aleister Crowley and the significance of the number 666. Iris suggested we hold a séance. Bernie and Carl were indifferent to the idea, but Dusty, Ken, Diana and Roger Yale were enthusiastic.

I was a little surprised that Dusty showed interest. I assumed she was Catholic, and knew such practices were highly discouraged by the Vatican. But then, as far as I recalled from past studies, spiritualism was frowned upon by all organised religions. In many cases it was forbidden, with draconian punishments for disobedience. However, it wasn't Dusty's religious persuasion – whatever that was, I never enquired – that made me wonder about her interest in the occult. I thought her too young for the subject. I mentioned it to Ken, who told me he had become interested in magic when he was about twelve, and shortly after had become fascinated with psychic phenomena. 'I would say youngsters get into all that stuff,' Ken opined in his Australian drawl. 'It doesn't last too long. That's coz nothin' much happens. People go back to it, I think, when they get older. When they lose someone close. No, Mike, I don't think Dusty is too young to be interested in the occult.'

The first séance took place in the club house, the hotel's multifunctional breakfast room. We got back a little later than usual, having eaten at the Sergeants' Club after the show. We rearranged the room, moving the pre-laid breakfast tables to the side and leaving just one table surrounded by six chairs in the centre. Carl, Bernie and the girl from the Iris Long Trio decided they would rather be spectators than participants. Iris lit six candles she had bought in readiness, and she and I placed them around the room.

At Iris's signal, Dusty switched off the lights. The room was immediately transformed into a place of shadows and mystery. The six
participants sat down close together around an empty table meant
for four. Iris instructed us to hold hands. In the flickering candle
light, the séance began.

'Is anybody there?' Iris's voice filled the silent room. She
repeated the question twice more. A voice answered.

'Yes. I am. Tell your spirit to bloody well speak up.' Naturally it
was Bernie. A few nervous giggles. Iris put a stop to that. 'That's
not funny, Bernie. This is serious.'

'Sorry,' Bernie apologised. 'I was just trying to give the spirit
a laugh.'

Iris ignored the remark. 'Come on, everyone, you must hold
hands. Now concentrate. Try to make contact. Sshh, everyone.
Mike, see if you can get a response.'

It was pretty obvious Iris had been through this routine before.
I never had. I took a deep breath and in a sombre voice intoned, 'Is
anyone there?'

I asked again. The room remained silent. I repeated the question
once more, adding, 'If you are here, give us a sign. We need you to
give us a sign.'

Silence.

I can only tell you what happened next – what all those in the
room saw happen. It started at my end of the table. There was a
movement; the table began to rise, tilting upward. There were
cries of 'Oh, my God. What's happening? Who's doing it?' Each
voice had an undertone of panic. Dusty called out to anyone
listening to put on the lights. Carl jumped up from his chair by the
wall and did so.

Iris was furious, and blamed me. 'You did it, didn't you? Well,
you ruined it. Spoilt everything. Just for a cheap laugh. You used
your knees to do it. I'm surprised at you.'

'I didn't do anything. My knees didn't touch the table.' I turned to Ken. 'You're very quiet. It was you, wasn't it?' I grinned at him. 'You got us all going, you bloody sneaky Australian.'

Ken firmly denied it. He said it must have been Roger, who shook his head. 'Hey, don't blame me. I was getting freaked out,' he said holding up his hands innocently.

Bernie got up and walked over to the door. He was leaving. 'I've had enough of this nonsense. You're all bleeding nuts. I'm going to bed. This is a load of old bollocks.'

The room cleared quickly, and Iris and I put the furniture back in order. 'Goodnight, Mike,' Iris said coldly as she left.

'Good night, Iris,' I said. 'I didn't do it, honestly.'

The work rate of the Unit picked up pace. Each evening, from our hotel headquarters in Munich, we would be driven to a military base or bases, depending on how many bookings we could fit in during the evening. If they were relatively close to each other we might fit in three shows. Sometimes, we would work the EM Club (Enlisted Men's Club), then maybe the Sergeants' Club or the Officers' Club. One night, we did five separate performances in three different bases. Mostly though it was a single base with just the one performance.

The audiences were normally good, though without question it was the ladies who got the best reception. Diana, with her great legs, stopped the show – her dancing wasn't bad either! And the talented and good-looking Iris Long Trio was the stuff isolated soldiers' dreams are made of. Bernie and I got a lot of laughs, not so much from our material, but from our ad-libbing and how we handled the mixed comments the audience sometimes threw at us. After a few such shows, we began to gain a good reputation, spread by club managers who called us 'troubleshooters' because we could handle rowdy audiences. When guys in the infantry came back from manoeuvres, and had downed about six beers before the show, they could be a problem. The yelling, and the whistles of appreciation when they saw the females in the show, were deafening. On those nights, Ken and the Yale Brothers, and Mike and Bernie Winters too, cut short their acts. The rule was: keep it fast, short, and get off before they realise they don't like you.

But most shows were fun and the troops well behaved. The Unit was popular, and there were no petty arguments among the cast. Carl Yale was in charge. He was cool, and ran things effortlessly. Transport to and from bases was on time, changing facilities at the bases were clean and secure. Carl dealt with the American in charge at the club, and handled any problems at the hotel.

The Yale Brothers were older than the rest of the show. Perhaps that was why they didn't get involved in our free time activities, which were pretty limited anyway – going to local historical sites, or eating wonderful cakes in the many patisseries in the centre of Munich. Magician Ken hung out with Bernie and me. Sometimes Dusty would join us, but she spent most of her time with Iris and the other lady in the trio. Perhaps they spent their time rehearsing or, as Ken said when I asked him where the girls were, 'Oh, I guess they're doin' girl things.'

After the show we ate at the club. American forces food was great. This was 1955; rationing in Britain had only ended the year before. We had seen and heard about hamburgers, fried chicken and hot dogs in the movies. But eat them? It was a new and enjoyable experience.

For us British in the Unit it was another world. Performing in the EM and sergeants' clubs was like playing a three-star hotel. And officers' clubs were a revelation. They looked as if they were exclusively for famous film stars, rich executives and royalty. Bernie and I had never seen anything like them. We knew we had even more grandiose and magnificent places back home, but we had never been inside them. The Ritz, the Dorchester, the Savoy weren't for young, struggling show people.

Back home in England, we had worked a few one-nighters for free, at British camps. There was a marked contrast between the social amenities on offer to the British Tommy and those available to American serviceman in Germany in 1955. In the American PX – a cross between NAAFI and a grand store – there were goods of all kinds you could not find in Oxford Street. I found myself with a mixed bag of feelings. Envy, admiration, anger and aspirations.

When Carl told us we were leaving Germany and moving to Austria, I was pleased, not only for the opportunity to visit a different country, but because I never felt at ease in Germany. Although I met many friendly Germans, and some were obviously too young to have participated actively in the war, I couldn't erase from my mind what Hitler and his followers had done to the Jews, gypsies, homosexuals and the mentally disabled, in fact anyone at all who opposed their evil philosophy.

Did I hate the Germans? Bernie, Ken, Dusty and I had discussed that very question. We agreed, we didn't hate the German people, we hated the people, no matter where they came from, who had committed or supported those heinous atrocities against their fellow human beings. And I should point out that, not too many years later, Bernie married a German girl, Siggi, one of the Lionel Blair Dancers. They remained married 'til the day he died.

So we moved to Salzburg, the birthplace of Mozart. It was only for a couple of days, and there was no time to think about another séance. Before we had fully unpacked we were on the move again – this time to Vienna, the capital of Austria.

To be in the Austrian capital at this historic time was strange. Like the rest of the country, it was still occupied by the Allies, America, Great Britain, France and Russia. Vienna was a city of contradictions. It was the home of the Hapsburgs, who dominated Europe for centuries, and of Albert Einstein, who revolutionised science. The River Danube flowed through the city, which was the birthplace of Johann Strauss and the waltz, of Sigmund Freud and psychoanalysis. And of Adolf Hitler – and we all know what he brought to the world!

To scramble my over-active mind even more, Mike and Bernie Winters, an unknown comedy act from London, were going to perform in front of American servicemen at the historic Vienna Opera House. For me, it was a great thrill, but no doubt some dead opera divas and famous tenors turned in their graves.

I don't know if anyone else got the same charge out of the event as I did, but I do know I blew Dusty's mind when I invited her to come for a walk to the British sector with Bernie and me. We had been advised not to go wandering out of the American sector, but what harm could it do to wave at a few Tommies?

According to the guys at the EM Club, the British sector was to the north of the city, the French to the south and the Russian to the east. 'Don't get lost in the Russian sector,' they warned us. 'You may never be seen again.'

Next morning, the three of us set out heading north; at least, we believed it was north. It was a bright and invigorating spring day, and as we walked we talked, fascinated by the amount of rebuilding we saw taking place. Indeed, within a few years of our visit the grand old Opera House itself was demolished and work on a new building began.

After forty minutes or so, we saw in the distance what looked to be a platoon of marching soldiers. We quickened our steps, wanting to wave and shout words of encouragement to our boys. We began jogging towards them. The soldiers took a left turn on to a wide main road, which made it easier to catch up. We cut down a couple of side streets and ended up just in front of them. Slightly out of breath, smiles on our faces, we waited for our boys to get a little closer before shouting, as planned, 'Rule Britannia' and 'God Save the Queen'. That would make them feel good. They'd know they had friends here.

Our soldier boys began to pass us. They were boys all right, and they were soldiers, but they weren't British soldiers. They were Russian.

We stood watching them march by. They looked so young. Bernie turned to Dusty and said, 'They look even younger than you.'

Dusty replied, 'They shouldn't be in the army, they should be in school.'

I said, remembering what we had been told at the EM Club, 'Let's get the hell out of here.'

Our Vienna hotel was similar to our previous digs in Munich – small, modest, near the town's centre, with few other guests, and with a dining room we could commandeer. That night after the show, we decided, we would hold another séance. Iris cleared it with Anna, who served as receptionist, telephonist and manager. The dining room would be ours all evening, but we had to leave it as we found it.

Our participants would be fewer than last time. Diana had a date with a good-looking army captain; Roger and Carl had been invited out to dinner by a South African journalist who was doing a story about Austria's imminent return to sovereignty. Bernie had other plans too. He had his eyes on the receptionist, Anna. She normally went to a nearby *gasthaus* – a kind of pub where you could drink, and eat the local food. So Bernie was off to the *gasthaus* hoping he'd get lucky.

The third member of the trio wasn't interested in a séance, preferring a good book. So, once again, in a dining room lit by flickering candlelight, the remaining intrepid exponents of the dark arts (it sounds creepy, although I'm not too sure what it means!) began their second séance.

This time we were better prepared. Iris and Dusty had written the letters of the alphabet on small white cards. Ken and I placed the lettered cards around the perimeter of the round table in a near-perfect circle. I took a medium-sized glass from one of the tables already laid for breakfast, and placed it in the centre of the circle of cards.

The four of us sat, not holding hands this time, but each placing the forefinger of our right hand lightly on the top of the upturned glass. We were silent, our breathing deeper. Then Iris's voice filled the room as she began her incantation. 'We are gathered here to meet you. We are friends. We wish to contact someone who has crossed over. Please give us a sign you are here with us.' Nothing happened. We waited a long moment. Again, nothing.

'Is anybody there? Please give us a sign,' I said in a sepulchral voice. Still nothing. I tried again, this time a little louder. 'If you are here, let us know. Contact us.' As the word 'us' left my lips, the glass began to move.

Was it Ken pushing it? I didn't think it was Dusty. Perhaps Iris? It wasn't me, I knew that. We kept quiet and watched the glass. It moved to the letter D and stopped. Dusty exclaimed, 'It's D! Is there a message for me?'

The glass moved erratically and stopped at the letter A. 'It's not you, dear,' Iris said to Dusty.

'Maybe it's a lousy speller.' I had no idea why I said that. Maybe it was nerves. The glass continued on its way, moving around the table in fits and starts. It stopped at N.

'Dan?' Ken blurted out. 'Anyone know a Dan?' No one answered. The glass sped away, racing around the table, nearly falling off. We all leaned as far forward in our chairs as possible, our right arms fully extended so we could keep our fingers on the glass.

There was no doubt in my mind that neither Iris nor Dusty was causing this to happen. If it wasn't a natural phenomenon, and if it wasn't a piece of mischievous magic by Ken, it was a phenomenon of the unnatural kind!

The erratic movement of the glass affected us all. I felt certain the other three were just as exhausted as I was. Tension can be tiring. Bernie's entrance was a welcome relief. We removed our fingers from the glass and slumped back in our chairs. 'It's like a bloody haunted house movie in here. Do you want the lights put on?' Bernie asked. With one voice, we answered, 'Yeah, put 'em on.'

In the bright light, we grinned sheepishly at each other. 'What's so funny?' Bernie asked, then added, 'Did you have any luck?' We shrugged, not knowing how to answer. Bernie studied us and the table. 'Well, I hope you were luckier than I was tonight. Ah! Your own Ouija board,' he added, pointing to the circle of letters on the table. He knew the routine. 'Did you get any good messages? I wouldn't be any good at this game, I can't spell. Come on, what happened?'

Dusty answered, 'At first I thought I had a message, but it was for someone named Dan. None of us know a Dan.'

'Dan?' Bernie repeated. 'Not Dan, Dan, the dirty old man?'

We laughed. The mood was broken. The séance was over. As we tidied the room I whispered to Bernie, 'How d'you get on with Anna? What happened?'

'Nothing. She disappeared with some Yank. These Yanks are everywhere.' Bernie paused for a moment, and then smiled. 'Thank goodness, otherwise we'd be out of work.'

There were no more séances in Vienna. The next few days we were busy doing shows in the far western reaches of the American sector. On the Sunday we had a free day, although we had to pack ready to leave for Italy early the following morning. Next stop, Rome.

We travelled by train. As we went through the border check entering Italy, it was as if someone up there had switched on the lights. The Italian border guards had a smile for us, the Italian crew came on board and the atmosphere changed. Lighter, happier, a feeling of fun. Maybe it was all in my mind, but whatever the reasons, I was glad to be in Italy.

On our first day in Rome, I talked Bernie into walking around the capital and seeing as many of the historic places as possible. We ended up with blisters, but we saw the Trevi Fountain – I even threw a coin in the water to ensure I'd return – we scaled the Spanish Steps, and had our first ever pizza. Bernie had seconds.

By my third day in Rome I had fallen in love with the place. I could speak a little Italian, which I'd learned from my Italian friends in London and from Ray, an old school chum who had been stationed in Italy during the war. That made it easier for me to get around. But my affection for Rome split me from the rest of the show, including Bernie.

I loved wandering the streets of the city and hanging out at the local cafés and restaurants, whereas the rest of the show loved the American base with its PX and canteen, where the food was American. I didn't blame them, but as far as I was concerned, I intended to take advantage of my stay in Rome.

That stay soon came to an end. Luckily, though, we weren't leaving Italy; we were going north to Livorno, a military port, then on to Verona, the fictitious home of Shakespeare's legendary Romeo and Juliet.

As soon as we had settled into the faded elegance of our venerable hotel, Dusty, Bernie, Diane and I took the opportunity to explore our new surroundings. By their reaction I knew I could be spending a lot of time there on my own. Verona was a quiet, tired old town, not the fashionable destination she would become. Cheap flights, holiday package deals and mass tourism hadn't yet changed the world. I liked Verona as it was.

By the second day, I'd discovered a friendly restaurant, Manetti's, I think it was called, where the prices were low and the food superb. I became a regular, while another regular, an American sergeant with the name of Aldo – guess which country his family came from! – had seen the show. He assumed I was of Italian extraction and a Catholic. He introduced me to the owner, Mr Manetti, and his two daughters, Katerina and Maria.

Aldo was engaged to the elder daughter, Maria. The unengaged daughter, Katerina, was gorgeous, and seemed to like me. We would spend time sitting in the restaurant trying to make conversation, though her English was even worse than my Italian.

Mr Manetti invited me to attend Sunday morning mass with the whole family. I don't know why I agreed, but I did. Katerina and I walked a little ahead of the two maidenly chaperones, probably aunts, and the rest of the family, including Aldo. As I entered the church I felt a sharp pang of guilt. I had recently become engaged to a non-practising Catholic, a young lady from London named Kathleen, and the similarity of the names was disconcerting. Of course, I hadn't mentioned to Katerina – or anyone else – that I was engaged.

After the service, the crowd mixed and exchanged family news and waited for their opportunity to give a personal greeting to the priest. Aldo pulled me aside. 'The family likes you. Katerina is taking your courtship seriously.' Courtship? Hey, hold it right there, I thought, but didn't interrupt him as he continued. 'Don't play games with her, Mike. This is family. I'd be very upset, and so would Mr Manetti. D'you know what I'm saying?'

'Listen to me, Aldo,' I began softly. 'I like Katerina very much, but I'm leaving in a couple of days and who knows if I'll be back. I have to face reality. I'm in show biz, you know what that's like.' I looked him in the eyes and said gravely, 'I want you to tell Katerina I'm not right for her. Explain to the family I'm just an actor, a gypsy, always travelling. I think it's best that after today, none of you see me again. I have to suffer the pain alone. I don't want to hurt her or disrespect the family. Will you help me, Aldo?'

'You got it, pal. You're doin' the right thing. Leave things to me. Say nothing.' We shook hands.

In regimental style, with Katerina and me leading the way, we walked past old Verona houses and down quiet medieval streets to the restaurant, where I made an excuse about having a rehearsal for that night's show. Ignoring the suspicion I saw in Mr Manetti's eyes, I left without a backward glance.

I felt a little embarrassed about my exit speech to Aldo, especially the bit about suffering the pain alone. But I never dreamed Katerina and her family were thinking marriage. I was just flirting with a pretty girl. She was a sweet and beautiful young lady, but I was in love with somebody else.

The tour was coming to an end. For the remaining days in Verona I hung out with the rest of the cast at the PX and ate American. We were leaving for France in a few days, where we had ten days' work lined up. Then it was back home to England. Ken suggested, as time was running out, that we should have another séance.

At first the warm Verona nights made the thought of spending time inside a hotel room unattractive to me. I liked to go to a sidewalk café after work, drink an espresso and people watch. But on our last day in Verona, the weather changed. The temperature had dropped, and it looked like rain. That morning Iris, Dusty, Ken and I decided over breakfast we would indeed have a séance. This time everyone said they wanted to come.

The old, once rather grand hotel where we were staying had seen better days. It had not only a lounge, but an oak-panelled reading room that cried out for a séance. Dusty and Iris chatted up the manager, who obviously fancied the young and innocent-looking Dusty. A smile did the trick. We could use the room from eight until ten.

That night, we all had supper in the hotel's dining room. The food was good, if you like lasagne, and I do. The rest of the Unit must have too, as they all kept shovelling pasta into their mouths. I guess it made a change from hamburgers and French fries.

At around eight we made our way to the reading room. No need to rearrange the furniture, we just had to place nine chairs around the large, heavy wooden table. If that baby rose off the ground I would be a sceptic no more.

Before we could start, Bernie decided he would sit on the sofa and watch. The young lady in the trio shook her head, wished every one goodnight and went to her room. Carl suddenly remembered he had some paperwork to do. We were again down to six.

The preliminary moves were carried out: the white cards with letters written on them were placed in a circle on the table with an upturned glass in the centre; flickering candles on saucers were strategically placed around the room; the lights were switched off; everyone was seated, arms outstretched, forefinger gently on top of the glass.

Iris began the incantation. She repeated her request for the spirit to contact us. Although there was no response, the mood was such that Bernie felt restrained from making a humorous remark. 'Give us a sign you are with us. Spell out "yes" if you are here,' I said. The glass started to move, slowly, and then gathered speed. It stopped at the letter Y, then at E. It came to a halt at S. There was an audible intake of breath around the table. Bernie stood watching in amazement. I said, as calmly as I could, 'Who is the message for?' The glass spun erratically. Dusty's finger came off the glass momentarily. The glass sped to the letter D, then A, then N, then G, then E, stopping abruptly at R.

Iris couldn't contain herself. 'Danger! Are you saying someone here is in danger? Who is it?'

The glass remained still. Dusty spoke up. 'Is it me? Am I in danger?' There was no movement.

Ken, his Australian accent more pronounced than usual, asked, 'OK, mate. No messing about. Am I in bloody danger?' There was no movement. Then the glass began racing round, stopping somewhere in the middle of the table.

I was getting annoyed. The glass had spelled out 'danger' and now refused to tell us who was in it.

'Are you still with us? If so, spell "yes".' I didn't try to hide my frustration. Once again, the glass spelled 'yes'.

'Right. Tell us who is in danger.' I felt the glass spin forward; I had to concentrate to keep my finger on the glass. Round the table it went, first quickly then slowly. It spelled out ALL.

'All?' I queried. 'That's terrific,' I said sarcastically.

'What d'you mean, all?' Iris asked. The glass remained still.

'This is ridiculous,' I said. 'You're playing games with us. If you really are a spirit, prove it. Do something other than moving this glass. That is, if you really are moving it. We're probably doing it ourselves, whether we know it or not.'

'Damn right,' Ken put in. 'If you're a bloody spirit, move something we can all see.' He paused, looking around the room. 'Like that old desk over there. Move that.'

If I had witnessed what happened next while on my own, I doubt if I would have believed it, but I wasn't alone. There were five other people in the room.

After Ken's words, there was complete silence as our eyes concentrated on the old desk. The silence was broken by gasps of astonishment, as the heavy wooden desk suddenly moved at least two feet forward.

'Jesus bloody Christ!' Ken said in disbelief.

'Holy shit!' Roger exclaimed.

'Bleedin' hell,' said Bernie, shaking his head.

'My God,' Diana intoned in shock.

Iris and Dusty held hands, dumbstruck. I was silent too. I couldn't believe my eyes. Strangely, there was no discussion after the event. As I remember it, the evening just disintegrated. We were all badly shaken. I can't remember the candles being put out and cleared away. I can't remember leaving the room and going to bed.

The next morning, over an early breakfast, we noisily discussed the trip to France. The thought of visiting Paris was indeed exciting. No one brought up the subject of the séance, except Bernie. He said confidentially to me. 'I don't know exactly what went on last night, but you'll never get me at one of those effing séances again.'

I suppose the others might have felt the same. Anyway, we never held another séance on the tour.

There is a coda to this story. It concerns the flight to France. We were flying in an army transport plane. No regular seats. It was stark and empty – we were the transport. We sat on two long benches either side of the plane, like parachutists.

Due to storms, we took off three hours late. The journey was rough, with continuous bad weather. At one point the co-pilot came out of the cockpit and instructed us to prepare for a possible crash landing. A what! We had straps to hold on to, that was it. Five minutes later he was back again. This time he told us to relax. We were going to make a forced landing at La Rochelle.

The landing was successful and we stayed overnight in the delightful town. But I can assure you that until we were safely down on the ground, the thought uppermost in the minds of five of the passengers in that army transport aircraft was the warning we had received during the séance in Verona. The warning of danger for all.

Bernie and I worked with Dusty again more than once over the years. By then she had become the famous Dusty Springfield who is so well remembered and loved. We shared a few laughs together, but we never went into the details of the Verona séance. And I never found out why, with four first names to choose from, she called herself Dusty.

9

Mafia, Kosher Style: Meyer Lansky

The celebrated authoress Jackie Collins, sister of actress Joan and daughter of our agent, Joe Collins, sometimes worked with Bernie and me on our TV show in the Sixties.

Every so often, during rehearsal breaks, I would talk to Jackie about a book I was reading by Peter Maas. It was the first book I had ever read about the inner workings of the Mafia. Until the early Sixties the Cosa Nostra/Mafia was unknown to most people. Jackie seemed as fascinated by the subject as I was.

Towards the end of 1969, while our TV series was on its winter break, Bernie and I were asked if we would attend a convention at the Hilton Hotel in Chicago. It was a strange offer and came out of the blue. We would receive no salary, but we and our wives would get four first-class return tickets to fly to Chicago for five days, including suites at the Hilton, all expenses paid. All we had to do, besides promotional interviews on television and radio, was one performance for the RoBo Car Wash Corporation.

It was a weird deal, as no one in Chicago had ever heard of us. But we didn't care. We were determined to enjoy the experience. For me personally, it was an opportunity to see the city of Al Capone, and the place where the St Valentine's Day Massacre took place. Our affable host, Ralph Hedges, showed us a wonderful time. We travelled with an entourage of at least fifteen people and visited a range of venues, from an exclusive nightclub where singer Jack Jones was appearing, and where Bernie and I were introduced as 'the most successful and famous act in Europe' (I wish!), to various downtown bars where we took our glasses with us when we left, still drinking as we headed to the next joint. Two stretch limos followed our every step and were ready to whisk us off to wherever Ralph thought might amuse us.

Each night we would meet for cocktails in Ralph's massive hotel suite, number 505. I'll never forget his instructions, 'Five o'clock in 505.'

The first evening in 505, somehow I was separated from Cassie, Bernie and Siggi, and was stuck at the back of the room surrounded by happy Americans. Across the room, standing by the large rented bar that came with a bartender and waitress, stood Ralph, guys on each side of him. He waved to me and shouted out 'Jack Daniel's'.

I barely heard him and didn't know if it was a question or not. Assuming he was introducing me to one of his friends, I yelled back, 'Hi,' with a smile and a friendly wave. Minutes later, the jolly, over-weight waitress came over and handed me a glass half full of ice and bourbon. And that is how I first met Jack Daniel's – we've been close friends ever since!

Ralph seemed to know everybody who was anybody in Chicago, so I asked him if he could arrange for me to meet someone in the Mob. He laughed, saying he'd take me to lunch tomorrow at a place where Mafia big shot Sam Giancana sometimes ate, and where probably every other man was either a Mafia member or connected. 'This is Chicago, Mike,' he told me. 'It's not what you know, it's who you know.'

Giancana wasn't there, but Ralph introduced me to Lew, a smartly dressed man who looked to be in his sixties and who, Ralph told me later, was a very important figure in the Mob. When told I was a famous entertainer from England, Lew proudly informed me his parents were Welsh.

We chatted at the bar for a while over our drinks. He was surprised that I, an Englishman, knew so many gangsters' names. He answered the few questions I asked about US crime, but he only had one question for me. Did I know Tom Jones? I told him Tom was a mate of mine. Lew was impressed.

Our time in Chicago was ending. The performance we gave to a packed ballroom of exuberant conventioneers went by in a haze of booze – imbibed not by Bernie or me, but by the audience.

Ralph and his entourage stood on unsteady feet in front of the stage, glasses in hand, smiling benignly at us. They understood very little, but they liked the sound of our accent. The crowd of two thousand clapped, whistled and cheered every time we mentioned America, Chicago, and the Chicago Bears, the local football team. We finished our drastically cut performance with the words, 'Thank you, and God bless you all, and God bless the United States of America.' We would have received a standing ovation, but most of them were in no state to stand up.

Months later, back in England, Jackie Collins called asking if she could borrow my Peter Maas book. She was writing her very first novel and needed background information. I readily agreed, telling her about my Chicago trip and saying I had written an article on the Mafia I'd been hoping to sell to the *Sunday Times*. They hadn't taken it, but if it would help her I would drop it in to her dad's flat along with the book.

There is a little twist to this tale. I first heard the name of Meyer Lansky from Lew in Chicago. Later I learned of the incredible influence Lansky had in the growth of organised crime. A little man who earned respect from both Italian and Jewish crime leaders, he became an underworld legend in his own lifetime. And I met him. It was in Miami...

I have been fascinated by gangsters since I was a schoolboy, when I watched James Cagney and Edward G. Robinson play them in the movies. In those days, there was no mention of the Mafia. The authorities knew little if anything about what was then truly a secret society.

My dad knew about it, however. In the early Twenties, he had a fight with a mafioso in a private gambling club in the West End of London. The guy ran out into the street, and my dad chased him down Shaftesbury Avenue. Mafioso or not, the guy wanted no part of my father. The mobster turned, took out a gun and fired off a wild shot at my dad, hitting him in the leg.

No charges were filed. Dad saw his private doctor and got fixed up. No permanent damage. The gunman went back to the States.

Dad never spoke about it. When I once asked about the scar on his calf, he brushed me off by answering that it was nothing, just an accident. He did talk about gangsters sometimes, but only in general. Once, when he was in a loquacious mood, he told Bernie and me some of his thoughts on crime and criminals. 'When you have bad laws, the kind people don't want, gangsters take care of their needs. Take gambling, drinking, prostitution, being a queer. Who voted to make any of that against the law? D'you know what I mean?'

He went on, 'Gangsters normally come from working-class families. They're uneducated. Not that they're stupid or anything, they just didn't go to the best schools. I never met one who even got to a grammar school. You know, boys, I'll tell you something, there are plenty of crooks who come from privileged backgrounds, but they become politicians, company bosses, bankers. For my money, they're gangsters too without breaking the laws they made to suit themselves.'

Dad took a rest. His cigarette was down to a half inch of ash, which dropped on to his jacket. He casually brushed it off, took another cigarette from his Player's packet and lit up. It was still mid-morning so he was probably on his tenth fag.

He had a little more to say. 'Most of the gangsters, the tough nuts who are considered criminals – and I suppose they are – that I know, would sooner do you a favour than a bad turn. That is, of course, if you've played the game and not pulled any strokes. There's good and bad everywhere. As long as you do the right thing, you'll always have respect.'

Bernie and I were always spellbound when Dad talked. He knew so much. He was well read, an authority on many card games, and could do complicated multiplication and work out percentages in his head. He rarely talked about his early life before he was married, though family and long-time friends would sometimes let a story or two slip out – like the shooting.

Although his name was Samuel, my dad was known by friends and enemies alike as Mougie, a name derived from a Russian word meaning 'bad boy'. He had a bad temper. It was rarely lost at home, except when he and Mum had a big row. He was normally quietly spoken, a loving father who never raised his hand in anger at anyone in the family. But in his gambling-orientated work environment, I once witnessed his violent side. He said very little beforehand, something like, 'Behave yourself, otherwise I'll hurt you.' Once he'd said that though, he immediately threw a punch. The time I was present, one punch finished the dispute.

On another occasion, as we were about to get off the 653 bus at Manor House Underground station in North London, we allowed a bunch of old Jewish ladies to alight first. A big man in a workman's outfit was waiting impatiently to get on the bus. 'Come on. I haven't got all f***ing day. You f***ing Jews think you own the world.'

'Watch your mouth,' Dad said menacingly as the ladies scurried off the bus.

'You can go and f*** yourself, Jew boy. Come on, yiddle, get off.' The man took a couple of steps back, sneering as he did so, daring Dad to get off the bus.

Dad calmly stepped off, and went towards the man. I followed, fists clenched. I wasn't going to stand by while this big bastard beat up my dad. The guy was at least four inches taller, and in his leather protective gear, he looked a lot heavier too. Dad, wearing his favourite raglan sleeve raincoat and grey trilby hat, looked outgunned. This is a mismatch, I thought.

I was right, but not in the way I imagined. The workman stood looking at Dad with complete contempt. 'Well, Jew boy, what d'you think you're going to do?'

Dad took a step closer to the man and threw a right hook to his jaw. The guy staggered back about three yards. His back hit the brick wall behind him and he slumped to the ground. Dad quickly grabbed hold of the man, holding him up.

'Now I told you to watch your mouth. You shouldn't pick on helpless women,' Dad said quietly.

'I'm sorry, sir. Sorry, sir.' The man said.

'Don't do it again.' Dad was right in his face. 'OK?' Dad straightened the front of the man's shirt collar and clothes where he had held him.

'Thank you, sir. Sorry, sir.'

Dad gave him a nod. Turning to me, he said, 'Come on, son, let's go.'

As we walked down the steps that led into the Underground station, I couldn't believe Dad was so cool and calm. My heart was still thumping like a rock band's bass guitar. I wanted to talk about what had just taken place, but Dad seemed oblivious to it. I couldn't stand it any longer.

'Dad, aren't you shaken up? I am.'

Dad looked at me and frowned. 'No,' he answered. 'Why should I be? It only took a minute.'

'You're not even breathing hard. What I mean is, weren't you scared at all? He was a big geezer. You just cracked him.' I shook my head, half in bafflement, half in admiration. 'I wish I was like you. How do you do it?'

Dad thought for a moment. 'I'm used to it.' He put his arm round my shoulder as we walked to the ticket counter. 'You don't want to be like me, son. Getting into fights isn't clever. Sometimes you can't help yourself, but using your brains is better. Remember that.' The inquest was over. We went to the platform and caught our train.

At various times in his youth Dad lived with an Italian family, the Mancinis. I had an Uncle Alf who was a Mancini, though I didn't know if he was a real uncle or not. When I was in my early twenties I asked my grandfather, Jack, who was a Bloomfield, where we originally came from. He told me Barry. I had no problem at all with my antecedents originally coming from Barry, in South Wales. Wasn't Gareth Edwards, the Welsh scrum-half, my idol? It wasn't until years later that I learned Grandad had meant Bari in southern Italy.

Dad hung out with a family of Italian criminals from Red Lion Square in London who were involved with off-track betting. I call them 'criminals' because bookmaking outside a race track was illegal at the time; there was no Ladbrokes, or any other betting shops. To make a halfway honest living Dad made a book at race tracks, was a bodyguard to some big-time bookmakers, and ran private games of Chemin de Fer and Faro – a favourite card game from the old Wild West days – at glamorous gambling parties.

Dad also played bridge and poker for money. He never seemed to lose at those games; only at betting on horses did his luck run out. He was friendly with London's rival top gang leaders, Jack Spot, who was Jewish, and Albert Dimeo, known as Albert Dimes, who was Catholic – though as far as I know, they, like my father, never practised their religion. I met both Spot and Dimes, and they seemed like nice guys. They always had time for a laugh with Mougie's two boys.

Some of Dad's various partners from his different enterprises used to make brief but regular visits to our home, though Dad didn't like his business associates to become too friendly with his wife and family. One such partner, known as 'Snouty' Parker, was the brother of Maxie Parker, the guy who started Ladbroke's. Pity Dad hadn't been Maxie's partner. The Winters family might have ended up as part owners of Ladbrokes!

All this, especially his involvement with an Italian gang, maybe explains why my dad would have known about the Mafia before the FBI. And perhaps his life explains my interest in gangsters and tough guys. Anyway, I thought my unique family background would be an asset when I became a partner in a nightclub on Miami Beach in the early Eighties.

I had been told by a friendly neighbour that nightclubs paid protection money to the Mob. Was that so? I thought of Dad, and wondered how I would react if I was approached. Some of the locals seemed to be inexplicably and perversely proud of Dade and Broward Counties' historic association with organised crime. Miami Beach had once been the home of legendary gangster and mafioso Al Capone, and it was the current home of the notorious Meyer Lansky, one of the most powerful mobsters in the history of the rackets. To me, the Beach was virtually controlled by greedy politicians and rich businessmen, who, I was told by my lawyer, had connections to the Mob.

But it didn't affect me. The Mike Winters Room, at the Versailles Hotel on the beach side of Collins Avenue, was a big success. My partner, Joe Hyman, a big-time tour operator associated with the iconic Harry Goodman, made sure the many British tourists who were coming to Miami through various tour companies booked to spend an evening at our club. I organised and produced the cabaret show, which was followed by dancing to live music. I was 'mine host' for the evening.

Good-looking and sophisticated, Joe was the ideal partner. He expertly did what he had to do, and left me to do what my experience allowed me to do. Our cabaret was terrific. An all-American cast, except for our British star, Derek Dean. Derek had settled in Fort Lauderdale, near Miami, and had the skill, talent and knowhow to entertain not only the British holidaymakers, but the American patrons too. The room was packed every night. Joe and I had a lot of fun, and just as importantly, had a big success.

Prior to 1980, the summers on Miami Beach were dead. From May until mid-November it was too hot and humid for tourists. In previous summers, the only life I used to see when taking an early evening stroll along Collins Avenue, where the main hotels were situated, was an occasional cockroach walking along looking for company.

The Mike Winters Room began to change all that. Through Joe's foresight and expertise, the British began visiting Miami Beach in their thousands. Many of them spent an evening at our club. We were the talk of the business community. The famous Fontainebleau Hotel wanted us to move our operation to their place. But we had other plans.

A larger club, that's what we needed. We would run the bars ourselves; that was where the money was. And we would have our own kitchen and serve our own meals. Could it be done? Yes. Were we capable of doing it? Therein lies the rub. I was a former entertainer and erstwhile writer, who knew nothing about running a bar and less about running a restaurant. And Joe? Man about town, travel expert, bon vivant, whose restaurant expertise was restricted to appreciating good food and knowing which West End eating establishment was 'in' or 'out'. Not the ideal couple to embark on the proposed venture. Joe came up with the idea of getting a partner. He also came up with a partner.

Hyman Ukitel was a local big shot. He owned three restaurants, including the well known Place for Steaks, frequented by the local movers and shakers. It was also there that, almost any night, you could find a mobster or a visiting showbiz personality.

Hyman, known as Hy, was a big man, around six foot two, with an expansive personality. His suite of offices took up the entire penthouse of the Sterling Bank Building on the 72nd Causeway. So, I had two partners now. After being a partner with Bernie for twenty-five years, partnerships weren't an arrangement I relished. Joe Hyman on his own was fine; he didn't interfere with my life, but now another Hyman. . .

When I first met Hy, though, I was impressed. He was in his large office, sitting in an authentic barber's chair being shaved by his personal barber. Two of Hy's associates were also present. One, a stocky guy with greying sideburns, looked to be in his fifties. I think his name was Benny or Lenny. The other guy was standing, arms folded across his chest, leaning against an exceptionally large desk. He looked sharp in a dark grey suit and a fashionable white, pin-collared shirt.

Joe introduced me to Hy, who in turn introduced me to his associates. Hy was covered in shaving soap and his head was tilted back, so I couldn't be sure of the names he gave. But I found out at later meetings that the younger, smarter one was called Bob.

As I got to know Hy better, it was obvious to me that he had some heavy friends. On a couple of occasions when I went to his office he would be on the phone to Las Vegas. Perfectly innocent in itself, but when I happened to overhear him tell whoever was on the other end of the line to make certain that the guy they were discussing was seriously hurt, I began to suspect he was not one of nature's gentlemen.

I already had some experience of the widespread influence exerted by Miami's crime culture. In the previous year I'd been part of a consortium that bought a football – soccer – club to Miami. We named it The Miami Americans. We were in the ASL, the American Soccer League. The major money and force behind the franchise came from an Italian-American named Mario. He and I were both big boxing and football fans. He suggested I should be his personal representative in running the football club when he was out of town. I was flattered, and we celebrated the arrangement over supper at one of Miami's best restaurants. Cassie and I, and our friends Dorothy and Peter Whitehead, an English couple living on Miami Beach who had introduced us to the sport-loving Mario, had a great night and agreed Mario was a charming and generous host.

To be part owner of a football club in Miami seemed surreal. The whole area was full of Spanish-speaking people. Everyone knew how much the Spanish and the Latinos of South America worshipped 'futbol'. I called my brother-in-law, Leslie, who had run the TV All Stars for Bernie and me, to tell him the news. I would make a fortune. What could go wrong? Just two little things.

First, the vast majority of Spanish-speaking people in Miami at the end of the Seventies were Cuban. Cubans didn't play football! Second, the charming and generous Mario was soon arrested in Ohio on drug smuggling charges. Not one of the small, personal smuggling deals that were prevalent at that time. Oh no. It was the single largest drug bust in American history up to that time.

I spoke with Mario's lawyer, who told me nearly all Mario's money was tied up in the drugs, and he would do heavy time. He didn't know what would happen regarding the Miami Americans. He berated Mario for personally going out of state. 'What can I do in friggin' Ohio? Here, we got connections. Mario got a dose off the stupids. He should have known better than to go there. How can I get to a judge in friggin' Ohio?'

I had more sense than to ask questions. Anyway, it was pretty self-explanatory. The team lasted just the one season. But truthfully, I felt sorrier for Mario doing hard time than I did for myself. At least, I had been a director of a football club, albeit not for long.

So, you can see disappointment had hit me before Hy Ukitel ever came on the scene. There was something about the man that rubbed me the wrong way. I got a nagging feeling in my gut about Ukitel when the kitchen he was going to install in the new club fell behind schedule. At a meeting, Joe and Hy, who were also tied up in another promotion – an outdoor Country & Western barbecue, with lots of beer and dancing – convinced me not to worry. The kitchen, for one reason or another, wouldn't be ready, but for less money we would prepare the food at Hy's restaurant and bus it over, like they were going to do at their barbecue. Fine with me. Hy was a restaurateur. As long as it worked, I had no problem.

Toppers, the new club's name, occupied the entire penthouse floor of the Saxony Hotel on Collins Avenue. We spent money on the room, although it was impressive when we took it over. We installed special lighting, and put in a stage for a band and artists.

We didn't have a kitchen, but no one seemed to notice. The food, laid out in a self-service buffet style, was plentiful and reasonably tasty. There was pasta, fried chicken and chips, and soup that remained hot on portable grills. I don't know what the food was like in the hotels where the British tourists were staying, but they kept going back to the buffet for seconds. In any case, my efforts were focused on organizing and producing a show. And what a great show it turned out to be.

One of Britain's finest double acts, Hope and Keen, were the comedy stars, and they were a big hit. As a star guest act, I booked the legendary Gerry and the Pacemakers. Known to both the tourists and the locals, they wowed the audience every night. To add glamour, we had a good-looking, young American singer and two former Miami Dolphins cheerleaders, who did two different dance routines during the evening in exotic costumes designed by my wife.

But I wasn't involved for long, because I walked out around six weeks after the club's opening. Why? A good question. It's difficult to remember exactly what pissed me off first. Ukitel's flashy and arrogant manner began to get under my skin, but I said nothing. The first actual face-to-face confrontation was over Gerry and the Pacemakers' bar bill. The boys would invariably go to the bar after their spot and have a few drinks. I wanted the lads to get a big discount. Hy disagreed. They were getting well paid, he said, and they didn't give us a discount. If they wanted a drink they should pay like everyone else. We were running a business, he insisted, not a charity for freeloaders.

I could see his point. . .just! But I thought he was wrong. Giving the performers a discount didn't cost us anything. We had plenty of booze to sell. It wasn't as if we would run out. Having the stars of the show around the bar area was good for the paying customers. They got a chance to speak to the boys, get an autograph, and buy a drink at the bar – at full price. I thought it gave the club a friendly atmosphere. And it made the performers feel they were working for nice guys, and were appreciated. As Bernie and I had found, a happy backstage atmosphere helped create a happy evening for performers and audience alike. Anyway, Gerry and the boys weren't big drinkers, so their bar bill at the end of the week was peanuts. But Hy didn't seem to get it.

Joe sided with me, explaining to Hy it was a British thing. But the discount was reduced so the club earned something on the drinks. I said sarcastically to Hy, 'Great. With your third of the money, you can set up a charity for greed control.' I did manage to smile to soften the insult, but from that time on, Hy hardly spoke to me, and I returned the favour.

I wasn't too put out by the conflict. These little arguments happen in most relationships. It's far from rare in show business. Mostly, they blow over. You get on with your work, and my work was proving to be pretty exciting.

One evening at the club, Patrick, the manager, came over to me accompanied by a small elderly man and a taller woman of similar age. The little man looked vaguely familiar. Patrick, showing great deference to the couple, introduced them as Mr and Mrs Meyer Lansky.

No wonder the man's face looked familiar. I had seen it in magazines and newspapers. He was known as the Boss of the Jewish Mafia. Meyer Lansky – friend and business associate of Lucky Luciano, one-time Capo di Capi of La Cosa Nostra, and of Benjamin 'Bugsy' Siegel, the tough Jewish mobster who helped create Las Vegas as we know it today before being shot to death there.

The media had labelled the three men as notorious gangsters, as killers, as kings of crime. I looked at the short, ageing man, in a sedate blue suit, standing alongside his wife, and for a moment could not believe that he was the infamous Meyer Lansky. I wanted to ask him a million questions about his life, but I said with a smile, 'Good evening. So glad you decided to give Toppers a visit. I'm sure Patrick will take good care of you. Please have your first drink on the house. It is a pleasure to meet you both.'

I probably went over the top. It wouldn't have taken much for me to have bowed at the waist. What an idiot I was, but he didn't seem to think so.

'Thank you, Mike, that's very nice of you. You're from England, right?' He turned to his wife, 'You see, Thelma, the English are very polite. Nice place you got here,' he said to me in a deep raspy voice. Patrick showed them to a table at the back, with a good view of the stage.

I made a quick stop at their table after the floor show. We exchanged pleasantries, and instead of me asking him any questions about his life and times, he had me telling him about my showbiz background, and how Angelo Dundee and Betty Mitchell, Angelo's office manager, had been good friends to me when I first arrived in Miami. Well, I guess most show people like talking about themselves!

The next day, I was annoyed I hadn't had a photograph taken with Mr and Mrs Lansky. What the club needed was a photographer on the premises. I called my good friends John and Irene Bell, owners of local newspaper *The British Tourist*. John gave me a number to call, and that same evening I had a photographer working at the club.

Carlos Ramos and his assistant, Anna, arrived at six o'clock. At seven, when the first customers began arriving, Carlos and Anna started work, canvassing the room for potential customers. Many welcomed the opportunity of having their photograph taken. Before the evening was over, the customers could pick up and pay for their photographs, which were encased in a cute little locket. A nice little keepsake. I was pleased with myself for getting the photo deal up and running. It should be a nice earner – far more than we would make on Gerry and the Pacemakers' bar bill.

I was standing welcoming customers as they arrived, when my attention was drawn by loud laughter coming from the entrance. It was Hy Ukitel with three other guys, probably enjoying a dirty joke. They came up to me, still chuckling.

'How's it going?' Hy asked me coldly.

'Not too bad. It's still early.' As I spoke Carlos appeared.

'Photo, señors?' Carlos asked, pointing his camera at the four men.

Hy looked Carlos up and down with distaste. 'Who the hell are you? Who let you in?' he asked in a bullying tone.

Carlos looked at him, then at me, and was lost for words. I was immediately angry at Ukitel's unnecessary rudeness.

'Hey, cool it,' I told my large, overbearing partner. 'Carlos works here. I hired him today. He's doing a good job.' I turned to Carlos. 'You're taking plenty of pictures, right, Carlos?' I shared my smile with Hy and his friends, and tried to sound pleasant.

'You hired him? You don't hire anybody without clearing it with me. Understand? I'll sort this crap out tomorrow. Send the boy home.' He turned his back on me and spoke to his companions.

'Come on, fellers, let's eat. We'll take a booth in the side room. I'll get Pat to arrange service for us. The room looks good, doesn't it?' Hy added as they walked away, ignoring me completely.

I stood there dumbstruck. Then the anger began to rise. I thought I said under my breath, 'The fucking pig.' Maybe it wasn't quite under enough, as Carlos gave me a nervous look and went right back to work.

I tried to calm down, but I was reaching boiling point. How dare he speak to me like that? I was too mad for analysis, too angry to remind myself to be cool and remember where I was. I strode purposefully into the side room, over to where the four men sat. I stood looking down at Hy, while he looked up at me with a supercilious expression on his immaculately shaven face. I pointed a finger at him. 'Who the fuck do you think you are? Don't you ever speak to me like that again, or as big as you are I'll fucking kill you.'

I paused as he made a move to get up. 'Stay where you are, you fat pig, otherwise I'll hurt you,' I said, my finger inches from his eyes.

I stared hard at his three companions. They were mute. They were taking no chances. This was Miami. They didn't know me. I could be a connected guy, even a 'made man'. There had been a shooting at the Newport Hotel last week. Maybe I was carrying. In Miami you didn't take anything for granted. Dead bodies showed up in Biscayne Bay, and the local fish liked human flesh. The three men wanted no part of this.

I was running out of steam. My temper evaporated at the lack of resistance. 'You had better understand one thing; I do not work for you. We are partners. Get it. You remember that.' I glared into his pale blue eyes. Unfortunately, I didn't see fear, only hatred. It was over. I walked away, ignoring the looks of the few people who witnessed the impromptu entertainment, and went to the bar and had a large Jack Daniel's.

I didn't stick around to see Joe. He called the following morning and we met. After a quick and civil discussion we agreed I would leave at the end of the month. He and Ukitel would buy my shares as soon as the construction costs were paid. I would receive 15 per cent of the profit at the end of six months. I would carry on for a few more weeks to ensure a smooth transition, and make arrangements for Mike Keen or Alby Hope to take my place as host. Then I was out of there.

The next night at the club, I was there as usual, smartly dressed and looking good. A smiling Patrick couldn't wait to tell me that the Lanskys had enjoyed themselves, and thought I was a charming guy. They were coming in to catch the show again tonight. Patrick made no mention of my words with Ukitel.

After the show, I joined Mr and Mrs Lansky. I was about to ask if they had liked Hope and Keen's new material, which I found very funny. But Meyer didn't believe in pussyfooting around.

'I hear you had a disagreement with Hy Ukitel last night.' He looked in my face, waiting for an answer.

'These things happen. No big deal.'

'What was it about?'

'Like most things, over nothing. You know how it goes,' I said with a smile.

'I had a good friend from England,' he said, abruptly changing the subject. 'He's from Leeds. In Yorkshire.' (He pronounced it *Yorkshyer*.)

'One of my best pals comes from Leeds, Ian Brill. Actually, I have a lot of friends from there.'

'My friend's name is Owney Madden. Maybe you know him?'

'He's too young to know Owney Madden. Talk about Tom Jones, why don't ya,' said Thelma.

'Listen to me, Mike, forget about Tom Jones.' Meyer gave his wife a quick look of exasperation. 'Owney Madden was a big shot, believe me. You could do business with that guy. He had a big piece of the Cotton Club. You've heard of the Cotton Club, right?'

Of course I had. 'Sure,' I said with enthusiasm. I hadn't heard of

Owney Madden, so later that night I asked Patrick about him. It seems the gangster from Leeds was really big time. He was a boss of the Irish Mob, part owner of many illegal gambling operations along the east coast, and a partner in the legendary Cotton Club in New York.

I don't know why Lansky even mentioned Madden to me. Because he was British? Perhaps he just wanted to talk, be friendly. Was he bringing up the fact that he had a big-shot English pal just for my benefit, to make it seem we had things in common? But as we talked a little more, I felt we did have a tenuous link – he reminded me of my dad.

Dad had said violent people should be treated with care, like wild animals. You may think they are trained, but you can never be certain. A dog can be a wonderful, loyal friend, but provoke him at the wrong time and he'll bite you. Dad also told Bernie and me that bad people are bad. And they can't help doing bad things. You stay away from them, they're trouble.

I should have remembered his words. I should have been aware that Hy Ukitel wouldn't forget being embarrassed in front of his friends. He would want to do bad things to me. What could I do? I'd have to wait and see what happened. Anyway, at this time, bad things were happening in Miami Beach.

Cuban dictator Fidel Castro had opened his prisons and asylums and released thousands of prisoners and mental patients, many of whom had flooded into Miami. It was the start of a crime and violence epidemic. Not an ideal situation for the tourist industry! From now on a sunny, fun-filled vacation in Miami Beach was going to be a very hard sell. My time in the club business was nearly up.

As business at Toppers fell, Hy's resentment against me grew. He wanted revenge. Of course, I didn't know what he was planning, and wouldn't until it happened. Then, of course, it would be too late. I wouldn't have known anything at all if it hadn't been for Bob

– the guy in a pin-collared shirt from Ukitel's office. We bumped into each other in laid-back Coconut Grove. We sat down at Market to Market, a small coffee and sandwich café owned by a friendly Frenchman, and ordered espressos.

'I gotta tell you, Mike, you are one lucky SOB,' Bob said as he manoeuvred his chair so the sun hit his face. Like me, he always had a sun tan.

'You mean getting out of the partnership?' I asked.

'Well, that too. But I'm talking serious injury time here.'

'What are you talking about?' My curiosity was growing.

'Hy wants to do a number on you, baby. It's eating him up. He called his contact in Vegas to send someone over to take care of you. The Vegas guy called a friend of Meyer Lansky here in North Miami, to save money by using a local guy for the job. You know what a piker Hy is – if you offer him something for free, he'll want two.' Bob grinned in amusement. He took a sip of his hot coffee and continued.

'Well, my friend, you know what a small town it is here, Lansky found out about it. I guess the guy in Miami told him. Let's face it, nothing goes down on the Beach without Lansky and his heir, Al Malnik, knowing about it. Anyway, here's the best part. Lansky called Hy and warned him to lay off, that you were a friend of his, and also thick with Chris and Angelo Dundee. Hy nearly crapped his pants. He went white. Whiter than he normally looks, and that's saying something. You should have been there. You got a lot of connections for a little Limey, don't you?' He laughed and slapped me on the shoulder.

I had been lucky. And it seems my dad was right all those years ago when he told me most gangsters would rather do you a favour than a bad turn. I guess there are good and bad in every walk of life.

10

Two Princes, Two Dinners and a Luncheon

Have you noticed how gangsters, hoodlums and members of the Mob are credited like royalty?

You've heard the expression 'King of the Underworld'. Was that Al Capone or Lucky Luciano? Benjamin 'Bugsy' Siegel 'ruled' Las Vegas, Vito Geneves ran an 'empire' of crime – the kings and princes of the 'rackets'. Meyer Lansky was the 'power behind the throne'; a good position to be in as long as you never try to take the throne. He was wise; he knew that with power came responsibility.

The British royals I met seemed to have an innate sense of duty and were also aware that with power came responsibility. And I learned through meeting them that being a member of the royal family is not only tea and cucumber sandwiches (which I happen to like) and keeping a stiff upper lip (which I admire), but having genuine affection for people. And, equally important, a good sense of humour...

When I was a kid at elementary school in Tottenham, my favourite game was one we called 'Cavaliers and Roundheads'. It was a simple game. Some of the kids would be Cavaliers, the others Roundheads. We would chase each other around the playground and have fights with toy swords.

The game had nothing to do with politics or class warfare, although, on reflection, the class monitors and nerdy pupils seemed more prone to be Roundheads – law and order and that sort of stuff – and the Cavaliers drew from the not-so-academic, and those most likely to gather lots of bad marks for misbehaving. I didn't really fit into any particular category, though I was a Cavalier because I liked the large feather plume the king's men wore in their flamboyant headgear. I suppose I had showbiz inclinations even back then.

This loyalty of mine to the throne has stayed with me ever since those early schooldays, which is rather surprising as in my late teens and early twenties I was a serious socialist. My political view-point changed over the years, but certain beliefs remained constant. A democratic royal family does not – well, should not – in any way conflict with social justice.

Having lived in America for long periods, I have come to the conclusion that having a Queen and royal family as we do is one of the best promotional assets Britain has, and it's value for money too.

If the Queen had been able to keep a percentage of the tourist money she brings in, plus a piece of the action her prestige brings to export deals, she would have her yacht back again, and certainly a private jet. The bankers and brokers who helped to economically rape our Sceptred Isle have them. The royals are a bargain.

The first royal I actually spent time speaking with was Prince Michael, Duke of Kent, the Queen's cousin (I love the title 'Duke' – unfortunately, Americans pronounce it 'Dook'!). The Duke was in Miami in 1989 to show the flag and to be Grand Marshal for the Miami Grand Prix international motor race, in which the Jaguar team were competing. His trip was arranged by Meg Clements, one of the Welsh stalwarts of the Miami British Chamber of Commerce. She ran the local British rugby team, so naturally we got on very well, even though I was well past my sell-by date as a player.

At that time, Burger King's CEO was Englishman Barry Gibbons, and a visit by Prince Michael to the fast food giant's headquarters in South Miami was arranged. I'm not sure how or why I was invited to go along, perhaps because the British Chamber wanted to have a local British celebrity around. Anyway, I'm glad I got involved. I became great friends with Barry, a straight-talking, fun-loving Lancastrian. Our wives, Barry's Judy and my Cassie, hit it off too. I also got to know Prince Michael.

Before Prince Michael's visit was over, we had a chance to talk. We had numerous interests in common. We were both members of the venerable theatrical lodge, the Grand Order of Water Rats. He had a lot of amusing stories about his many friends in show business, and he proved to be an interesting and witty conversationalist. The description of him that first comes to my mind is 'an English gentleman of the old school'. Not the kind of description I had ever read in the press, who always seem to cover his glamorous wife rather than him. Well, that's showbiz!

There is no doubt he won the admiration of the Miamians on the day of the Grand Prix. The summer heat was brutal even for Miami. All the spectators were in shorts and T-shirts, and many – at least the males – were topless.

It was a long walk through the pits and along the track to the stands. A scorching sun was burning down on the Prince's uncovered head as he made his way past the crowds. In his beautifully tailored, buttoned suit jacket and his immaculate hand-made shirt from Pinks in London, he won the admiration of the semi-naked crowd as he nonchalantly walked towards the enclosed stands, impervious to the blistering heat. Every few steps, he would give the applauding race fans a friendly smile and an appreciative wave.

The other members of his entourage, including me, all had our jackets on, but we had either removed our ties or loosened them and undone the top shirt button. The Prince in contrast, shirt button done up, pure silk tie with its large knot perfectly tied, walked as if he was strolling through his Gloucestershire garden on a spring day, hosting a garden party. Of course, he was well aware that it wasn't so. The Prince knew what he was doing. Stiff upper lip! The Americans appreciated it.

Barry Gibbons told me later that admiration for the British prince and his stiff upper lip was a talking point around the business community. You can't buy publicity like that.

Prior to Prince Michael's visit in 1989, I received the bad news that my brother Bernie had been diagnosed with cancer. The news affected me more than I realised. My consumption of bourbon went up, and my behaviour deteriorated in proportion. I needed something to occupy my mind. Writing or performing weren't in the frame, so becoming involved with Prince Michael's visit and being asked to help organise his gala dinner had been the perfect antidote for my personal headaches. I'd also worked with Walter Bowen of Center Stage in Orlando on a film about Jaguar's participation in the Grand Prix, and now, knowing of my friendship with Angelo Dundee, Walter asked if I would work with him on a couple of boxing productions in Orlando. I agreed. I had nothing better to do.

My marriage, if not exactly dead, was in desperate need of life support. Cassie and I were living apart. Somehow, one Friday lunchtime, she and I had got into what could be considered one of our all-time top ten rows. In keeping with my regular and, according to Cassie, annoying habit of refusing to get into a drawn-out shouting match, I grabbed my overnight bag, which I kept ready for such emergencies, and checked into the hip Mutiny Hotel in Coconut Grove.

My good friend Peter Stringfellow, the Peter Pan of the nightclub world, had opened the hottest club in town just across the street from my hotel. All I can say is that a good time was had by all! I arrived home around four o'clock on Monday afternoon, bleary eyed, slightly hung over, looking to resume my usual pleasant relationship with my wonderful but tempestuous wife.

I placed my key in the lock. It didn't work. Putting down my overnight bag, I concentrated on the keys, making certain I had the right one in my clammy fingers. I tried again. No result. This called for another examination of the keys. It was the right one. Slowly, deliberately, I tried again. No good! I pressed harder. I practically twisted the key out of shape. I told myself, don't panic, locks can warp, especially in hot weather − not knowing if that was true or not.

I took a deep breath. Calmly, I began knocking on the door. Not so calmly, I continued to bang. It wasn't that I was angry − though I was. I was getting worried. Her car was still there, parked in its usual place. Where was she? Cassie just didn't go for walks in the afternoon heat. She was too worried about sunstroke.

I banged a few more times on the door, but the noise and the effort made my poor head ache. Was she OK? I tightly closed my eyes, gritted my teeth and banged on the door even louder as I shouted out her name. 'Cassie! Cassie!' Hysteria was beginning to creep into my voice.

'Yes? Who is it?' My wife's well-articulated, English-accented voice came from behind the locked door.

'It's me, Mike. I can't get in. My key doesn't work. Are you all right?'

'I'm fine. I've changed all the locks. I don't want you here. You want to be a bachelor, well, go ahead and be one.'

'What are you talking about? Who wants to be a bachelor? Come on Cassie, let me in.'

'No. You aren't wanted here.'

'Come on, let's talk about this. . .'

'Go away. Call me and we'll make arrangements about your things. I have nothing more to say. Don't waste your time standing out there. Go back to your hotel. Goodbye.'

Living full time in a hotel had its good points, but cost wasn't one of them. After a month of swanning it in the cafés and restaurants of the Grove and living it up in Stringfellow's, I took the news of the Mutiny Hotel's imminent closure with mixed emotions. I'd miss having my room cleaned and my bed made daily, and its central location was a boon, but I missed Cassie and hoped this would be the right time for reconciliation. I was wrong. Cassie didn't want to know.

With the Mutiny Hotel about to close and Cassie wanting nothing to do with me, Walter's suggestion that I come to work in Orlando was looking better every day. Walter came up with the clincher: He lived in a large three-bedroom house in Kissimmee, on the outskirts of Orlando. Why didn't I stay with him? His last wife, his second, was long gone. It sounded good to me. 'I'll be there,' I told him, and within two days, I was.

By the time I had fully unpacked, knew my way around the house and had investigated the orange groves bordering the development, there was a change of plans. Pinklon Thomas, former heavyweight boxing champion of the world and a great pal of mine, was on drug rehab and wanted to leave Miami and its seductive nightlife scene. I talked it over with Walt. Within days Pinklon had moved in with us.

We called our home the Halfway House. For the next fifteen months we laughed a lot, talked a lot, I stopped drinking and we worked on getting our lives together. I began a campaign to win back Cassie, driving from Orlando to Miami every week until, with one excuse or another, I got to see her. After a while we went to supper together. It was a very subtle courtship. It took over a year and a lot of driving, but it paid off; by the beginning of 1991 we were back together. We still argue, but we're still together. And I no longer have an overnight bag standing by ready to go.

Walter meantime got himself another wife, and moved to Gulf Shores, Alabama. I decided, with Cassie's input, to stop my gypsy lifestyle and stay at home in Miami Beach. I began work on a thriller, but progress was slow, and was eventually halted by a phone call from Leeds. It was from my oldest friend Ian Brill, suggesting I might be interested in organising a fundraising visit to Miami for Prince Philip on behalf of his charity, the Duke of Edinburgh Awards Foundation.

To get involved with such a worthy charity sounded good, not to mention that I would be meeting Prince Philip. I told Ian I'd love to do it. He was pleased, but warned me it wasn't easy. I had to be sure the event would be financially viable, as I had to guarantee the Foundation a substantial sum of money.

One other thing, Ian pointed out; I would have to go to London for an interview so they could see if I was a suitable person to promote a fundraising event for a member of the royal family. Ian would make the appointment, suggesting that a cordial meeting over lunch would be a good idea.

'They'll want to meet you. See what kind of person you are. Of course, they know who you are, but they may ask a few questions about your background.' So it was arranged that I would meet two of the top directors of the Awards Foundation, Hugh and Carol (not their real names; one must be circumspect when dealing with major people who work for royalty).

In the late summer of 1994 a meeting was confirmed. I took my daughter, Chaney, with me. She spoke their language, unspoiled by Americanisms or showbiz jargon. We met for lunch at the

Lanesborough Hotel in Hyde Park, London. Hugh and Carol were charming, and were in turn charmed by my daughter. It was agreed that I would organise the fundraising promotion in Miami early in 1995, and my business, WINC (When In Need Care), would take 20 per cent of the revenue raised after all expenses were paid. The Foundation would receive its agreed guarantee plus 80 per cent of revenue after expenses. Ian would work with the Awards Foundation in England, and I would handle the Miami end. It was an exciting prospect. Although I had never done anything quite like it before, I was confident I could handle it. What could possibly go wrong?

There was a change to the original plan Ian had given me. It would not be Prince Philip who would be coming over, but the Queen's youngest son, Prince Edward.

Back in Miami, I began making plans, the most important of which was figuring out how I would raise the money I had guaranteed. But before I could begin nailing anything down, Carole was coming over to, as she put it, 'do a rec' – a reconnaissance of the hotel where the Prince would be staying, and the various places he might visit to raise money for the Foundation.

Problem was, Carole hadn't given me a definitive date for Prince Edward's arrival, which made it impossible to confirm anything. She would let me know shortly. But what did that mean? This wasn't exactly a flying start!

Miami in November is normally a good month for weather, dry and not too hot. So when Carole arrived from London, she fell in love with Miami Beach immediately. She loved the sheer beauty of the place, the waterways, bays, ocean views, a profundity of palm trees, bougainvillea and a skyline of striking high rises.

I showed Carole the hotel I had tentatively chosen for the gala ball, and where the Prince and his entourage of two (his equerry and a Scotland Yard detective bodyguard) would stay. She approved.

I explained that the hotel was eager to have us stay there, but the ballroom was rapidly being booked for Saturday nights, the obvious night for a gala ball. We would have to confirm the date soon. I suggested the second Saturday in April. That would give us nearly six months to organise and confirm everything.

I also explained that mid-November was the start of the Miami Beach Season, which continued until Easter. If we put back Prince Edward's visit any later we might miss the wealthy 'snow birds' — northerners who had second homes in Miami Beach and other expensive neighbourhoods. We needed them to buy the costly tickets for the ball. Even more importantly, they were the people who could afford to attend the exclusive private dinners I intended to arrange. It was a pity Carole couldn't have stayed longer. She really loved the place, and everyone who met her, especially Americans, found her warm and friendly.

I received a call from Carole the following week. Everything was fine. The first and second weeks in April weren't possible, but the third week looked good. The Prince would arrive at Miami Airport on Monday 17 April from New York. I would have him for a whole week. She would give me full details as soon as they were finalised. But none of this information could be released yet. She'd let me know when.

Concerned that I couldn't release any information, I conferred with Ian. He assured me it was all going well. We didn't need any press yet. He had been through all this before. But he had been organising in England where everyone he dealt with knew him. I was in Miami where I could count my contacts on one hand.

Two of those contacts. . .Let me rephrase that, two of Cassie's and my dearest friends, whom we had met through Danny La Rue, were my first source for advice. Sandra Holiday, a lovely lady from London, and her partner Anita Priest, one of Miami Beach's most renowned interior designers, were two of the kindest and most genuine people we knew.

Anita, an experienced businesswoman, was concerned I hadn't given myself enough time. From now until April every charity organisation would be chasing the 'deep pockets' for donations. Sure, Prince Edward was a fresh name for Miami, but not many Americans knew about him.

And she had another worry for me. I would have to work with an American charity, preferably one with a prestigious name, because Americans would get no tax relief on donations to an overseas charity. Without that tax incentive, Anita didn't think I'd raise sixty dollars, let alone six figures.

Sandra suggested I contact the Joe DiMaggio Children's Hospital. She had read recently that they had helped an English child, so it would be a nice gesture if Prince Edward made a personal appearance at the hospital. Perhaps I could come to some arrangement with them.

I got hold of my American associate, Tricia Naron, a former director of the Coconut Grove Chamber of Commerce, and asked her to make me an appointment as soon as possible with the marketing director of the hospital. I also prevailed upon her to use her considerable charms on the manager of the Grand Bay Hotel and get him to hold the ballroom for 22 April, and to reserve the presidential suite for the preceding week.

When Tricia rang back, the news was good. The hotel had agreed to hold the ballroom and presidential suite. She had also arranged a meeting for me at the DiMaggio Hospital for the following day. I asked her to come with me. I'm glad I did.

The hospital's marketing offices were across the road from the main building. It had its own car park. Tricia – I called her Trish, short for Trish the Dish; she didn't object, I think she rather liked it – pointed out the expensive cars parked around us. 'I guess you get a richer bunch of people working for Joe DiMaggio than we had at the Coconut Grove Chamber of Commerce,' she said.

Mary Lynn Cohen was in charge, and appeared to be in her

early thirties. There was a no-nonsense aura about her. No question, she was all business. Trish had given her a short indication of what we had in mind when they had spoken over the phone, astutely emphasising the prospect of Prince Edward making a personal visit to the children's wing.

Mary turned to her second in command, a large, dark-haired Irish-American who hadn't lost his brogue. 'Having the Prince personally visit the children would be wonderful PR, wouldn't it, Pat?' she asked.

'Yes, it would. He'll get a lot of publicity out of it too. So will the English. They certainly need some good publicity, what with their murderous policy in Northern Ireland.'

I was more than a little taken aback at the remark. I knew Northern Ireland a little, having played there many times. My last visit had been to entertain the British troops stationed there. I certainly didn't consider them murderers.

'Well,' I said. 'When the Republicans and the Loyalists stop murdering each other I think the government policy will change.' I gave Pat a tight-lipped smile. He flushed and was about to respond when Trish jumped in. 'My mother's family came from Ireland. They tell me it's a beautiful place. Have you ever been to Ireland, Mary? Mary? Sounds so Irish, is it?'

I thought Mary might sound Irish, but I wasn't too sure about Cohen!

Mary shook her head impatiently. 'I don't know. I think we should get on with the business in hand, don't you?' she said, giving Pat a meaningful look. 'I would like to show Mike . . .' She paused, and with a twinkle in her eye added, 'Mike! It sounds so Irish. As I was saying, I'd like to show you around the hospital. It's quite a place. Now, let's discuss dates. . .'

Except for the Irishman's dislike of the English, the meeting went well. The children's hospital would be a beneficiary. It would receive a percentage of all revenue raised and would have no cost or risk in the promotion, and I agreed to Prince Edward making a visit. All revenue cheques would be made out to the hospital, giving the payer a legal tax deduction. The hospital would deduct its percentage and forward the balance to me to pay the multitude of expenses, after which I would send the profit to the Awards Foundation.

On the drive back to Miami, Trish and I discussed the deal. 'It all went pretty well, don't you think?' I asked Trish, who was driving.

'I hope the big Irish guy lightens up next time.' she said. 'We certainly don't need him making remarks like that to the Prince.'

'I had no idea your mother's family came from Ireland. You look Scandinavian,' I said.

'My mother's family came from Germany and Dad is a true-blue American boy. I thought I had better say something before you and Paddy came to blows. Shall we send Mary and Paddy boy a bottle of Irish whiskey each, part of the Christmas spirit thing?' she said.

'Hmmm. . .Maybe we should make it whiskey for him and a Hanukkah bottle of wine for Mary. Her name is Cohen, not Cohan.'

Unlike in England, Christmas in Miami is over before you know it. That year Cassie and I stayed home and enjoyed each other's company. Cassie had sold quite a few paintings, and I had Prince Edward's visit to look forward to. Early in January 1995, I heard from Carole in London. First the good news – Prince Edward would arrive in Miami on 17 April. Then the bad news – I still couldn't release the date to the media.

I told her about the tax deduction problems and about the special relationship we would have with legendary baseball player Joe DiMaggio. 'Was he the man who was once married to Marilyn Monroe?' Carole asked. I told her yes. I asked her, how could I sell the visit if I couldn't publicise the date?

'No problem,' she said. 'You can confirm the date with your sponsors and the businesses HRH is to visit. The media coverage won't affect them. In fact, Michael, some companies don't want media coverage. Anyway, you will have clearance in a week or so.'

Trish and I were putting in all sorts of hours. There were meetings with Burger King, Barclays Bank, British Airways, Virgin Airways, Arby's, a couple of supermarkets, more meetings with the DiMaggio people, who on their part had arranged meetings with potential sponsors. I also had to find someone to produce invitations and gala night brochures, so I met with many printers. Eventually I got a great deal through Betty Mitchell, Angelo Dundee's office manager. She introduced me to the CEO of a large printing firm who was a big fan of Joe DiMaggio, and had fond memories of England from his service days when he was stationed near Norwich in Norfolk. When I assured him that in return for giving us a special price he could have a complimentary table and would definitely meet His Royal Highness, Prince Edward, he was satisfied. 'You mean this Prince guy is a genuine Royal Highness? Hey, that's really sumthin'.'

Ian Brill kept in contact, though he didn't have the Prince's flight plans yet. He had set up the whole project, had attended numerous meetings travelling up and down to London from Leeds, all at his own expense, without any remuneration whatsoever. He also had a menswear business and a new wife. Both had demands. I was keen for him to fly out and help me, but he couldn't get over until the day before the Prince was expected.

By February we had received a few deposits from the gala ball ticket sales, and had a couple of potential sponsors. I hoped my meeting with the Fisher Island marketing people would improve that situation.

Fisher Island is arguably the most expensive chunk of real estate in Dade County. At our meeting, the marketing director and I agreed to hold an exclusive dinner for twenty-five couples at $1,500 per couple. The director, a sharp, no-nonsense type of guy, suggested Saturday 22 April as the best date, but the gala was on that night, so we settled on Monday the 17th, the day the Prince arrived. That shouldn't be a problem.

Six weeks before D-Day – Prince Edward's arrival – Carole called. Almost her first words warned me she was either about to inform me of a catastrophe, or tell me something fabulous was going to happen. I'm an average optimist, but I would have bet on the former.

'Are you standing or sitting?' she asked. I told her I was standing.

'I think you had better sit down,' she said with no hint of humour.

'That's OK, go ahead. I'm a big boy.' I didn't know what to expect. I just knew it was nothing to do with my family, so I was pretty calm.

'HRH will not be arriving on Monday,' she said. There was silence while I let that sink in.

'When will he be arriving?' I was scared of hearing the answer.

'Well, it seems it won't be until late Tuesday, or more probably Wednesday morning. He has personal business he has to attend to.'

'Personal business! I would think this fundraiser was personal business. So he won't be here until Wednesday, eh? This means I'll have to cancel quite a few important fundraising events, including the lunchtime visit to the Joe DiMaggio Children's Hospital on the Tuesday. That won't go down too well!'

I couldn't believe this was happening. It seemed so ridiculous. Personal business? I kept my voice controlled, which was a struggle, but I didn't want to blame the messenger.

There really was nothing I could say. Carole understood my position. She told me to forget about the amount I had guaranteed to the Awards Foundation. Whatever we did would be fine. I told her I just hoped we could cover the expenses now that we would lose the Fisher Island dinner, and who knew what repercussions there would be over having to cancel the Tuesday visit to the children's hospital. After I had hung up the phone, I did sit down.

There wasn't anything I could do but get on with it, but the thought of telling the people we had let down made me feel a little sick.

The reaction I got from the marketing director and his team at Fisher Island wasn't pretty. They blamed me. I apologised, but my credibility was ruined. As for the Joe DiMaggio people, they had a good reason to be furious, and they were. They had been ready for Joe to be there in person to meet the Prince. For American baseball fans, letting down Joe was a national insult, a far better reason for going to war than rumours of weapons of mass destruction in Iraq.

At least Mary Lynn Cohen didn't blame me personally. She saw how upset I was. Of course, Paddy's views were as expected. He ended his rant with 'What else can you expect from the duplicitous English?'

I couldn't let it go. 'Look, Paddy, whatever the reasons Prince Edward has let us down, I apologise for him. However, I am English, and resent being termed duplicitous. You really must control your prejudices. It is as stupid as me hating the Irish because of your offensive remarks.' There was a moment of hush caused by the sharp intake of air into lungs. It was broken by Trish's calm voice. 'Pat, did you know Mike's wife's family originally came from Cork? It's a small world, isn't it?' It was true, and it cooled the atmosphere a bit.

Mary agreed all we could do was carry on and do our best. Before Trish and I left, I handed Mary a personal letter from me apologising to Mr DiMaggio. Pat and I shook hands, and managed a smile.

With only three weeks to go, Carole called. This time there was no warning to sit down. Everything was on schedule. Arrival date was Wednesday, 19 April at approximately 1pm. Ian Brill would confirm. I could bring in the media.

All the aggravation and worry was getting to me. I called Chaney, my daughter, and asked if she would fly over and help me. I also needed someone who knew the publicity angles and could work with the media. I didn't want the expense of taking on a high-powered PR firm. Luckily, I knew just the man. My friend and erstwhile TV associate, Walter Bowen, said he would fly down from Gulf Shores, Alabama, the following week, and do it for expenses only.

With Chaney and Walter working alongside Trish and me, things began to come together. It was too late to hope for a financial success – the loss of Fisher Island and cancellations from the DiMaggio Hospital supporters was too big a handicap – but it looked possible we might at least cover our costs.

I formed a Duke of Edinburgh Awards Foundation Miami Beach Committee, inviting Barry and Linda Gibb to join. It was a big plus having one of the Bee Gees involved. It was a pity Dwina Gibb was away, as we had worked on Prince Michael's dinner together. I also invited Gillian Donnerstein, a bright young Englishwoman, highly regarded in Miami's social circles. She was keen, and immediately took an active role in the promotion. The tables for the gala ball began to sell.

But time was our enemy. Walter and I met with the US Secret Service to confirm arrangements for Prince Edward's arrival. Before we knew it the day had arrived.

On Wednesday, around midday, Walter and I drove around Miami Airport's perimeter until we found the entrance to the designated private runway. The Secret Service guys were already there. Not long afterwards the small four-seater, twin-engined plane came in to land. I breathed a sigh of relief. Prince Edward was here.

The passenger door of the plane opened. First down the few steps was a pleasant-looking, well-built man in his forties. We learned later that his name was Brian and he was from Scotland Yard, assigned as Prince Edward's bodyguard. He stood aside and watched a tall, slim young man, whom I recognised immediately, come down the steps.

Prince Edward gave me a friendly wave. Was he old enough to have remembered me from television? Wearing a big smile on his good-looking face, he bounded over, hand outstretched. 'Hello, Mike, so nice to meet you,' he said as we shook hands.

'Welcome to Miami, sir.' I felt Walter's presence edging closer to my side. 'May I introduce my associate, Walter Bowen.'

They shook hands like they knew one another, which of course they didn't. For a second I wondered if the Prince had mistaken Walt for the singer Kenny Rogers – they did look alike.

'I understand we're in the same business, Prince,' Walt said confidently.

'Oh really, what's that?'

'Television. We both make programmes.'

'Oh splendid. So you're a producer, eh?' The Prince sounded interested.

'Maybe we could do some business. . .' said Walt.

'Isn't it marvellous,' I said to the Prince, breaking into the conversation. 'You've been here two minutes and the bloody Yank is trying to do a deal.' We laughed, and that set the tone for the rest of the Prince's visit.

Lieutenant Colonel Sean O'Dwyer, HRH's equerry – or, in today's terminology, private secretary – had arrived a few days earlier to double-check the arrangements. He had a droll sense of humour, and enjoyed a good laugh. To me, he was from another era, not that he was old, he wasn't – maybe in his late thirties. With long, bushy side whiskers, a strong jaw and clear, honest eyes, Sean had an aura of quiet confidence. He looked heroic, rather how I imagined the eldest brother in P.C. Wren's novel *Beau Geste* would look.

What remained of the first day was spent settling in at the Grand Bay Hotel and letting Brian satisfy himself that security was up to scratch. The second day began mid-morning with a drive of an hour-and-a-half to one of South Florida's most prestigious all-girls' schools. The drive would have been uneventful, but we had made a change in the driving arrangements

An hour or so before we set off, Sean called me aside. 'Would it be a problem for Walter to drive HRH? The fellow we had yesterday, nice enough chap and all that, but his English was a little. . .you know. He didn't sort of add to the party. Not like Walter, if you understand me? So, if you have no objection and Walter doesn't mind. . .'

Of course Walter didn't mind; in fact, he was flattered. 'Pity the Prince isn't next in line to the throne, then I could tell my grand-children, when I get any, I used to drive the King of England around. Hey, I'll settle for a Prince. The grandkids wouldn't believe me anyway.'

Our new chauffeur was in a loquacious mood. He told the Prince that he ought to visit Gulf Shores, Alabama, where he and his wife, Cindy lived with their two children. 'Gulf Shores! Thirty-two miles of white sandy beach,' Walt informed us. Not once, or twice, but so many times we were saying it in unison – 'Thirty-two miles of white sandy beach.'

We were in fine spirits when we got to the school. After a warm welcome and a large dose of deference towards the Prince, we had lunch. The school was out of the very top drawer. I would imagine its fees would have been astronomical. Besides making a donation to the Foundation, some of the students had participated in the Duke of Edinburgh Awards programme. In fact, one athletic-looking young lady we met, a teacher no less, had been a proud participant. Members of the faculty, mainly women, were under-standably fascinated by the young, good-looking Prince, who was charm personified as he answered their many questions.

I couldn't help noticing the sideways looks Walter was getting from staff and students alike. He was obviously an American; an Englishman wouldn't dress in tight blue jeans, cowboy boots, a plain white shirt, a string tie fastened by a silver emblem of

Alabama, and a tan-coloured western-style jacket – unless it was for a bet! I was pleased he'd left his Stetson back in Gulf Shores. But I'm sure they could tell he wasn't Kenny Rogers – they didn't look that much alike.

When we eventually left after a busy afternoon, the senior staff saw us to our car parked outside the main entrance. One teacher, unable to curb her curiosity any longer, asked Walter hesitatingly, 'Tell me, sir, where do you, er, come from?'

'Gulf Shores, ma'am,' Walter answered as we took a step toward the Lincoln.

'Gulf Shores? Gulf Shores?' she repeated.

'Yes, ma'am. Gulf Shores, Alabama, It has . . .'

In one voice, Sean, the Prince and I finished the sentence with him, 'Thirty-two miles of white sandy beach.'

We dropped HRH and Sean at the hotel, where we met Chaney and Trish for a quick drink and a news update.

'Mike,' Trish began, fiddling with her small red notebook. 'I know you don't want to hear this, but you must pay the deposit for the band, and for the flowers and decorations Gillian ordered for the tables. And the Mayor is confirmed for Sunday. Julio from La Voile Rouge called and gave me the good news.' The Voile Rouge, a beach club, overlooking the Atlantic Ocean, was to host a luncheon for the benefit of the Dominican Red Cross, with Prince Edward as guest of honour.

Walter chimed in. 'Well, Mike, you're goin' out with a bang. You finally got the Mayor of Miami Beach to get involved in something.'

The fundraising evening was to be held on a yacht, which according to all reports was magnificent. Movers and shakers from Fort Lauderdale and the Palm Beach area, all supporters of the Joe DiMaggio Children's Hospital, were attending.

I had contacted the owner, an Englishman known as the Commander, as soon as I knew about the Prince's change of plan.

He and his wife decided to go ahead with their fundraising dinner anyway. The Commander, who knew of me from TV and happened to be a fan, put a seat aside for my daughter, adding her to Prince Edward's party of four – the Prince, his private secretary, and the Miami Duke of Edinburgh Awards Committee chairman and his wife (Cassie and me).

Not going to the dinner didn't bother Walter. As he so aptly put it as he drove us to the yacht, 'Why would I pay to meet Prince Edward? I've met him. I drive him. And I bet they serve all that fancy-schmancy food I don't like. For fifteen hundred bucks I can eat like a king for a week in Gulf Shores, and . . .' Taking his eyes off the road for a couple of seconds, he turned his head and grinned at the Prince, setting up his punchline. 'And enjoy thirty-two miles of white sandy beach.'

How do I describe the evening on the yacht? Excuse me while I check out my thesaurus!

Diamonds. Opulent jewellery. Wildly expensive watches. Specially coiffured hair – and that was just the men! It was a little mind-boggling. The yacht had the tallest mast I had ever seen, while its length dwarfed all the other expensive yachts moored near it.

Several young cadets from a military academy, looking very smart in their dress uniform, were standing by to escort the ladies up the carpeted gangplank. But first, all the guests had to remove their shoes, which were then laid out neatly on a black tarpaulin.

Inside, the yacht had been divided into separate areas. The main lounge, wood panelled, with the feel of an elegant English country house, had been turned into a beautiful dining room. Staff circulated serving drinks. Outside on the wide, railed deck, there were three strolling musicians: a guitarist, a bassist and a clarinettist. I knew the clarinettist from the local jazz club where I had occasionally sat in with the band. He must have spent the evening trying to figure out what the heck I was doing there as a guest!

Two other custom-designed lounges had also been converted into dining rooms, with fully laid tables, immaculate white table-cloths and silver cutlery. At dinner, Prince Edward, looking very cool in a white dinner jacket and black trousers – no shoes – was the centre of attraction. He was dining in the main room, where the Commander and his good lady hosted their very special guests.

Cassie, Chaney and I were seated in the first lounge. At the table, they were separated by Sean, with men either side. They looked as if they were enjoying themselves sitting next to Sean, who in his Irish Guards traditional, full dress uniform and his mutton-chop side whiskers, looked as if he had stepped out of a casting call for the movie *The Four Feathers*.

I sat at the far end of the table with friendly, middle-aged ladies either side. I think I talked incessantly. They seemed amused, and told me they just loved my accent. I reminded them of Dudley Moore in the movie *Arthur*. Perhaps this was because after a couple of glasses of wine with my dinner, to go with the three I'd downed already, I sounded a little sloshed.

I have no idea what time we left. I got the impression everyone had a good time. Days later, when I received a cheque from the children's hospital, I found out it had been very successful financially too.

When Trish called at eight the following morning, I tried to convince her I had left for England and wouldn't be home for a couple of hours. She didn't buy it. 'You sound as if you had a good time last night. Was it fun?'

'I'm sure it was. I don't remember.' I looked at my watch lying on the bedside table. 'Trish, do you realise it's only eight o'clock? This is Miami Beach, we don't start until midday.'

'You don't today, Buster! You have a meeting at the Grand Bay at nine thirty with the band leader, who's coming up from Kendal to go over the music you want. Then you and Gillian are meeting with the flower woman to confirm floral decorations. OK, party boy? See ya at the hotel. Don't be late.'

I woke up Chaney. She wanted to be there to choose the music – scared I would insist on all big band swing numbers that no one under fifty would know.

By eleven o'clock we were done. Gillian handled the floral arrangements, and Chaney dealt with the music, at least the contemporary stuff. When she and Hal the bandleader started talking about Hootie and the Blowfish and Pearl Jam I lost the plot.

Prince Edward, Brian and Ian Brill joined us for coffee in the lounge – Ian's wife Jackie was shopping in the Grove. Before I left, Trish called me to one side. 'I didn't want to say anything in front of anyone. You did ask me not to mention it in case we got a negative. Well, we got a positive.' She gave a silent cheer.

'Great! Let's keep it to ourselves. Make it a surprise.'

'OK, but I have told Walter. . .we have to make arrangements to pick them up at the theatre.'

'Right. I'll ask Walt to say nothing. It's good news, isn't it?' I said.

And it was good news. Having David Cassidy and Petula Clark make an appearance at the ball would be the icing on the cake. Too late, unfortunately, to help ticket sales, but it certainly would add glamour to the evening, and please HRH.

I hadn't had much opportunity to talk to the Prince, but like Prince Michael, he was interested in showbiz. After all, he did run a television production company.

During the limited time we spent together talking, I discovered he was far more accomplished than I had thought. While a student, he had achieved his glider wings, earned his private pilot's licence and gained a Royal Air Force pilot's preliminary flying badge. He and I were both former rugby union players, and both loved sporting activities, though not always the same sports. I was into football, boxing and swimming. He snow skied, played tennis and sailed. We both enjoyed horse riding, but he was far more skilled at it than I.

The Prince had a Bachelor of Arts degree, so it was logical he and my artist wife would discuss art. Cassie held strong views. I'm not sure they always agreed – their discussions looked pretty animated. But there was plenty of laughter, and no blows were exchanged!

On the drive back from the Grand Bay Hotel, Chaney was curious about my upbeat mood. She soon got out of me the news about David Cassidy and Petula Clark – Chaney had been a fan of David Cassidy ever since his *Partridge Family* TV show.

She wanted to know how I had managed to get them to attend the ball. It was simple, I explained. 'I knew Petula from the old days. She's a terrific lady. Well, I called her and invited her to be my guest at the gala this coming Saturday night. She mentioned her co-star David Cassidy. I said please invite him too. I told Petula we would lay on transport and have a meal and a bottle of French champagne waiting for them when they arrived.'

Chaney was thrilled. 'So I'll get to meet David Cassidy! I hope nothing goes wrong.'

'Don't worry, Walter will take care of everything. He'll most likely talk them into going to Gulf Shores for a holiday.'

'Right. And enjoy. . .what is it? Thirty . . .' Chaney said, laughing.

'Thirty-two miles of white sandy beach,' I said, also laughing as I helped her out.

Before we could go home for a rest, Chaney and I had to go to a meeting on Miami Beach with Michael Cambar, one of the organisers of the next day's luncheon for the Dominican Red Cross.

It had been a little hairy dealing with the sharp, Spanish-speaking young men from the island of Dominica. They were cool, immaculately dressed, and members of every hip nightspot on the Beach. Problem was, they weren't too eager to pay the up-front fee for the Prince's personal appearance.

They had kept putting off paying, and then offered me a cheque yesterday, which wouldn't have cleared until after the Sunday luncheon. I told the bilingual Cambar, a schoolboy friend of my son, that unless I had the cash in my hand before Saturday afternoon Prince Edward would not, I repeat, not appear at their function.

Michael got the picture, but his partners didn't fully understand. They thought the fee was going into my pocket, and what was to prevent me from skipping off and screwing them and the Prince? Fair enough. I had similar thoughts about them. What was to prevent them skipping out after HRH's appearance without paying the Red Cross, La Voile Rouge, or more to the point, me? This was Miami!

I had explained the previous day to young Mr Cambar that the money went to the Duke of Edinburgh's Awards Foundation. Yeah? What did this Duke do with the money? I was no expert, but I tried to explain. 'It's a non-profit, non-competitive leisure programme for young people worldwide aged between fourteen and twenty-five. The programme helps them achieve their best in each of the programme's four sections – community service, expeditions, skills and physical recreation. It has a special relevance to those with disabilities, or kids from disadvantaged backgrounds, as well as those in the workplace. It develops character, and it's open to boys and girls. Listen, Michael, the Red Cross will know about the programme. Remember, it develops self-worth in these youngsters, and makes them better human beings.'

My explanation must have worked, because when Chaney and I reached the magnificent home of his friend and fellow organiser, Michael handed me a large brown envelope containing the money I had asked for.

As we drove home, I asked Chaney if she would go with Mum to the gala tonight, as I wanted to get to the hotel early. I rested for a while thinking of how lucky I was. A loving wife, my beautiful daughter here helping me, and in a short time I'd see my son and his lovely wife Erin. Their flight from New York had probably landed, and they were settling in to their hotel room on the Beach.

They wanted to be on the ocean. Tomorrow morning they would be swimming in it. Who knows, I might join them. But first, let's get tonight over with.

The dining room looked spectacular, the floral arrangements superb. Gillian Donnerstein, who had done a great job, looked stunning in her evening gown. Trish too looked glamorous; in fact, the ladies had pulled out all the stops. Walter had risen to the occasion too, wearing an expensive hired tuxedo with a black silk shirt and matching bow tie. I wore my Harrods dress suit, the one I had used for stage appearances. As I dressed that night, I felt a pang of sadness; my suit reminded me of my brother, Bernie, my stage partner. But this was no time for sorrow.

At the top of the hotel stairway, Walt, Trish and I held a quick conference. Everything seemed under control. As we chatted, Brian came out of the elevator and joined us. I hardly recognised him in his smart tuxedo. 'You look nice,' Trish told him.

'I am nice, darlin'. But not as nice as you. You look smashin',' Brian replied in his inimitable London accent.

'You carrying?' I asked with a grin. He tapped the left side of his jacket, beneath which he wore his gun holster, and smiled knowingly.

We checked with the maitre d'. Special dinner arrangements had been made for Mr Cassidy and Miss Clark, who would be arriving late. No problem. And Cassie's original watercolour, one of the paintings she exhibited in top galleries in Miami Beach and Palm Beach and was being presented as a gift to HRH, was on display.

Walter and I took the elevator to the presidential suite to check that all was well with the Prince. We found Sean, who like HRH was wearing an expensive, hand-made traditional black tuxedo. The Prince asked if we'd like a drink. The toast was 'A happy and successful night'.

Let me tell you, the evening was, to use showbiz parlance, a smash hit. And what a cast! The London Palladium should be so lucky! Superstar Barry Gibb of the Bee Gees, the one and only Danny La Rue, the fabulous Petula Clark and our American guest star, David Cassidy. And, of course, there was the compère, Mr Wonderful, one half of Britain's favourite double act – at least, in his home! A legend in his own mind, Mike Winters!

After an excellent meal the stars mingled with guests and signed autographs. Earlier, I had introduced them from the stage, and they had stood up and taken a bow. The biggest laugh of the night came when I introduced Danny La Rue as the king of showbiz's most prestigious charitable society, the Grand Order of Water Rats. Danny stood up and shouted out, 'Not the bloody king, I was the queen!'

To my surprise and delight, Prince Edward, instead of having the microphone brought to the table for his speech, went up on to the stage. He thanked everyone for their support, and gave a short monologue about royal tennis. A strange choice, perhaps, but his natural charm carried it off, and I don't think anyone cared what he spoke about. The Americans were absolutely knocked out by his English public school accent.

The band finished at midnight, and hundreds of tired, but happy faces began the exodus. HRH left shortly thereafter, accompanied by Sean and Brian. After endless thank yous and goodbyes, I told Cassie I was going home. To say I was tired was inadequate – I was shattered. I gave Anthony and Erin hugs – they were exhausted too. Chaney gave my cheek a peck and wished me goodnight. It was time for bed. I had another exciting day ahead of me. This one would have a hot Latin beat to it!

I made the morning pot of tea and toasted the raisin muffins as usual, but instead of taking them to Cassie in bed, I talked her into having breakfast in our secluded garden.

It was one of those Miami mornings travel writers drool about. The world seemed bathed in extra bright colours. The sky was bluer, the fronds of the palm trees greener, the paving stones whiter. And the water in our swimming pool looked an even richer blue. I did a couple of laps, stopping when Cassie called out, 'Your tea will get cold.' Dripping wet I let the warm sun dry me, and joined her on the patio. She smiled contentedly at me as she sipped her tea.

I had to get ready to leave. I wanted to make sure I was at the club to check things out before the Prince arrived. Chaney would drive Cassie to La Voile Rouge in time for the lunch.

Everything was down to the Dominicans now. Prince Edward was their guest of honour and we had received their donation. All we had to do was make certain HRH was correctly looked after, his security was as required, and he reached the venue and got back to his hotel safely. That was up to Walter, Sean and Brian.

I had no worries that the Dominican event would be successful, glamorous, slick and sophisticated. That is how the young, Dominican guys running the function were. They lived the high life, both at home, and in Miami Beach. Sean and I had checked out La Voile Rouge a few days earlier, at mid-morning when the club had not opened yet. Empty except for a few staff, it looked tired, kind of hung-over. It reminded me of a hot model just out of bed without her face on. Sean was surprised the place seemed so secure – Brian would double check it anyway.

Julio, the young manager, told us in a slight Latin accent, 'Of course we got good security. Do you think we let people in without paying? And if some fool doesn't pay his bill, believe me, señors; it is not easy to leave. Not even if you try to swim in the Atlantic Ocean. Don't worry; we will look after your Prince and the Mayor of Miami Beach too.'

When I arrived at the La Voile Rouge on Sunday, the place had got her act together. She had her face on and was looking good. On the outside walls, there were coloured ribbons everywhere. Flags – British, American, Cuban and a larger Dominican one – were flying on the roof. Brightly painted pots holding red roses hung from the second-floor windows. The place looked as if it was throwing a party for two of Miami's favourite residents, Julio Inglesias and Gloria Estefan, the hottest humans in the city's universe in 1995.

It both amazed and annoyed me to see a couple of boutique television crews and a bunch of photographers waiting outside the club. When Walt had contacted the local press they were indifferent, or so it seemed. Now they were here on our last day. Where had they been when we needed them? The PR people for La Voile Rouge must have some clout.

As I was entering the club, the paparazzi left me alone. They wanted Prince Edward and local celebrities. At the door I showed my VIP invitation to one of the two muscular Hispanic doormen, and with a flashing smile he ushered me in.

A few people I didn't know were having an animated conversation in Spanish by the large bar. I made my way to the restaurant where the luncheon was to take place. It was a sea of white tablecloths, punctuated by the vivid red of the roses individually laid out on the table tops as gifts for the ladies. On the walls were magnificent paintings.

The Dominican Republic's national music, the merengue, with its pounding tambara drum beat, dominated the place, creating its own special atmosphere. I found myself raising my voice as I spoke to La Voile Rouge's manager, Julio, and the club's PR guru, a young lady who could have only been in her early twenties. Her name was Mimi. She was Dominican, and her father was a big shot back home. She had been in Miami Beach for eight months. Mimi had the art of seeming to be completely interested in whatever you said, whether in English, Spanish or French. I congratulated her in getting the media out. She smiled – naturally, she had perfect white teeth, though her English was a little imperfect.

'Gracias. Thank you. It ees still early. Many more will be to come. From Palm Beach and Tampa I make contact. From 'ome too, newspaper come. Dominican Red Cross ees popular, so ees the Engleesh Prince. Every table full. Thank you, Señor Michael, for working weeth us.'

I mumbled something humble and went to the entrance to wait for the Prince. The crowd had grown bigger with locals and tourists curious to see what was going on. When Walter parked the black Lincoln outside the club, they sensed someone important was arriving and moved in closer, pushing the paparazzi out of their way.

Brian jumped out and stood guard at the side of the car. One of the club's car valets, wearing an all-black outfit with a red rose emblem on the chest, came over and took the car keys from Walter, who got out and let the valet get in. At that moment, Brian opened the car's kerb-side back door and out stepped Sean, followed by HRH. The paparazzi and the TV units went crazy, battling with the public to get to Prince Edward.

Walter, Brian and Sean acted as a defensive shield, surrounding the Prince. I was about to go to his aid when I was stopped by a doorman who jumped down the couple of steps on to the street, authoritatively clearing a space for HRH and his defensive unit to follow him down a side alley to a back entrance. Cameras flashed, shouts in Spanish rang out, but the royal team made it safely into the club.

'Where were you?' Prince Edward asked when we met up in the manager's office. 'We could have done with an old rugger player like you.'

'Not so much of the old, if you don't mind,' I said with a grin. 'By the looks of things you needed the whole bloody rugby team. Actually, the doorman was quite impressive, don't you think?'

'Rather,' HRH agreed. 'Perhaps the paparazzi will have gone by the time we leave?'

'I don't theenk so, Señor Prince,' Mimi said. 'Everyone weeth a camera will be coming off the beach about that time. And, the Mayor's office will remind the media that he will be here weeth you, Señor Prince.' She gave him a dazzling smile. 'I theenk we should take our seats for lunch, Mayor Gelber ees already seated, as are your wife and daughter, Señor Michael. They are very lovely, no? I had them shown straight to their tables. I will arrange their car to be waiting when they leave.' This time I got the dazzling smile. She touched Prince Edward's arm. 'Come weeth me, Señor Prince. You are at the top table. Gentlemen, your table and seating numbers are on your invitations. I'll leave you in the capable 'ands of Julio.'

We watched HRH and Mimi walk away. Walter couldn't take his eyes off Mimi's retreating figure. She was no more than five feet two, with long, dark brown hair – just his type. I was about to say to him, 'You're already on your third wife, are you trying for a fourth?' But I didn't say a word.

Walter sat with Brian at a small table set up in a space behind where HRH was sitting. Chaney was seated with Sean near Cassie and me, who were at a table with three young couples from the Dominican Republic. Our table, like most of the others, was animated with chatter and laughter. Youth dominated the scene. You could have won a prize if you had spotted anyone over fifty! Well, not quite. Besides myself, there was the Mayor of Miami Beach, Seymour Gelber. Now in his third term, he was rapidly kissing middle age goodbye.

A female dressed in the uniform of a high-ranking Red Cross officer gave a short speech in Spanish to an appreciative audience. I didn't catch her name or understand a word of what she said. Then it was Mayor Gelber's turn.

He thanked everyone for such a warm welcome, then continued . . .and continued. . .and continued. It was probably no more than twenty minutes, but it seemed like an hour. The captive audience listened politely while the Mayor droned on. They wanted to hear, and get a good look at, the British Prince. Mayor Gelber carried on regardless, mentioning how pleased he was that an English prince had honoured Miami Beach with a visit. Somehow the remark was taken to be the start of an introduction to Prince Edward.

The Prince left his table and took the few steps to the stage. The crowd went wild, cheering, applauding and whistling. HRH and Mayor Gelber stood together on the small stage a few feet apart, looking at each other – the Prince expectantly, the Mayor baffled. As the exuberant yelling and applause died down, the Mayor, not quite hiding his annoyance, said, 'Sit down, Prince. I ain't finished yet.'

The people laughed, hooted and whistled. HRH grinned, shrugged and made a dignified exit back to his table. Gelber got the message. Having given a short account of the special relationship between Great Britain and America, adding how fortunate America was to have friends like the wonderful Dominican Republic, he quickly followed with a glowing introduction to the Prince. No matter what his age, he was still a smart politician.

Prince Edward was smart too. His speech was short and concentrated on the great time he he'd had in Miami Beach. He intended to return, he said, and when he did nothing would stop him going to the Dominican Republic. He graciously thanked everyone, even the serving staff, not only in English but in Spanish too. He was a big hit.

Mimi came over to the table and quietly suggested I take my wife and daughter and leave before the crowd started departing. Outside was like a scene from the Oscars in Hollywood. There were more cameramen and women than I thought existed in Miami Beach – maybe in the whole of South Florida.

Two doormen stood guard at the entrance, but the space between them and the roadside where Chaney's car was waiting was packed with people, leaving its driver just enough room to stand, arms folded, leaning against the vehicle. As soon as he saw my two gorgeous women at the entrance he got in and started the engine. With the help of the doormen we pushed through the crowd. Our man jumped out of the car and Chaney took his place. I helped Cassie into the back, simultaneously jabbing an elbow into a persistent cameraman who was leaning on me trying to see who was sitting in the vehicle.

I managed a 'See you later' before Chaney began to pull away. Both my ladies had big smiles on their faces. They loved a bit of excitement, and were probably remembering Mayor Gelber's immortal words: 'Sit down, Prince, I ain't finished yet.'

The club employees and I muscled our way back to the entrance without much effort. Before I made it back inside, there was bedlam in the street.

There was a wild rush towards the alley at the side of the building. Behind a phalanx of English royalists, two Dominicans in black uniforms bearing the sign of the red rose, and Prince Edward pushed their way to the road and their transport. It was a battle. Unfortunately the English contingent consisted of just two members, Sean and Brian. Walter had already slipped out and now sat in the black Lincoln, engine running, fortuitously parked in the space left by Chaney's car.

I rushed to their aid, imagining I was wearing the plumed hat of a Cavalier. It seemed a far more exciting game than the one I'd played in my boyhood. We were completely outnumbered, but heroically we Royalists fought our way through the unruly mob, oblivious to the dangers of the deadly cameras manned by fanatical paparazzi who pressed ever closer. Fearlessly, and urged on by our royal Prince, the phalanx surged forward – forward to the car, forward to freedom!

We had made it. The Prince, pushing away a ferocious paparazzo, entered the sanctity of the solid vehicle. Two loyal followers quickly joined him and the mechanised chariot sped off, scattering innocent onlookers and forcing frustrated paparazzi to abandon any thought of chase.

There was nothing more I could do. I accompanied the two Dominicans back to the club, where guests were leaving in numbers. The car valets were rushed off their feet fetching the parked vehicles.

I had parked my car a block away. But the traffic would be horrific for a while yet, so I went to the pool and had a large Jack Daniel's, relaxing while I waited for the traffic to clear.

An hour later I was at the Grove Bay Hotel, knocking on the door of the presidential suite. Brian, after ascertaining it was me, opened the door and let me in. 'Did you get out OK?' Sean asked me, but it was Brian who answered.

'Never seen anything like it in my born days. It was bleedin' worse than leaving West Ham after a Saturday home game.' he said, and went back to the beer he'd left on the coffee table.

'It was all those damned cameramen and tourists. I am quite sure most of them had no idea who I was,' said the Prince, putting down his nearly empty champagne glass before getting up from a deep armchair and stretching his arms.

'Oh, I wouldn't say that, sir,' I began. 'In fact, a few of your admirers are outside the door waiting to meet you. They say they're old friends, and you'll know them immediately.'

That got his attention. He straightened his tie. In public, he never looked anything but correctly dressed.

'Really?' he said. 'I know them? What are their names?'

'Paparazzi, sir. You met them at La Voile Rouge. Shall I let them in?' I said pleasantly.

It took a minute for it to sink in. 'You bloody bastard,' he said, laughing and waving his fist at me.

'Well done, Mike. I think that calls for drinks all round, don't you, sir?' Sean said, turning to the Prince.

And that is exactly what we did. The toast was 'To Queen and Country. . .'

11

Red Leather, Yellow Leather: Helen Mirren

Dick Haymes was one of my favourite singers of the Forties and Fifties. Besides his recording career he made movies, and he was married to screen goddess Rita Hayworth for a while – well, you know what these Hollywood marriages are like!

He and I met in a lift at the Piccadilly Hotel in Manchester. I was in pantomime, and he was doing cabaret at the aptly named Cabaret Club in the city centre.

Dick was wearing a tuxedo beneath his smart open coat. I thought I recognised him from his movies, but more than likely it was from publicity shots of him when he sang with big swing band legends – Benny Goodman, Harry James and Tommy Dorsey. Dick had one of the best light baritone voices of his time, but it wasn't his voice which had originally made me so interested in him. While I was a student I'd been a fan of another of his wives besides Rita Hayworth, the actress Joanne Dru. I guess we had a similar taste in women, although I had only one wife. Dick took two shots at it!

'You look like you're going out on the town tonight,' I said with a smile.

'Not really,' he said, smiling back. 'I'm going to work.' His voice and American accent convinced me.

Without standing on ceremony I introduced myself. As it happened, he recognised me from the pantomime publicity around the town and outside the Empire Theatre, which was practically opposite the Cabaret Club.

I asked if he had time for a drink before his show. He politely declined. However, he did invite me to his show the following night. Before I could answer, the lift stopped and we stepped out into the lobby. As we walked to the entrance I thanked him for the invitation and told him I looked forward to seeing him tomorrow night. Perhaps we could have a drink afterwards. He smiled. 'Sure,' he said.

After my show the following evening I took my time leaving the theatre and strolled the short distance to the Cabaret Club. I didn't bother to call first and reserve a table. I knew the owner, a former wrestler, would find a spot for me if the club was packed. When I arrived, the rotund, powerfully built owner greeted me warmly and took me to a table on the elevated level of the room with a good view of the stage.

The room was practically empty. I thought it was because there was at least half an hour before show time.

I ordered a drink and waited patiently, wondering when the club would fill up. It didn't. The lights dimmed. A spot hit the stage. Music began as an offstage voice introduced Dick Haymes. Looking every inch a star, he walked on and began his act.

The fact that the audience consisted of only seven people, including me, didn't seem to bother him. He sang and chatted in between the songs for an hour. He was terrific. As he left the stage, the audience of seven gave him a standing ovation. He came back on, did an encore, and finally exited to another standing ovation.

Ten minutes later, after signing autographs for the six fans, he joined me. He ordered a coffee, telling me he didn't drink. He hadn't told me he was on the wagon. I congratulated him on his wonderful performance and told him I admired his professionalism, saying it must have been tough with such a small audience.

Dick said thoughtfully, 'In the movies I learned to try my best without an audience or any reaction. Why should I short-change these nice folk who paid to come and see me tonight? It's those who didn't come I got a problem with.'

He smiled ruefully and added, 'I'm grateful to be here. I drank myself out of a great career and six marriages. I left Hollywood. I live in Ireland now. I quit the booze and quit looking for wife number seven. Hearing the applause gives me a good feeling, and I don't have to pay alimony,' he said with a grin.

Later, reflecting on Dick's performance, I couldn't imagine many comics doing their full act and an encore to such a small audience. Actors and actresses are different. I don't know many, but my old friend Edward Hardwick, one of the stars of the TV series *Sherlock Holmes*, comes from a prestigious theatrical family and would give his best if lit only by a candle to an audience of one. The same goes, I believe, for Dame Helen Mirren. Both are true thespians.

I used to play football with Edward. I never had that pleasure with Helen, but I did know her, if only a little. Let me tell you about it. . .

D o you ever really know what people think of you? I don't think so. I always saw myself as a quiet, reasonably minded, sensitive man, with a deep sense of honour and fair play. Indeed, my wife told me many times that her friends and respective husbands or boyfriends thought I was a nice chap.

Friends and showbiz acquaintances of brother Bernie had a rather different opinion of me, so he told me, most commonly expressed as 'stuck up'. Cassie's – and my family's – opinion of me was as follows: vain, vague, inept and – I couldn't believe this one – charming!

Who am I to disagree with any of those opinions? Yet no one

mentioned, though I feel no one would argue with the statement, that I liked pretty girls.

That being said, anyone who really knows me wouldn't have been surprised that while walking along the platform to board the Manchester train, I noticed ahead of me a young lady with long, luxurious blonde hair, wearing a trendy woollen coat with a fur collar. She seemed to be accompanied by three young men, with hair and clothing typical of the late Sixties fashion scene. I wondered idly what she looked like.

Because of my leisurely gait, the blonde and the three guys had lengthened the distance between us. I watched as she got on the train. Only two of the men boarded with her; the third guy walked to the next entrance. So, they weren't all together. As she boarded I got a quick look of her profile. Very attractive. I was too far away to really judge, but she had something about her.

Within minutes the train noisily began pulling out. I had been one of the last passengers to get on, having no appetite for being pushed and shoved. I lit my pipe and waited until the mad rush was over, then boarded at the last moment.

The train was crowded, but there were some compartments with the odd free seat or two. A main corridor ran the length of the train and off it were separate compartments, each of which could seat eight persons on comfortable, well-upholstered benches. Each bench was divided into four seats separated by adjustable arm rests. On the far side from the corridor was a door that opened directly on to the railway track, or when the train was in a station, on to the platform. Over the seats were full-length luggage racks capable of holding large suitcases. Gentlemen always assisted in lifting a lady's luggage.

I walked down the corridor, peering through the glass top half of the wooden sliding doors that enclosed the compartments, searching for a compartment with an unoccupied seat. The first thing that caught my eye when I peered through the window of one compartment door was a head of thick, luxuriant blonde hair. I didn't hesitate. Sliding open the door I took a tentative step inside. 'Is that seat free?' I asked the compartment in general as I pointed at the single empty seat opposite the blonde.

'Yes, help yourself,' said the young man sitting to the right of the blonde. He had an unusual voice. I looked at him and murmured thanks. He looked familiar. Did I know him from somewhere? I went towards the empty seat, surreptitiously glancing at the blonde who was openly watching me. I smiled. Cool and assured. As I stepped forward I tripped over the outstretched legs of a bearded young man sitting reading a paper. I went tumbling towards the door, the one that opened on to the railway lines. I was only saved from hitting it by someone on the opposite bench grabbing my expensive Burberry wool-lined raincoat.

Falling arse over tip, assisted by the rocking and rolling of the train, somehow I ended up sprawled half on the floor and half in the empty seat.

Everyone was silent. A lone voice quietly asked if I was all right. I uttered a 'Yes, thank you,' but my dignity was shattered. I pulled myself up on to my seat and tried to act as if nothing had happened.

I put a name to the man with the unusual voice. I was sure it was actor Tom Courtenay (now, of course, Sir Tom). The lady with the luxurious locks (I couldn't resist the alliteration) looked as if she could be a theatrical too, but I didn't recognise her or any of the four other people in the compartment. One, probably another actor, was travelling with Tom and the blonde; the other three were regular people, or as some theatricals would say, 'civilians'.

Amazingly, within a minute, or so, my embarrassing mishap was history. . .as if it had never happened. The civilians were reading their newspapers – one the *Daily Mirror*, two *The Times*. The actor was glancing through the showbiz bible, *The Stage*. Tom Courtenay and the blonde were talking quietly together. The train kept up its regular rhythm, and I tried to ignore the slight pain in my shoulder.

One of my fellow passengers had kindly handed me back my *Motor Classics* magazine, which had fallen with me to the floor. I opened it and hid my embarrassment behind its pages. I felt so stupid. Fancy falling like that. I could hear my plaintive voice saying 'Sorry' to nobody in particular. What a wimp! Why hadn't I made a joke out of it? It was funny. But no, I'd been a prat who had done a prat fall! It was so uncool.

Between visits to the toilet and a solitary lunch in the dining carriage, the time went quickly. Back in my seat, I reckoned we had an hour or so left before reaching Manchester. I glanced over at the blonde, trying not to stare. She must have sensed my eyes on her. She looked up from the book she was reading and gave me a quick smile.

'About an hour-and-a-half to go,' I said. She nodded her head slightly and gave me a half smile, which I felt was more sympathetic than friendly. It was somewhat as if she thought me a little retarded. I gave her more ammunition. 'That is Tom Courtenay, the actor, isn't it? I mean, I recognise him. I've seen him in the films. *Billy Liar*. You know, in the cinema. Not personally, but you know, in a film in the cinema.' Scintillating stuff!

She nudged Tom, who was slumped in his seat, either dozing or pretending to be, so that he wouldn't be bothered by idiots like me. He sat up, eyes alert, and looked at the blonde.

'This chap is a fan of yours. Seen all your films,' she said mischievously.

'Really?' Tom said, grinning at me. 'Well, that is nice. I'm a fan of you and your brother. I used to watch *Blackpool Night Out* whenever I could. I'm from the North. Hull, actually.'

'We all have a cross to bear,' I joked. My confidence had returned. Being recognised can do that to you.

'I think I saw you with Tommy Steele playing a cinema there when I was a kid,' Tom said. 'I saw you play football too, with the TV All Stars. I play, you know.'

Play football! That was all that was needed. The conversation flowed. He was doing a play at the Royal Exchange Theatre in Manchester. Sitting next to him was his leading lady, whom he introduced as Helen Mirren. She was undoubtedly very attractive, and now, without her coat on, I could see she had a great figure. I thought to myself, 'She doesn't have to be much of an actress with her looks.' But the longer we talked the more conscious I became of her wonderful voice. I revised my earlier assumption; with her looks and that voice she would probably become a big name. I couldn't help thinking she would make a great Cinderella. I wondered if she could sing and dance. I never did find out.

Before we said goodbye at Manchester Station, I had asked Tom to turn out for the TV All Stars football team (which later on he did), and I asked Helen to come and see tomorrow's matinée performance of our pantomime, *Robin Hood*. Tom was otherwise occupied, but she accepted.

Sometimes I speak without thinking the subject through. Why invite Helen – or anyone, come to that – to watch you in a matinée you know will be at best only half full, and with an audience whose average age is between sixty-five and death? Of course, we were professionals and we tried to get a big result with every audience. But a half-empty house of pensioners can be tough. And on the afternoon Helen Mirren came to see the show, that applied in spades.

I could see her sitting in the stalls, about a dozen rows up on the side. There were a few empty seats around her. In fact, the whole cast couldn't fail to notice this good-looking blonde woman – she was like a golden summer flower set in a field of ancient, snow-covered winter trees.

By the end of the show, the word had got around backstage: the blonde was a friend of Mike Winters! When Helen popped back-stage to say goodbye and thanks for the ticket, I introduced her to Bernie and tenor John Hanson, our co-star. Backstage gossip was in overdrive.

Helen and I arranged to meet for coffee the following morning. There had been no time to talk about the pantomime, which was fortunate as far as I was concerned. Bernie and I had struggled. The evening show was different. First, it was practically full; second, the audience was enthusiastic and we got big laughs. But Helen hadn't seen that show!

At coffee the next morning, I steered the conversation away from the panto. I wanted to know about her. I learned very quickly that she was a serious actress and already successful in the 'straight' theatre. I hadn't seen a straight play since my days at the Royal Academy of Music when, with a few students, I went to see Oscar Wilde's *Lady Windermere's Fan* and a Somerset Maugham play about divorce. I had however seen nearly every hit musical since *Annie Get Your Gun* and *Kismet*. More my style, after all, I was in variety or as the Americans called it, vaudeville. The snobbish barrier between variety and straight theatre was beginning to crumble, but with all due respect, the straight theatre still called themselves the 'legitimate' theatre. So I guess that made me and my fellow performers illegitimate.

Helen had recently made a film with James Mason, one of my favourite actors. 'What kind of man was he to work with?' I asked, thinking he was sure to be serious.

Not so, it seemed. She told me, 'He was a lot of fun. Always joking around. And such a good actor. I learned a lot working with him. He has such a wonderful voice.'

I told her I thought she had a beautiful voice. Study and practice, she told me. She leaned across the table. 'I think you have a slight impediment in your speech.'

'Oh,' I said, trying not to sound shattered. What else could happen to extinguish my ego? She had seen me trip over a shoe, struggle to get laughs in front of an audience who had probably come to the show in the first place to hear John Hanson sing something by Ivor Novello. Now, she tells me I have a speech problem.

I asked innocently, 'Could you be more specific?' I spoke perfectly, enunciating every word, in a way reminiscent of my days at the City of Oxford School.

'You don't finish your words. You can do it, as you just demonstrated, but you need to practise. Exercise,' she said.

Didn't she realise that the audiences who came to watch Bernie and me weren't expecting to hear Laurence Olivier or some Shakespearian actor? They were looking for a bit of fun from a couple of lads with no pretensions. But I knew she was right about my lazy speech. Bad diction was nothing to be proud of. I asked if she knew what kind of exercises I should do.

She knew all right! She had once been a speech therapist. 'I'll show you,' she said, pushing the pot of coffee to the side of the table. For a moment I wondered what she was going to do.

'Repeat after me,' she began, 'Red leather, yellow leather. Again, after me. Red leather, yellow leather. Again. Red leather, yellow. . .'

There we were, sitting in the lounge of the prestigious Piccadilly Hotel, looking earnestly at each other across a small table, continually repeating to each other Red leather, yellow leather. So endeth the first lesson.

We met for supper a couple of times, and I believe we went to the cinema one afternoon. We enjoyed each other's company, mainly because she talked about the theatre. . .The names of famous playwrights, classic and contemporary, gushed from her lips like water from a fountain. If I recognised more than one from my school days I was doing well. Not wanting to look a philistine, I extolled the genius of Artie Shaw, Charlie Parker, Bill Evans and Miles Davis. It sort of evened up the conversation. Anyway, I think we both just liked to hear our own voices. Granted, hers was far more attractive than mine.

Helen gave me other voice exercises to practice, which I used gratefully until I quit the stage. I let her into my secret wish to become a writer. She was appalled that I read Harold Robbins and wasn't conversant with the Brontë sisters, H.E. Bates or Proust. She was more impressed when I told her my reading tastes lay with works by Upton Sinclair, Somerset Maugham, Sinclair Lewis, Sir Arthur Conan Doyle, and perhaps my favourite writer, Evelyn Waugh – she most certainly approved of him.

One night, after our shows were over, we met at my hotel to watch a black and white film we both wanted to see. We went to my room, where we watched *The Third Man*. Bernie happened to see us leave the hotel after the movie had finished. It was late, but if you're thinking what Bernie was thinking you are wrong! Nothing happened. We were both in very happy relationships.

On her last day in Manchester, Helen dropped by the theatre and left me a present. It was a book by H.E. Bates. That was very sweet of her. I had no idea if we would meet again, but she had made what could have been a dull and boring week in Manchester an interesting and pleasant one. I was just sorry she hadn't seen Bernie and me at our best.

The opportunity to redeem that impression came along about eighteen months later. Bernie and I were doing a one-night stand at a club. . . well, more like a restaurant really. There was no stage, the lighting was a solitary spot, and the seating was at round tables, so some of the patrons had to turn their chairs around to see us. It was hardly the Talk of the Town.

My heart dropped when I reached the small dance floor in the middle of the room where Bern and I were going to work. Directly to my right, practically on the dance floor, was a table of eight young people, looking at us expectantly. Sitting in the middle of the group, with a questioning smile on her face, was Helen Mirren.

Do I have to paint the picture for you? To use theatrical terminology, Bern and I bombed. You could hear more laughter at a funeral service. There was an upside though. Because of the tiny space we had to work in, we had cut our dance routine and closed on a singalong. Songs everyone knew, including the audience that had just won the staring contest with us.

Our act finally finished. We exited to generous applause from the audience, though they were actually applauding themselves for doing most of the singing. Even Helen's group, who hadn't cracked a smile throughout our comedy routines, sang the old tunes with gusto – though how Gusto got into the place is a mystery! (I thought I'd throw in that old Groucho Marxism.)

Bernie was out of the place before I had changed. I went into the main room to say hello and goodbye to Helen before I left. She introduced her fellow actors and actresses, all from the Royal Shakespeare Company. A man sporting a chiselled beard was sitting next to Helen. I got the impression from his proprietary manner that he was her boyfriend. I listened to a few congratulations from a couple of the more compassionate RSC members, wished Helen good luck and thanked her for coming, and then got the hell out of the place.

Once again Helen had seen us when we weren't at our best. I can only think she must have wondered how come we were stars.

In spite of the occasional bad night, our career continued to prosper. In 1971 we were the honoured celebrities on the TV show *This Is Your Life*. At that time we were probably at the height of our popularity. The following year we returned from a three-month tour of South Africa and Zimbabwe, which was then still known as Rhodesia – and what a great place it was then. The racism was a fraction of what I found in South Africa, though of course it was still unacceptable. Bernie and I were soon booked for another panto and for a one-off Christmas TV special for London Weekend Television.

Meanwhile, Helen Mirren had been getting quite a lot of publicity not only over her fine acting ability, but also over her great figure. She was becoming the sex goddess of the 'legitimate' theatre. I admit, I always found Helen very attractive, but when I bumped into her at London Weekend's canteen, goddess didn't immediately come to mind.

Bernie and I saw her sitting alone nursing a cup of coffee. We exchanged greetings and asked if we could join her. She smiled a 'Please do'. She has a beautiful smile that lights up her face, which at the previous moment had looked rather sad.

Helen was there rehearsing a play. She seemed tired, and her glorious mane of hair was limp. She wore practically no make-up. . . She was in typical rehearsal mode. The glamour, if the part called for it, would miraculously materialise at show time. She pushed a few loose strands of hair from her forehead and with the palm of her hand tried to smooth one side into shape.

'Been away? You got a little colour. Southend?' Bernie asked jokingly, purposely pronouncing it 'Soufend'.

Helen smiled. 'No. I was in Mustique.'

'With the Princess? Not bad at all. Was John Binden there? Was he having it off with Margaret or Roddy?' Bernie could get away with saying things like that. He had a magical way about him. I never heard anyone get annoyed over a dicey remark he made. If Bernie wanted to insult you for real, you'd know it.

Helen smiled and said, 'Sorry, Bernie, I've nothing to report. I don't gossip. I'm taking the high ground. It's a beautiful island and it was fun, but it's a long flight.'

'That trip must have cost a few quid,' Bern said.

'I shouldn't have thought you two would be concerned with how much things cost, not with all the money you must make. I'm really getting sick at the lousy money actresses make. It's unfair. It's ridiculous.'

It was a strange conversation. Bernie and I looked at each other when Helen left to go back to rehearsals.

'She didn't seem too happy, did she?' Bernie observed.

'No. She didn't seem the same girl I knew in Manchester.'

'I thought you and she were sort of, pretty close.'

'I know what you thought. I told you at the time, there was nothing going on.' I reflected a moment. 'To tell you the truth, Bernie, I don't think she reckons us. Both times she saw us work we struggled. You can't blame her.'

'True,' Bernie said. He screwed his mouth up, as he often did when thinking.

'I've never seen her work, but from what I've read she is a terrific actress. But we've worked hard and earned our reputation. Not everybody loves us, but we're a famous pair!'

I haven't seen Helen again, in person that is. However, I have followed her career with interest, and in some weird way with pride. I suppose it's a form of reflected glory. I knew her before she became a star.

12

Eventually, Jack Benny

Not many comics become stars of stage, radio and television. The few who do achieve that kind of success usually end up making a movie or two as well, giving them even greater visibility.

Bernie and I had the pleasure of working with one such artiste. One of England's most popular comics, Arthur Askey, known as 'Big-Hearted Arthur', was a household name for many years. He is still remembered today with great affection.

We did a summer season together at Southsea, in Hampshire, in 1963. Arthur was the star of the show and we were just beginning our first TV series, *Big Night Out*. He was more than kind, even helping us with material for the TV shows, always advising us to cut out anything smutty.

'Your show is on around dinner time. Children will be watching. You won't get laughs from dirty material from kids, they won't under-stand it, and parents will appreciate it that you aren't smutty. Remember, boys, audiences have a long memory. They won't take their kids to see a dirty comic in a summer show or a pantomime, and they are integral parts of how we make our living.'

Arthur often invited us into his dressing room for a chat. After one matinée when Bernie and I struggled to get a laugh, he told us that a tough audience was just a part of the business. We shouldn't push, or get annoyed, or panic. We were professionals and we should do our best. After all, the public had paid to see us. Just because we couldn't hear them laughing didn't mean they weren't smiling. Bernie and I listened to what Arthur told us and tried to follow his advice. Arthur was a credit to show business. He really was 'Big-Hearted Arthur'.

As I mentioned at the top of this chapter, very few entertainers become stars of theatre, radio and television, and also make their mark in the movies. One American did and became an international star. It so happens that he was my favourite comedian, the one I admired most of all.

When a bunch of comics get together and talk about comedy and other comics, invariably the art of 'timing' is mentioned. And the comic who is acknowledged as the master of that most important and difficult of skills is Jack Benny.

He was the idol of so many comedians. When I found out I was going to meet him I wondered if he would have feet of clay. What would Jack Benny really be like? Let me tell you about it . . .

In the early Fifties, Bernie and I were booked for a week's work at the Ardwick Hippodrome in Manchester as a supporting act to the beautiful American singer Helen Morgan. She was a terrific performer.

Considering we were one of the least known acts on the bill, Ms Morgan was always charming to Bernie and me. We fancied her like mad, but neither of us got beyond a pleasant exchange of 'Hello, how are you?' and a friendly smile.

That week, across town, Frank Sinatra was playing the Palace Theatre to so-so business, whereas Helen was playing to packed houses. Being big fans of Sinatra, Bernie and I felt sorry he wasn't doing sell-out business. Of course, we had no idea that in a few years' time he would be even bigger than he had been before. But we did know that he was struggling that particular week in Manchester.

By Wednesday stories were going around that Frank wasn't happy. He was arriving at the theatre just before he was due on stage, changing hats ready to go on and do his spot. I don't know how true the rumours were, but it seemed certain that Frank wasn't enjoying his week in Manchester.

On Thursday morning, Bernie and I stood by the stage door telephone, debating whether or not to make a call to the Palace Theatre and leave a message for Mr Sinatra to contact us. If he did, we would invite him for a drink after the show, or maybe for a morning coffee.

We chickened out. Maybe he would think we were two weirdos. It made more sense to wait until he would have at least heard of us before calling him. It goes without saying we didn't call him that week. In fact, we never did, though we wished we had.

Years later, Sinatra was doing a one-night concert at the London Palladium. It was televised by Thames Television and produced and directed by Philip Jones, the director and producer of our TV series. The following week, I asked Phil what Frank Sinatra had been like to work with. I was surprised by his answer.

'Frank was absolutely no trouble at all,' Phil began. 'In fact, I never had to give him a single note. Not like you, Mike,' he said with a grin. 'His musical director, a lovely chap, worked directly with our musical director, and he stood in for Frank at rehearsals.'

Philip sighed and added rather sadly, 'I was in the technical van when Mr Sinatra eventually turned up just before show time. To tell the truth, I was getting a little worried, but one of Frank's team told me to relax. Frank never missed a show. He was a real pro. Anyhow, I didn't get to speak to Frank when he arrived.'

Philip shook his head in admiration as he continued, 'It was a great show. Frank made it all look so easy. The audience loved him. What a night!'

'I bet it was. But what was Frank like in person?' I asked.

'Ah yes. Well. . . as soon as the show was over, and it was technically cleared, I hurried backstage; I wanted to congratulate Frank . . .' Philip paused. I think it might have been for dramatic effect.

'Well? What was he like?' I pressed.

'I can't really say. You see, the bugger had already left. But I can honestly say, he was no trouble at all!' he said, keeping a straight face before chuckling to himself.

Although I never worked with Frank Sinatra, there were other wonderful American artists with whom I did work, either on television or in the theatre. Because they were my father's favourites, I begin with the Mills Brothers. Enormous stars from an earlier era, they were great to work with.

Then there was Billy Eckstein. He was cool, a sharp guy. I loved his voice. His pianist, Bobby Tucker, and his bassist, Colridge Goole, jammed with Bernie and me most mornings in the theatre. Bobby gave me one of his American tuxedo shirts I had admired during the two-week tour we did together.

Buddy Greco was very friendly, and a great jazz pianist. He even recorded one of my compositions, 'There's a Place Called London'. We did a TV show with Sarah Vaughan together, but never got to meet her. Nor did we get a chance to meet gospel group the Deep River Boys. They were always surrounded by their management team. And we only exchanged a few words with Lena Horne. She was a dedicated, wonderful performer though.

Pat Boone, meanwhile, was a lot of fun and easy to speak to. And Patti Page was charming. A big star from an earlier era, she wasn't as well known in Britain as she was in the States, but Dad thought she was sensational, and I didn't blame him. Jayne Mansfield was very nice – unassuming and kind of sweet. Everyone liked her. Vikki

Carr was a delight to work with. One of the most underrated singers in show biz, she was terrific. And of course I met Rosemary Clooney and Eartha Kitt when Bernie and I did the Royal Variety Performance at the Palladium. In one of our later shows, Bernie did a comedy bit with Eartha which was very funny. Bernie and I were fans of Eartha and Rosemary before we met them, and always remained so. And Sophie Tucker was one of the all-time greats – but more about her in a moment.

There were some extraordinary encounters. We played the Palace Theatre in London with Johnny Ray. We met and discussed a TV appearance he would make on our show. He was the hottest name in town and filled the theatre, but he seemed to be in another world.

Supporting Gene Vincent was a wild experience! We arrived at the theatre, did our spot and got the hell out, with a leather-clad audience calling for Gene all through our act. We never met Gene. Freddie Bell and the Bell Boys were a genuine rock 'n' roll band and a good act. We toured together in the Tommy Steele Show, which culminated in playing the Dominion Theatre in London. And Tiny Tim was unique, the same off stage as on.

The vast majority of American artists Bernie and I worked with were singers, but our main interest was in the great American comics. As youngsters, we were big fans of comedy acts – Abbott and Costello, the Marx Brothers, Laurel and Hardy, and the underrated Ritz Brothers. When we became fully fledged performers we greatly admired the more contemporary acts such as zany Dick Shawn, the polished Danny Thomas, and Bernie's particular favourite Jerry Lewis, not only when he was partnered by Dean Martin, a fabulous all-round performer in his own right, but also when Jerry went solo.

And then there was the great Bob Hope. The sum of my interaction with him happened when I passed by him backstage at the London Palladium. We were both appearing in the Royal Variety show. 'Hi, Bob,' I said. He responded with 'Hi there', and gave me a friendly grin. He hadn't a clue who I was. Later in his life, he became a fellow member of the Grand Order of Water Rats. Those artists who had worked with him said he was a good guy. He often had young, funny comics in his show. To me, that's a sign of a confident and generous nature. But the American comic I most admired was Jack Benny.

That I would ever work with Jack and that we would become friends never entered my mind. But it happened. The indirect catalyst was one of the American singers I mentioned, Sophie Tucker. She was my mother's favourite singer, and it was because Bernie and I worked with her that I got to meet my favourite comedian.

My mum was also a fan of Ann Shelton, a good Catholic girl who sang 'My Yiddishe Mama'. With Italian ancestors, Mum had a foot in both camps. Sophie Tucker sang 'My Yiddishe Mama' too, but it was her trademark song, 'Some of These Days', that was Mum's particular favourite. I always think of my mother whenever I hear that song.

My mother Rachel was a beautiful woman. Tall for the times at five foot seven, with a natural dazzling smile, even after five children – of whom only three lived – she retained her fine figure. Once, shortly after Cassie and I were married, we went furniture shopping with Mum at Heal's, the prestigious store in Tottenham Court Road in London. As we strolled through the store, Mum, in a happy mood, began humming 'Some of These Days'. Cassie and I stopped to inspect a piece of furniture. Mum, still softly humming, sat on a display armchair and casually watched us. Her humming segued into singing. Quietly at first, it gradually developed into a full-blown performance. She gave the number all she had, including plenty of hand and arm movements.

Mum was oblivious to my reproving frowns and not in the least self-conscious. Cassie and I were embarrassed. . .After all, it was our first time in such an expensive shop. Having one's mother give a Sophie Tucker impersonation in a posh furniture store was, to say the least, unusual.

Other shoppers and staff looked a little shocked at first, but when Mum finished everyone was smiling and nodding in approval. One smartly dressed lady gave Mum some polite applause.

We continued our stroll through the store, Cassie and I acting as if nothing untoward had happened. When Mum began softly humming 'My Yiddishe Mama' I decided to cut our shopping expedition short in case Sophie did an encore. But I was never even slightly embarrassed by my mother again. From that afternoon onward I realised Mum had a rare gift – an independent spirit. She feared no one and offered her friendship to everyone.

I knew I was lucky to have such a loving mother. When Bernie and I worked with Sophie Tucker in our show, *Blackpool Night Out*, it wasn't surprising we had an immediate rapport with her. For some reason, she seemed to reciprocate the feeling.

Sitting in her dressing room before the show, we told her the story about Heal's and Mum's singing. Sophie smiled. 'I think I would have gotten on with your mom. Sounds like my kinda woman.'

As we chatted, we found little things we had in common. Our dad's family originally came from Russia; Sophie had been born there. Dad's mother had had three husbands; so had Sophie.

'How about your mum? How many husbands did she have? She sounds like a real red-hot mama.' Sophie shifted her large frame in her chair so she could see herself better in the dressing-room mirror. It was getting close to show time and she had to go to the make-up room.

'Mum had just the one husband,' Bernie told her. 'They seemed pretty happy, though they had lots of loud rows over money. Dad was a professional gambler, a bookmaker, and had been a boxer and a bodyguard before we were born. He made a very precarious living. Sometimes we were well off, next month Mum would be pawning her rings.'

'Just like being in show business,' Sophie said reflectively. 'I started out playing piano for my sister. They said I was too fat to ever make it. I even worked in "black face" minstrel style when I first went solo. The booker told me I was too ugly and needed the black face. I don't know how I made a living, but I had to work. No social security when I started, no way. Mind you, they were completely different times. Tough times.' She reflected for a moment then added, 'But maybe a more fun time.'

Before every major show since mother's death we had found a quiet spot, normally somewhere in the darkness on the side of the stage, where we would say a short, private prayer to her. Being with Sophie Tucker had made us far more emotional than normal. Thoughts of our mother flooded our minds. What a shame she hadn't lived to experience this day. . .her two boys working with the great Sophie Tucker.

Her opening music began. I knew the song well. That night, from the moment I heard 'Some of These Days', I saw my mum smiling as she sang the song.

The following year, on 9 February 1966, Sophie Tucker died. For some reason or other I didn't hear about it 'til days later. It was a sad moment. She had made eighty-two, and when you aren't yet forty, living to eighty-two seems an awfully long life. As you pass seventy-five that opinion sure changes.

The following year, we received a letter from the Variety Club inviting us to take part in a tribute concert to Sophie at the Victoria Palace in London. We were only required to do fifteen minutes, as there were so many artists appearing. We would go on directly before the closing act, the star of the evening, who was flying in specially.

I read the letter twice. I was thrilled. I was actually going to be working with Jack Benny.

We arrived at the Victoria Palace just before the interval. After a cheery greeting from the stage doorman, we went to our allotted dressing room, which we were sharing with Alfred Marks and Bernard Spear. We had decided weeks ago that as we only had fifteen minutes we should cut most of the musical content and our dance routine. The comedy routine we had rehearsed seemed right for Sophie Tucker's audience – elderly and middle-aged.

In the dressing room, Bernie and I freshened up, changed into our tuxedos, and slapped on a little make-up over our beard line. Bernie used eyeliner to define his eyes – eyes were one of the most important tools for his comedy. Ready for action, we made our way to the Green Room.

'You go ahead. I'll go and let the stage manager know we've arrived,' I said to Bernie.

'Right. Do you realise, Mike, this is our first time we've played here. Of course, I know the place well. I've been here enough bloody times. Mind you, mainly waiting at the stage door,' he said grinning. I knew what he meant. His wife Siggi had been one of the principal dancers here before they were married.

The stage manager was standing in the darkened wings watching Alfred Marks do his stuff. I got up close and softly introduced myself. He told me his name was Sid. I asked him who we followed.

'Not a hundred per cent certain yet. You're goin' to the Green Room, right?'

He spoke quietly in his north London accent. I nodded an affirmative.

'Right, my old son,' Sid said. 'Peter Scott is the *gunza mucker* here tonight.' I think that was the name he gave me, Peter something or other. As for '*gunza mucker*', I thought it was a name from the Middle East or India, brought back to the UK by British serv-icemen, but I have been told it is Yiddish and means 'boss'.

'Well,' Sid went on, 'Peter is sortin' things out. 'Ave a word with 'im, OK?'

I remained in the wings listening to Alfred Marks. A fine actor who had branched out into comedy, he was getting big laughs with clever, topical material. When Alfred began singing, I knew he was coming to the end of his act. Although he was a fine singer, I was only interested in the comedy. I went to join Bernie in the Green Room, where hopefully I would meet Jack Benny.

The Green Room was crowded and alive with chatter. Bernie, holding a glass of Coke, was talking to Bernard Spears, a talented actor with a flair for comedy characters.

Bernard and I exchanged greetings, then he asked Bernie and me if we knew who was standing at the far end of the room in the corner.

'There's a lot of people standing there. Who d'you mean?' Bernie responded.

'For goodness sake!' Bernard said, standing on his toes. 'He's hidden behind Keith Devon. Oh, he's clear now. Look! It's the man not in an evening suit. Don't you recognise him? It's Jack Benny.'

Bernie and I looked again across the crowded room. Bernard was right. Of course we recognised Jack Benny.

'Have you met him?' I asked Bernard.

'Sure. He's a charming man. Actually, he knew who I was. I was very flattered,' said Bernard, puffing out his chest.

'I'm going over to meet him. Coming?' I asked Bernie.

'I'll wait and see how you get on. I feel embarrassed about just going over to introduce myself.'

'Well, you could always ask him to lend you a few quid,' Bernard quipped. Benny's miserly stage persona was well known.

I wasn't wasting any more time discussing the matter. I asked Bernie if he was coming or not; he shook his head. I was off. I gently but firmly pushed by closely knit bunches of showbiz people, some of whom I knew. But I wasn't stopping for anyone.

Just before I reached Jack Benny, a tall man next to him in an expensive, beautifully tailored tuxedo leaned in and said something in Jack's ear. I wasn't deterred.

'Excuse me, Mr Benny,' I began. 'You don't know me, but I just wanted to come over and tell you how much I admire your work. I'm in tonight's show, and . . .'

'Of course you are,' Jack smiled warmly. 'I know who you are, for goodness sakes. You're Mike Winters. I'm a fan of you and your brother, Bernie. So nice to meet you.' We shook hands. He looked and sounded just like he did on TV and the stage, but I was a little surprised to find that I was slightly taller than he was. I guess it was the way he carried himself and his big personality that gave me the impression he would be at least as tall as Bernie, who was just under six foot.

'I hear you're a musician like me.' Jack delivered the line perfectly. . . I couldn't resist the temptation. 'Oh no, I really can play,' I said deadpan.

Jack laughed, and so did the man in the immaculately cut tuxedo. At that point, Jack introduced me to him. He was the big shot, the *gunzer mucker*.

We chatted easily and Jack told me the Variety Club of Great Britain was honouring him with a luncheon in ten days' time. I mentioned that Bernie, my brother, was a member, and we spoke about the great charity work done by the Variety Club. Jack brought up the name of a good friend of mine, Dickie Henderson, whom he had met on a previous visit and whom he was hoping to meet up with again with while he was over here. Gunzer Mucker said Dickie and he played golf together, and did I play? I told him no, but Bernie did.

As if on cue, Bernie was practically upon us. Gunzer Mucker quickly whispered something into Jack's ear – it sounded very much like 'Bernie Winters'.

Bernie gave Jack a toothy grin and began to introduce himself. Interrupting him, Jack said, 'For goodness sakes! I know who you are, Bernie. We were just talking about you. I hear you're quite a golfer.'

'No, not really, but I do like to play,' Bernie said with a touch of humility. 'Do you play, Jack?'

'Just the violin,' he said, folding his arms and giving me one of his trademark looks.

We were chatting away like old friends about this and that when Gunzer said to Bernie and me, 'Jack and I were talking earlier about the running order for the second half of the show. . .'

'Yeah,' I said jumping in, 'I asked Sid, the stage manager, who we followed but he wasn't sure. In fact, he said I should ask you.'

'Right. Well, Mike, we would like you to follow Jack,' he said.

'What do you mean exactly?' Bernie asked with a frown.

Jack took up the conversation. 'Look, boys, I didn't come over to do my stage act. I said to the Charity Committee, I would be delighted to make an appearance. You know what I mean? It's out of respect for my dear friend, Sophie. Look, boys, I've heard what a powerhouse act you fellows have. Without Dennis Day and Rochester or suitable substitutes and proper rehearsals, I'm just not prepared. Listen, if we could switch spots it would be a far better show, and I would sure appreciate it. I didn't even bring my violin with me tonight.' Tenor Dennis Day and sidekick Rochester, played by Eddie Anderson, were an integral part of Benny's show. He looked at us with what I could only call a hangdog expression.

I was sold. I would have gone on anywhere for him. Bernie wasn't convinced. 'Come on, Jack, be fair. Once they've seen you, for most of them, the show is over. We can't follow you.'

'Hmmm! That's very flattering, thank you. I have to tell you you are putting yourself down. Look, I will only do about five minutes or so. I'll be talking about Sophie. Then I'll introduce you boys. I'll tell the audience how much Sophie thought of you two. How she wanted you for her show in Las Vegas. For goodness sakes, of course you can follow me.'

Bernie was sold too. We would follow Jack.

That's how it went down. Jack went to freshen up, while we returned to the dressing room where Barry, our musical director, was sitting reading. We let him know about the switching of spots, and that we would be closing the show.

When we got to the side of the stage so we could watch Jack, there he was in the wings waiting to go on. He turned to us. 'Five or six minutes. That's it.' He smiled, but I could see the concentration on his face.

Bernard Spear had been drafted in to introduce Jack. Applause burst out at the mention of his name. We wished him luck, and in his inimitable style he walked on stage.

Five minutes flew by. I glanced quickly at my watch, not wanting to take my eyes off Jack. Bernie and I found ourselves chuckling, then trying to suppress our laughter. I don't know why. The audience wouldn't have heard us, they were too busy laughing themselves.

I glanced at my watch again when Jack began telling the audience how much Sophie had admired 'these two young men' and how much he admired them too. We were finally going to get on stage. Jack had been on for nearly twenty-five minutes!

Jack had wowed the audience. They were sure to be exhausted and ready to leave.

Bernie was resigned. 'Let's cut the act. You give them some hearts and flowers.' I nodded in agreement. Short and sweet.

Jack finished his flattering introduction. We made our entrance. The applause was substantial and Jack gave us both a quick hug before exiting. I began telling the audience how supportive they had been, explaining that because they had been so good we were running late. Bernie had been standing just behind me, slightly to one side, while he silently made fun of how I spoke, indicating that my hair was false, my shoes had large lifts in them, my teeth were false, and not to laugh as I would get cross. Every time I turned to see what he was doing he would stop and smile sweetly at me.

After less than five minutes, Bernie gave me the scissors signal, two fingers placed like scissors cutting – without the audience seeing, of course. It was time to finish.

'You've been a lovely audience and I thank you so much. And may God keep you all,' I said.

'I only wish I could afford to,' Bernie said, getting the laugh. We'd first heard that line at Al Burnet's Stork Club in London, circa 1950. Bernie followed up with a great ad lib. 'I would have liked to have done a lot more, but Jack Benny did my act. Did all my material. Problem was, he did it better than I could.'

I gave a nod to Barry, who was waiting, baton raised, in the orchestra pit, and he struck up the band for our singalong medley. Old standards. Everyone knew them. We thought it would be just the thing for this audience. Fortunately, we were right

After the show, Jack and Gunzer Mucker congratulated us, and thanked us for closing the show. Jack apologised for doing such a long spot, saying the audience were so good he'd lost sense of time. Lost sense of time? An old pro like him? Bernie and I looked at each other. We didn't have to say anything. So he overran. Who cared? He was Jack Benny. We told him to forget it.

Jack asked if we would join him for supper. Bernie said, 'Who's paying?' Jack folded his arms, looking at Bernie as if the question was ludicrous, and took an age to answer. 'You are!'

Alas, we had to decline his invitation, explaining that we had an early morning and a full day as we were opening at the Palladium tomorrow. But why didn't he come round and say hello? We were there for two weeks. He said he'd try. We made our goodbyes. And so ended one of the most memorable evenings of my showbiz career.

This would have been an ideal spot to finish the chapter, but on the Tuesday evening of our second week at the Palladium, we got a message in between shows from George, the stage door man. 'Mr Benny is at the stage door.'

At first the message didn't register. Mr Benny? Who the hell. . .?

Oh! Mr Benny! Jack Benny! We immediately sent our roadie to bring him in.

As soon as he came into the dressing room, Jack told us he had seen the show. 'I really enjoyed it. A kinda English vaudeville! I didn't know you boys could dance. I mean, I can tap dance, well, I used to, but you guys are so. . .er, physical. It's a great finish. And that drum routine. You know Bernie, the shtick when you knock down all the drums. For goodness sakes! At first I thought it was for real. Boy, did I laugh.'

'I saw you when you played the Palladium. You had Teddy Johnson do a wonderful bit with you,' I said enthusiastically, somehow feeling proud of myself. Let me describe that part of the show. . .

Jack is telling a long joke and as he gets close to the tag line, Dennis Day – or in this case Teddy Johnson, deputising for Dennis who was in the States – walks on stage. The orchestra strikes up, and Teddy goes into a popular ballad. Teddy, centre stage and belting out the song, has completely ignored Jack who stands about two feet away looking on, expressionless, with his arms folded across his chest. Two to three minutes later, Teddy finishes. There is massive applause. Jack hasn't moved a muscle, still standing there arms folded, showing no emotion. Teddy takes an extra bow, and finally exits. Jack gives it another moment or two, then takes a step to the centre of the stage, unfolds his arms, and carries on with the joke from where he left off as if nothing had happened. The audience goes crazy, applauding and laughing.

'That's right. Teddy Johnson! A nice man. You see, Dennis Day was working at the time. Teddy was recommended to me as his replacement. I wanted to keep that bit in the act.'

After about five minutes we were interrupted by a call from George at the stage door. There was another surprise visitor – our Auntie Lily.

Within minutes, our roadie ushered our charismatic aunt into our dressing room. Wearing a warm smile, and carrying a brown paper shopping bag, she immediately came over to Bernie, then me, and planted a wet kiss on our cheeks. Without wasting a moment she put down the paper bag on one of the chairs as she said, 'I thought you might fancy something.'

Bernie put his arm around her shoulders affectionately. 'Aunt, do you know who this is?' He didn't wait for an answer. 'It's Jack Benny,' he said proudly.

She turned to look at Jack, who seemed fascinated by her raw energy. 'Of course I know Jack Benny,' she said giving him a friendly nod of her head. 'How's Mary?' she asked.

Jack looked bemused. 'Mary?'

'Yes. Mary, your wife. Mary Livingston.'

Now Bernie and I looked bemused. Jack wondered the same thing.

'You know my wife?'

'No, not personally, but you're married to the actress Mary Livingston. Right?'

'Yes, I am. January 1927,' Jack answered with pride. His eyes showed uncertainty as Auntie Lily went to the chair and picked up the brown shopping bag.

'I got something here for you, Jackala [that's how the word sounded],' she told him. 'The boys love them. My Rae' – her sister and my mother, Rachel – 'loved them too. Probably the best in London.'

She wasted no time in opening the bag and offering Jack one of the warm, well-wrapped sandwiches. 'Wait 'til you taste these salt beef sandwiches,' she said.

Jack held up his hands to his chest and took a step backwards. 'Salt beef! Hey, I, er. . .I've never eaten that before. I'm supposed to watch my salt input.'

'Listen, Jack, I've been to America, I can't believe you have never had a salt beef sandwich. Every deli makes them. Do me a favour, take a bite. One bite. If you don't like it, leave it. My choochie face' – she meant me – 'will finish it. He doesn't look it, but believe me, he can eat.'

She handed Jack a sandwich. He obviously didn't want it, but Auntie Lily was difficult to deny. Gingerly he opened the wrapping, and the smell wafted out. Jack's expression changed to one of interest. He half smiled, then took a fair-sized bite. We all waited until his mouth was empty. He gave us a look of derision. 'Salt beef! For heaven's sake! Don't you English know anything? This is a good old American corned beef sandwich. And yes, Auntie Lily, it certainly is delicious.'

Before our two special guests left, Jack stood up to stretch his legs. As if drawn by a magnet, he ended up standing beneath one of the small spotlights that were dotted about the ceiling. It was as if he was on stage with the spotlight shining on him and a captive audience in tow.

Jack began to talk about his life and career. I wanted to ask questions, but had been told by my mother it was rude to ask people lots of questions. Auntie Lily had no such qualms. In short order she learned what his real name was. 'Benny Kubelsky.' What his father did for a living. 'Saloonkeeper.'

Auntie Lily was far too discreet, though, to ask him his real age; she just told him he looked great for his age. Now Jack, every year, always insisted he was thirty-nine years old. When he died eight years later, I worked out he must have been over seventy when we met. He really did look good for his age. Maybe not thirty-nine, but who's arguing!

13

The One and Only Tarby

One Saturday afternoon in October at the beginning of the Swinging Sixties, my brother-in-law Freddie and I arranged to meet outside the main entrance of Chelsea Football Club twenty minutes before kick-off.

We were both Chelsea supporters and were going to make a night of it. We always had a laugh together and had arranged to meet our wives, who were sisters, after the game at the exclusive nightclub Della Trusa for cocktails and supper.

Fred was at the entrance gate when I arrived. The crowd was already large and its excitement palpable, and we were no exception. We muscled our way to our seats. They were terrific; just below the directors' section, thanks to Peter Osgood, one of the Chelsea players and a pal of mine. The game turned out to be a thriller, and to top things off Chelsea won.

Fred and I left the ground in elation, surrounded by a happy mob of Chelsea fans, many wearing blue scarves and all animated, like Fred and I, reliving the highlights of the game. Without a break in our conversation we went along with the flow of the crowd until we were clear of the stadium. After a while, we joined a less dense stream of local supporters, still in celebratory mood, spilling into the road, indifferent to the impatient traffic.

Freddie, who was always great company, was telling me about some of the older Chelsea players he knew. I didn't notice the time passing or the crowd thinning out. He finished his story and glanced at his watch. 'Bloody hell! We've been walkin' for over twenty minutes. How much further?'

'How much further?' I repeated, not knowing what he meant.

'Your car. Where d'you leave it?'

'Cassie's got it. It'll be at the Della Trusa.'

'You mean you haven't got your car with you? Then where were you going?'

'With you, to your car,' I answered.

'I didn't bring a car. Maddy's taking her car to the club. We don't need two cars, do we? She'll drive us home.'

I smiled, shaking my head in amusement. The penny had dropped – we were stuck three miles or so from the club without a car between us.

'Why didn't you tell me you didn't have a car? You walked so confidently. As if you knew where you were going.' Fred sounded a little aggrieved.

'So did you,' I answered. We looked at each other and burst into laughter.

We had to wait for a while before we picked up a taxi that took us to the club and our waiting wives. After we had settled down to enjoy our cocktails, our wives asked with a hint of suspicion why it had taken us so long to get there. Sheepishly we told them the saga of the cars. They laughed their heads off. We were the butt of the joke. As I mentioned earlier, Fred and I always had a laugh together.

It was about that time, in the early Sixties, that I met Jimmy Tarbuck. It was no surprise that Jimmy hit it off with Freddie, and we have all remained pals to this day. You could rely on Jimmy always being good for a laugh. . .

I have been friends with Jimmy Tarbuck for over forty-six years and have never called him 'Tarby'. It just didn't feel right to me – for reasons I'll explain later.

From the first show we did together at the North Pier, Blackpool in 1964, Jimmy, Bernie and I became pals. Bernie and I had never met Jimmy, though we had seen him on TV hosting *Sunday Night at the London Palladium*. We were impressed. He was young, good looking, confident and distinctive. We found when it came to live theatre shows that TV names were often not quite up to scratch – or, to be completely blunt, that they weren't in our class. Personally, I thought an on-form Bernie was the funniest comic around. But Jimmy was different. I remember speaking to him after the first week and telling him I was a little surprised he was so good, and he was going to be a big star for a long time.

Though we didn't know it, Jimmy had similar thoughts. He admitted we were a much stronger act than he had imagined from seeing us on TV, and said that in his opinion, we were funnier than Morecambe and Wise. Of course, after saying that, Jimmy automatically became a valued friend! It may seem an unlikely basis for friendship, but we were three relatively young guys who were grateful to be doing as well as we were. Knowing Jimmy as I do now, I would have expected that he'd agree with me. There was always a refreshing lack of B.S. between us.

Being the eldest, and because I smoked a pipe that gave me a look of gravitas, I became a kind of monitor, trying to curb the exuberant and mischievous pranks of two unruly schoolboys. As a monitor I made no impact at all. I was a lousy example.

For reasons known only to Jimmy, he called me Trelawny, way before the name (spelt a little differently) turned up in a Harry Potter book. I assumed Jimmy was thinking of the Cornishman, Edward Trelawny, the nineteenth-century author and adventurer who was described as handsome, dashing and quixotic. He was a friend of Lord Byron and Shelley, and fought for the independence of Greece.

Trelawny was also a supporter of the Abolitionists in America, and personally paid for the freedom of a slave. Oh yes! I could live with being called Trelawny. However, I did wonder if Jimmy knew these historical facts. To this day, I have never asked him, but I like to think he did.

The name Trelawny has a certain dignity to it. And in keeping with that dignity, I addressed Jimmy for a while as James or Tarbuck. Calling him 'Tarby' may have been fine for his fans and others, but not for Trelawny, who in his role of monitor had to confront the pranks perpetrated by the naughty Bernie and James.

For example, one of my duties in the show was to introduce the singer Danny Williams, who had quickly risen to popularity with his hit record 'Moon River'. During some performances, mainly first house matinées when the audience was predominantly elderly. When I introduced Danny, Bernie and Jimmy who were hidden by the closed curtain behind me, would call out stupid and insulting remarks: 'Speak up. . .You're too loud. . .Give us a song, Mike. . . Get off the stage. . .You're an impostor.' Anything to distract me or make me laugh.

They weren't too concerned if the audience heard them or not. Strangely enough, if they did hear, the audience might break out into a giggle, though laughter would be far too strong a word. Danny Williams was a sensitive lad, and I asked him if the fooling around during his introduction was upsetting him. But he said he didn't mind, in fact, he found it funny.

Actually, the first couple of times, so did I. But after three or four repeats of this juvenile behaviour, I confronted Jimmy and Bernie just before I went on stage to introduce Danny. They were standing in the wings waiting to do their behind-the-curtain heckling.

'Listen, fellers, this messing about while I'm introducing Danny isn't right. It isn't fair to Danny, and it isn't fair to the audience.

We're paid to do our job. Let us do it properly. Remember, we are professionals.'

Silently they nodded their heads in agreement, keeping quiet throughout my speech. Not even one snigger. I had the ludicrous thought that they would applaud. My 'play on' music began, and I proudly walked on stage. The two erstwhile hecklers didn't move to their accustomed position, but stayed where they were to watch me. I had a surprise for them. Instead of my usual introduction I started talking about the Congo River – most of it was made up, including quotes from fictitious scientists with complicated Russian and African names, and my favourite, 'an ancestor of James Tarbuck, Sir Rodney Tookus-Bottomly, discoverer of the famous Berk Diamond'.

While I was spouting this nonsense, Danny, who was in on the joke, came round to the opposite side of the stage instead of making his usual entrance from the prompt side much to Jimmy and Bernie's surprise. They then realised I hadn't lost my mind.

The whole episode lasted no more than a couple of minutes. The audience had no idea why I had told them about Jimmy's non-existent ancestor, the Berk Diamond or the equatorial Congo River. They may have thought it just an overlong, boring introduction to 'Moon River'. Who understood these young comedians, anyway?

When I left the stage, Danny, in fine voice, had begun belting away. Jimmy and Bernie, arms folded across their chests, were waiting for me.

Bernie spoke over the sound of Danny's singing. 'Very professional!' Sarcasm dripped from his lips.

Jimmy followed, in his unmistakable Liverpool accent. 'Bloody paid to do our job, are we? A right load of bollocks, Trelawny. Tookus-Bottomly! I hope nobody out there speaks Yiddish. It was disgraceful.' Then he added, grinning, 'But it was funny.'

There was no more heckling from behind the curtain, but my status as monitor was ruined. It was finally put to rest entirely over what I call the 'First-Half Finale Episode'.

The show's director had come up with the idea of closing the first half of the show with a 'Naughty Nineties' production number in tribute to Randolph Sutton, another of the show's supporting stars. It made some sense: Randolph, who was seventy-eight years of age, had been born in the 1890s. But he hadn't attained his considerable fame until the late Twenties and Thirties, so the selection of songs in the pre-interval scene were kind of eclectic.

Bristol-born Randolph was a charming fellow and a privilege to work with, although he thought Jimmy, Bernie and I were a little crazy with a lot to learn. He wasn't wrong about that.

The matinée audience seemed to appreciate Randolph more than they did us new boys, and he didn't mess around self-indulgently as we sometimes did. The senior citizens sat politely through our performances, but as soon as Randolph began the first few bars of his big hit, 'On Mother Kelly's Doorstep', originally recorded in 1930, spontaneous applause would break out. (It would be many years before the song became synonymous with my dear friend Danny La Rue.)

The first-half finale featured the dancers in appropriate period costumes. Bernie and I, and Jimmy too, would come on in ill-fitting Edwardian costumes and each of us would do a number from that era.

I really disliked doing it. Please don't ask me the name of the song I sang – I have erased it from my memory. I didn't like putting on a silly costume and prancing around the stage singing a song that anyone in the audience under the age of sixty had probably never heard before.

Jimmy, Bernie and I, rightly or wrongly, were considered part of the new wave of comedy that had come in with the Beatles, the Rolling Stones and the other popular boy bands. Our fans wanted us to make them laugh; our singing, and in Bernie's and my case, dancing, was a bonus. It was perfectly fine for Randolph Sutton to come on in the first-half finale and sing a good old song from the past, but I felt it was a waste of time for me, and a distraction from what I presented in the act. I would have had no problem wearing a well-cut Edwardian suit for a good role in a sketch, a play or a film, but I was unhappy and embarrassed about doing that stupid song. I felt I had to do something about it.

Well. . .during one matinée, I didn't go on stage for my number. My music played and the eight chorus girls danced as usual, but this time without me singing and looking like a prat.

Bernie's music followed. He went on stage, did his song and then hurried back to the dressing room to find out what had happened to me. Jimmy arrived in the wings ready for his entrance during Bernie's number and was unaware that I hadn't gone on.

The stage manager came round during the interval, worried I was ill and wouldn't be able to finish the show. He was relieved when I told him I had missed my cue. And, surprisingly enough, he wasn't at all perturbed when I told him from now on I was cutting my song as it was too much for me. My excuse was the live TV show I had to do every week. He didn't believe me for a minute, but why should he care? It wasn't his show, and anyway, there were no lighting changes except to cut my follow spot.

Bernie had similar feelings about the first-half finale, but was worried there would be repercussions from the Bernard Delfont office if he cut his number too. I told him to forget about it. We were doing good business and the advance bookings were terrific, so the house manager had told me. The Delfont people wouldn't worry about us cutting a song or two as long as the business was good and the cuts didn't ruin the production number. Anyway, as far as I was concerned, taking me out of it improved it. Bernie and I decided that if we had to be in a first-half finale again we would do a comedy bit.

After a week or so, Bernie cut his song. No word came from the office. And no comments from anyone in the show, including

Jimmy, who had been having a right old time going to practically every big local afternoon social function in town.

At these do's, you would meet the mayor and other dignitaries, and many of the stars who were working in other shows through the summer. I think it fair to say that Blackpool at that time was the most popular holiday destination in Britain, and had more major shows than any other summer resort.

Bernie and I had previously done a summer season in Blackpool – our first –when we played at the Palace Theatre with a great North Country comedian, Albert Modley. A big name and a very funny man, he didn't mind having two young London comics in his show. He was always friendly and encouraging. Admittedly, we were absolutely no competition to him. Our act, twelve minutes of torture for us, died twice a night for six nights a week, plus matinées.

It was so embarrassing that we went to the producer, Alfred Black (or it may have been George. There were two brothers, George and Alfred Black, who were both big-time producers. We only ever called them Mr Black), and pleaded with him to let us change our material. He wouldn't hear of it and assured us how pleased he was with our act. All his friends really enjoyed our comedy, he assured us. We shouldn't worry that the North Country audiences didn't laugh at us as they did for Mr Modley. He was one of them. We were different; they didn't exactly die laughing, but they smiled.

We knew B.S. when we heard it. But we didn't change our act and continued to die until the show closed.

It wasn't until quite a few years later that we found out Mr Black had been inviting friends to the Palace just to watch us. He would tell his pals, as they stood at the back of the stalls relishing our torment, 'You've never seen a comedy act die like this one. It's a scream. It's the same every night. They wanted to change their patter but I talked them out of it. It's the best laugh in Blackpool. I ought to make a book on when they'll get their first laugh.' When we heard this account, later confirmed by Mr Black himself, we were able to laugh about it ourselves. But it was far from funny at the time.

That season, in 1956, the social function circuit was already in full swing. Bernie and I didn't get invited, because we weren't a big name – or even a small one! – but we went to a few events with Frankie Vaughan, one of the biggest stars in Blackpool. Because I had been in Albert Modley's Blackpool show when I was about the same age as Jimmy was now, I felt I should caution him about attending so many of Blackpool's social functions.

It was a casual conversation held in the number-one dressing room that Bernie and I shared. The three of us were drinking tea in between shows on a Saturday night. First house had been eighty per cent full and second house was sold out. What was more, our first two shows had made the top three in the TV ratings. Bernie and I were in high spirits.

'Did I ever tell you what Frankie told me about all these functions they have here?' I asked.

Jimmy shook his head, his Beatles-style hair hardly moving.

'You know, we were in Blackpool for sixteen weeks together,' I began. 'I think it was Frankie's first big summer season. Anyway, he told me for the first six weeks he never turned down an invitation to a function. He thought he would be appreciated for his support, but he learned there were rumours going around that he was a big head and just wanted to be in the limelight.'

'Who told him that?'

'His pal Charlie, who not only worked at the North Pier show as a stage hand at the time but got the stories from mates who worked at the town hall. Charlie is as straight as an arrow. He wouldn't make up stories. He just wanted to tip off his mate.' I paused and gave Jimmy a direct look. 'That's why I'm telling you.'

Jimmy took his time answering. 'Right. Thanks,' he said with half a smile. We didn't need to say anything more on the subject.

The following week, there was a big social luncheon at the town hall. Some of the Blackpool football team were going to be there. Jimmy went too.

The matinée was well into its first half when Jimmy arrived backstage. He popped his head into our dressing room and with a big grin, saying, 'I'm here,' and went to change for his act.

It was a tough audience. Jimmy got through his spot rather sharpish. The first-half finale followed. He had a fairly quick change into the Edwardian outfit he wore for his number.

Bernie and I, for some unknown reason, decided to stand in the wings and watch. Jimmy went on for his song full of energy. The first chorus went fine. It was when he joined the girl prancing around the stage that things went, shall we say, a little wrong. As Jimmy skipped along the edge of the stage, he tripped over his own foot and – wham! – he fell into the orchestra pit.

The audience loved it, thinking it was part of the show, and it got the biggest laugh and applause of the afternoon. Thank goodness Jimmy hadn't hurt himself. With the help of the musical conductor, he managed to scramble back up to the stage. Like a true performer he kept a big smile on his face and made a funny-walk exit.

We didn't see Jimmy until the following night, as he stayed in his dressing room before his act and left immediately after the show. Bernie and I thought it better not to go to his room and talk about it. The stage manager did go and check on him and he told us Jimmy was fine, if a little shaken up. He wouldn't be going on for his song in the first-half finale.

The following evening the old irrepressible Tarbuck came to our dressing room before the show. We looked at each other and grinned. Jimmy said, 'Why didn't Frankie warn you about the bloody sherry!'

I suppose I should mention that Jimmy never went on for the first-half finale again. For the rest of the season the three of us sat in the dressing room and watched television together.

The three of us were in that Blackpool show for nearly six months – six nights a week and some afternoon matinées. It's a long time to be stuck with someone. You can end up unable to stand the sight of each other, but if you're lucky you can end up being good mates for ever. Fortunately we were in the second category. It helped that Jimmy, Bernie and I were sports fans. Jimmy was a diehard Liverpool supporter and Bernie a fanatical supporter of Arsenal. I followed Chelsea, although the love of my life was rugby. And although the three of us had different personalities, we had similar backgrounds. Our dads were both gambling men who at some time in their lives had been bookmakers.

Having a dad who makes his living by gambling is like growing up in a land of feast and famine. The pay packet depends on the turn of a card, or the speed of a greyhound or a racehorse. Not what one could call a secure income! Yet I think it was a good background. It prepared us for the uncertain and precarious nature of show business. Jimmy's family, like Bernie's and mine, were down to earth, straight talking, and appreciative of the good things in life. When life was tough they didn't roll over, they just got on with it.

Considering the times in which Jimmy, Bernie and I grew up, the temptations our profession afforded us were formidable. It was the era of the chauvinist. Yet we managed to raise wonderful families and remain married. Even if our ability at picking the winner of a horse race may not have been much good, the three of us certainly picked winners in our wives.

The three wives got on well together and became friends – and they still are. The fact that, five or so years later, the Tarbuck family moved nearby made it easier for Cassie and Pauline's friendship to grow. And it was fun for me having Jimmy as a neighbour over the years. Our sons became good friends, and my son Anthony, influenced by Jimmy junior, became a Liverpool supporter. My London-born son a Liverpool supporter! Oh, the embarrassment!

My daughter Chaney, who now lives in Gloucestershire, and Jimmy's daughter Cheryl are still close friends. My son Anthony lives in upstate New York, so his schoolboy friendship with young Jimmy has been difficult to maintain. But Anthony is still a Liverpool supporter. . .

Cassie and I have a sense of pride that pretty little Liza Tarbuck has made a name for herself as a talented actress. Living on Kingston Hill with the Tarbucks as neighbours was a lot of fun, I must tell you. At least once a week, Jimmy would drop in for a morning cuppa and tell Cassie and me a new joke. I don't know how he managed it. Maybe they came from his chums at the golf club, or perhaps his pals from around the country phoned them through – Jimmy had golfing pals everywhere. Cassie was always laughing at his jokes. No one tells a joke better than Jimmy.

By now Jimmy's great affection for football had morphed into an even greater devotion for golf. Indeed, the Tarbucks' move to my neighbourhood was, I believe, motivated by golf; their beautiful Georgian house backed on to a fairway. His golfing pals included showbiz names by the dozen, many footballers – including, naturally, Liverpool players old and new – and charity organisations. And I must mention a mutual friend, 'Our 'Enery', Sir Henry Cooper.

Within a short time, Jimmy became a very good player and a tough competitor. I was told by many of his golfing pals he was good playing under pressure, especially when sizeable side bets were at stake – could it have been the residue from his dad's gambling days?

The time-consuming devotion Jimmy gave to golf understandably began to annoy Pauline. I had suffered the same reaction when I spent all week away working and played football on Sundays. I'm not certain who gave Pauline the idea to play golf. It could have been Cassie, but I can't be sure. At the time, it seemed a silly idea to me. Pauline didn't seem the type. She seemed too ladylike, too sweet for such a competitive, frustrating sport. I had tried it, but I didn't have the patience, the time – or the skill, damn it!

Pauline's story ends differently. She loved the game and became a very good player. I hear she can give Jimmy a run for his money.

But being married to a successful entertainer can be hard on any wife. In my humble opinion, it's absolutely necessary for a showbiz wife to have a good sense of humour, plus an understanding of what life is like for a celebrity alone on the road. She must understand the temptations and the potential loneliness. Having good mates who share your husband's interests, be it golf, rugby, football or stamp collecting, ornithology or charity work, is an understated benefit that might even save a marriage.

Jimmy was lucky in having good friends all over Britain. I think he comes second to Ian Brill, former rugby player, golfer, four-time chairman of the Yorkshire Variety Club and all-round good bloke, in having the largest network of mates around the country. There was always a golfing pal to have a chat or a drink with. You never needed to be alone unless you wanted to be. Golf is the perfect sport, the nineteenth hole the perfect place to meet new friends. At least, that's what my golfing friends tell me.

Because Ian Brill lived in Leeds and had been chairman of the Yorkshire Variety Club, plus the fact he was a golf nut and sports freak, Leeds became the centre of a lot of social and sporting charity events. One, an upcoming charity function, involved a visit by Princess Margaret. Jimmy, Bernie and I were part-time consultants.

I happened to be staying with Ian in Leeds when a meeting to discuss the royal visit and its programme was arranged. It was for eleven o'clock on the Sunday morning at the Wakefield Theatre Club. Ian and the committee were contemplating putting on a royal gala show at the club, which was about a thirty-minute drive from Leeds, in aid of charity in the presence of Princess Margaret.

I readily agreed to attend the meeting, even though it would mean getting up early after a late night. Bernie and I were playing

Batley's Night Club, another of the big new nightclubs in York-shire. Like the Wakefield Theatre Club, stars of the stature of Louis Armstrong and Tony Bennett played these amazing venues.

On the Saturday, the night before the Variety Club meeting, Bern and I remained late to drink and relax after a good week. Bernie stayed later than I did, which accounted for his absence on the Sunday morning. But as I was staying with Ian, there was no way I could avoid going to the meeting. We arrived to find the other people involved ready and eager to begin. Variety Club member comedian Dickie Henderson Junior, who was one of my favourite people in show biz, was his usual smiling, laid-back self. He would oversee the entertainment content for the evening. The other person at the meeting was Steve Burtle, the owner of the club and a tireless worker for various charities.

Jimmy hadn't yet arrived. Ian explained that Jimmy had told him he was driving up from the Midlands after a one-night gig in Coventry, and would probably stay at the motel on the A1, near Towcester. He'd see us all in the morning.

No one expected Jimmy to be on time. This wasn't a golf match, or a stage or TV show. We all knew and loved Jimmy, but I bet no one in the club's conference room would have been shocked if he didn't turn up at all.

After coffee was brought into the conference room, Ian brought the meeting to order. As the committee began its discussion, I sat back in my chair at the far end of the long table, listening to the chat and half reading the sports section of the *Sunday Express*.

The discussion was interrupted by the ringing of a phone. Steve put down his notebook and picked up the receiver. He listened for a moment or two, and then quickly covered the speaker with his hand.

'It's the switchboard. They have Pauline Tarbuck on the phone. Sounds dicey. I don't like it.'

'You're right,' Dickie Henderson agreed. 'I mean, why didn't she ring the motel?'

'Maybe Jimmy forgot to tell Pauline where he was staying,' I said lamely.

'Of course he wouldn't forget,' Ian said. We all looked at each other, thinking the same things. Why not tell Pauline where he was staying? Where was he now?

'Maybe we should call the motel,' Dickie suggested. Nobody moved. That wouldn't help. Pauline was on the line now! What should we tell her?

None of us thought Jimmy had been in an accident. We would have heard about that. Maybe he was on his way here as we spoke. But Ian and I agreed it wasn't like Jimmy to stay in a motel and not drive the extra few miles to Leeds. He knew he was welcome to stay with his golfing pal Marshall Bellow at any time – he usually did.

'There has to be a logical explanation,' I said.

'Is there a golf tournament around here we don't know about?' Dickie asked.

'No,' Steve told him. 'There's only one explanation I can think of why he didn't tell Pauline where he was staying.'

'Yeah? What's that?' I asked.

'He's got to be with a bird,' Steve answered.

'I doubt that. Anyway, we can't leave Pauline waiting. Let me speak to her,' Dickie said.

Steve nodded, relieved not to have to make up a story to tell Pauline. 'Put Mrs Tarbuck through, please,' he asked and quickly handed the phone to Dickie.

'We can't put Jimmy in it,' Ian said urgently. 'Think of something, Dickie.'

The three of us watched and listened to our spokesman. This was important. Our friend Jimmy's future happiness could be at stake.

'Hello, Pauline.' Dickie's voice was calm and friendly as always. 'It's nice speaking with you. We're up to our eyes trying to work out exactly what we want at Princess Margaret's function. It's going to be the best one we've done. We hope to get David Niven to join us. Of course, you and Jimmy will be there. Hey, I'm sorry for going on so long. You want to speak to Jimmy, of course. Well, it's bad timing. Jimmy's just left the room to go with Steve to his office, the one he has the other side of the club, the one backstage. They need to pick up figures from last year's function.'

Pauline's voice was loud and clear as we crowded round the telephone. 'Gone to Steve's office? Are you sure?'

'Oh yes. You just missed him. Yep, he's gone to Steve's office,' Dickie assured her.

'Well, that's nice. A little strange, though. You see, Dickie, Jimmy is here with me. Actually, he's in bed. He felt bad after the show in Coventry last night so he drove straight home. I made him go to bed right away. He's still resting. Jimmy asked me to call Steve at the club at around eleven thirty to let you all know what had happened. I didn't want you all to start worrying. Say hello to the other lads. It's nice to know Jimmy has such loyal friends.'

So spoke Pauline Tarbuck. As I mentioned earlier, a wife needs a good sense of humour.

14

Should Have Been Six of Us: The Beatles

Show business can be tough. Some of the people who run the business side can be utterly ruthless, thinking about the profits more than the artist.

But – except for a small minority – most of the entertainers I met throughout my showbiz career had a generosity of spirit. Bernie and I were lucky to meet many fellow artists who gave us a helping hand, often taking time to teach us and always ready to give invaluable advice.

I remember when we were booked to appear in the Benny Hill stage show. It was a four-week gig, and we dreaded doing it. He was the hottest comic around at that particular time, and we thought there was no way he would allow us to get too many laughs. We were completely wrong. Benny gave us carte blanche, letting us get all the laughs we could. I should add that it didn't prevent Benny getting all the big laughs he deserved. His show was a big success too, and a happy one.

Years later, when Bernie and I were riding high with our own TV series, we were asked by our TV producer, Philip Jones, if we had any objection to having another comedian on our show for four consecutive weeks. Phil told us the guy wouldn't clash with our style and was very funny. We remembered our good fortune with Benny Hill, and immediately agreed. We had no objection of opening a door for another comedian. So we had the pleasure of working with and encouraging a very funny and talented new comedian. His name was Les Dawson.

In a second-hand way we were also able to lend a helping hand to the Beatles, the subject of my next story. We were friendly with Brian Epstein, who before he became the group's manager owned a record shop in Liverpool. Whenever we played there, Bern and I used to spend hours in his shop chatting and listening to the latest big band records.

After the Beatles made their first guest appearance on our TV show, *Big Night Out*, Brian asked us if we could help get the lads a prestigious date in London to show off their talent. Bernie and I called our agent, Joe Collins, to see if he was interested. Joe jumped at the chance and booked them into a major London venue. The four lads wowed the audience. Brian was delighted, while Joe had a successful production – so much so that he offered Bern and me a booking fee. We told him to forget it. You don't get paid for doing a mate a favour.

Yet on reflection, I guess we did get repaid. When the lads were the hottest group in the world they did two guest appearances on our show that certainly helped our ratings. And Paul, John and George gave Bernie tips on playing the guitar. I believe Bernie and Ringo, two drummers, talked drums. I offered clarinet tips, but no one was interested.

So let me tell you how Bernie and I first met the Beatles...

I n the summer of 1963 it was a long, hard drive from Southsea in Hampshire to Didsbury in Lancashire – it probably still is. Especially overnight, and even more so after doing two shows. Bernie and I were appearing in summer season with the great Arthur Askey, and each Sunday we drove from Southsea to the studio in Didsbury for our live TV show, *Big Night Out*.

On this particular morning – it was the third show of the thirteen-week series – we arrived at nearly ten o'clock, just in time for rehearsals. Outside the studio, a small crowd of teenagers, mostly girls, stood waiting in palpable anticipation. Bernie gave me a big grin. 'D'you see 'em? Fans! We've made it, Mike. We've made it. Eeeee!'

I got out of the car and sauntered towards the crowd, eagerly awaiting that first autograph request. Boy, did I get a reality check! I was overwhelmed by complete indifference. Bernie's smile left his face as he too was ignored. We walked up the few stairs to the studio entrance and nodded at Paddy, the doorman. He jabbed a thumb in the direction of the crowd. 'Beatles fans.'

I suddenly remembered that the Beatles were one of the guests on the show that night. I hadn't realised how popular they were. Giving Bernie a sour look, I said, 'So we've made it, have we? Rather premature, don't you think?'

'I don't know.'

'What do you mean, you don't know?' I asked, sounding a little like Oliver Hardy.

'I don't know what premature means,' he said.

The Beatles arrived late for rehearsals. The actress Jane Asher was carrying Paul's guitar. Ringo and George looked a little disappointed as they took in the less than salubrious studio. John, with his pretty wife Cynthia a step behind, headed straight for me. 'I'm John Lennon,' he said. 'Sorry we're late, like. It's not easy to find, is it, sir?'

'Don't call him "sir", he'll want more money,' Bernie said. Everyone laughed and the mood was set. The show went well and was a lot of fun.

The following year, the new *Big Night Out* series was being shot at Thames Television's studios in Teddington. Now internationally famous, the Beatles were once again booked to do the show. Bernie and I had decided to ask every guest star to play some part in our comedy sketches. The Beatles readily agreed. They were so famous now, yet they were about to make their comedy début on the fifth show of our series – and it would be live!

The first comedy sketch in every show took place before the opening music or credits. It always resulted in Bernie getting blown up by some devious means, after which, covered in dust, clothes in rags, he would join me for the opening line: 'It's *Big Night Out!*' OK, so it wasn't exactly *University Challenge!*

I wrote some special material to include the lads in the first sketch. They were to be blown up as well and then we would all do the opening line together. They loved the idea.

The storyline was simple: we were six guys trying to choose a name for our new band. Getting frustrated, everyone except me goes offstage into the imaginary kitchen to make a cup of tea. Left behind, I call out instructions on how I want my tea, giving them time to change into tattered shirts and get covered in dust. Suddenly, I shout, 'Hold it! I left the gas cooker on. Don't strike a match.' Naturally, I'm too late. BANG!

The animated buzz from the audience hushed as the studio house lights dimmed, the TV lights flared up and the floor manager began the five-second countdown to start the show. Bernie and I, wearing Beatles wigs, sat with the band on the set – a lounge in a working-class home. Pumped up with nervous energy, grinning, we gave each other the thumbs-up sign. Five, four, three, two, one. Action!

John had the first line: 'We gotta get a good name for the group. Right, lads?' We all nodded sagely and Bernie jumped in. 'How about "The Fish and Chips"?' The audience laughed, but we cried out, 'No! Rubbish.' Next it was Paul's turn. 'What about "The Sexy Slugs"?' We all shouted him down, and did the same to Ringo's suggestion of 'The Pickled Onions'. Now it was my turn. The script called for me to say 'How about "The Rolling Bones"?' George would then answer, 'Not bad, but how about "The Beatles"?' Then we would all vociferously shout him down.

However, on the actual show, for a gag, I changed the script. 'I've got a good name,' I said, smiling straight at George. 'How about "The Mike Winters Six"?'

John, Ringo and Paul began to giggle. Bernie shook his head reprovingly at me, while grinning at the audience. 'Brother Michael is being naughty. He's ad-libbing. He changed the script.' Everybody laughed – everybody that is except George. He sat poker-faced. Was he mad at me? After all, this was live. No retakes!

George gave me an enigmatic smile and then calmly, with complete confidence, said, 'I don't think so. For me, "The Eric Morecambe Six" sounds much better.' There was a roar of laughter and appreciation from the audience. It was a heck of a start to the show. To coin a phrase, a great time was had by all.

The Beatles were probably the hottest band in the world at the time, and this was their first show in Britain since their triumphs in America. The crowds outside the Twickenham studio were monumental and their enthusiasm whenever a large car pulled up to the entrance gates was intimidating. The VIPs inside the vehicles must have been scared out of their minds, and relieved that they weren't the Fab Four. Of course, that they weren't only aggravated the mob.

Wisely, the producers had the Beatles arrive by launch on the River Thames – which fortuitously ran behind the large studio lot. The crowd of fans were disappointed but it saved what could have turned out to be a dangerous situation.

I had my wife Cassie and baby daughter Chaney with me, and made sure they were safely ensconced before the show in the large trailer that served as a Green Room. During rehearsals, Paul dropped in and showed surprising paternal instincts by having Chaney on his lap and captivating her. Well, captivating women of all ages was one of his gifts.

Bernie and I worked with the Beatles one more time. They were our special guests on *Blackpool Night Out*, and needless to say the ratings were great. We were ecstatic that they were doing the show, but this time they didn't do any comedy with us.

There were a couple of factors that made it impossible for us to do more comedy together. First, Bernie and I were playing in a summer show in Yarmouth and flew to Blackpool on Saturday night after our second house, from an isolated runway on an uneven field somewhere in the twilight zone of Norfolk. Matt Monro, one of the nicest men I have ever known, was co-starring with us in Yarmouth, and his daughter Michele, in her terrific book about her late dad, tells of one of those nocturnal flights he took with us. Two shows a night, the flight from hell, recovery time, writing and rehearsing our own routines, didn't make us too eager to try talking the Beatles into doing stuff together.

Second, the Beatles had changed. When we met at rehearsals at the ABC Theatre in Blackpool, it was like seeing old friends. The four lads were a pleasure to work with. But it would be stupid of me to say they hadn't changed – how many young musicians from an everyday background in Liverpool find themselves, in the space of a few years, not only rich and famous, but the most famous and most popular entertainers in the world? Of course they had changed. They were still nice guys, only now they had clout. Now they could undo any straps they felt were restricting them. Wealth and power have a way of freeing the imagination.

Ringo told me he had enjoyed doing comedy with Bernie and me, but John had his own ideas of what comedy would suit the band. He told me, as we sat in the stalls half-watching Paul show Bernie different chord positions on the guitar, that he liked less structured comedy; he preferred it more 'off-the-wall', bizarre. I understood what he was saying. He was avant-garde. His ideas preceded *Monty Python's Flying Circus*. I didn't talk to George or Paul about it, but I guess they sided with John, though I must add that Ringo didn't altogether agree with him. But it wasn't to be.

I never dreamed in 1965, the last time I saw the four of them together, that I would still be around today and two of the Beatles, John and George, would be gone. I feel fortunate to have known them, but in life, there is no 'advance programme' printed. We don't know who or what is on or off stage next. Life has a programme of its own.

You Need a Finale

At the end of a show when the applause has died down and before the final curtain falls, Bernie and I, like other 'top of the bills', would give our 'thank yous' to all those talented people who had been involved in the show. The following is my version of that time-honoured tradition.

I have met many terrific people during my thirty-plus years in show business. There are so many I'd like to thank for their kindness. Too many in fact, to mention them all, so here are just a few.

Thank you to: Val Doonican for helping me write jazz solos for clarinet; Bert Weeden, who helped teach Bernie guitar; Danny La Rue for so many kindnesses; Arthur Askey, who always found time to listen and advise, likewise Dickie Henderson and Kenny Earle. There was also Kenneth Moore and Anthony Newley who recognised my lack of confidence and helped me overcome it; the impressionist, Johnny Moore, who offered a helping hand when I needed it; the hand of friendship offered by legends, Cary Grant, and Jack Benny; the open heartedness and sense of fun shared by Tom Jones; and, I cannot forget, at the start of my career, the example given on how a 'Headliner' should behave by a master comedian, Norman Evans.

So many wonderful people. How fortunate I was to have known them, and how blessed I was having such a talented and loving brother. If I was forced to make the impossible task of choosing the six best mates who helped make my career an exciting and pleasurable experience, I guess I wouldn't want to leave out Frankie Vaughan, Matt Monro, Jimmy Tarbuck, Bernard Bresslaw, Tommy Steele and Philip Jones (TV director and producer).

OK folks, Champagne all round. The toast is 'To good Friends, and good Memories'. I hope you enjoyed the book.